CW00421040

Swifter than the Arrow

Frontispiece The Hemaka disc, First Dynasty, c. 3000 BC.

Swifter than the Arrow

The Golden Hunting Hounds of Ancient Egypt

———————————

MICHAEL RICE

I.B. TAURIS

LONDON · NEW YORK

Published in 2006 by
I.B.Tauris & Co. Ltd
6 Salem Rd, London W2 4BU
175 Fifth Avenue, New York NY 10010
www.ibtauris.com

In the United States and Canada distributed by Palgrave Macmillan,
a division of St. Martin's Press, 175 Fifth Avenue, New York, NY 10010

Copyright © Michael Rice 2006

The right of Michael Rice to be identified as the author of this work
has been asserted by him in accordance with the Copyright, Designs
and Patents Act, 1988

All rights reserved. Except for brief quotations in a review, this book, or any part
thereof, may not be reproduced, stored in or introduced into a retrieval system, or
transmitted, in any form or by any means, electronic, mechanical, photocopying,
recording or otherwise, without the prior written permission of the publisher.

ISBN 10   1 84511 116 8 (Hb)
ISBN 13   978 1 84511 116 8 (Hb)

A full CIP record for this book is available from the British Library
A full CIP record for this book is available from the Library of Congress
Library of Congress catalog card: available

Designed and typeset in Monotype Joanna by illuminati, Grosmont,
www.illuminatibooks.co.uk
Printed and bound in Great Britain by
TJ International Ltd, Padstow, Cornwall

Contents

List of Illustrations

Acknowledgements

The first acknowledgement that I wish to record here is to my friend Arthur Meade, who was really responsible for this book being written. In the late 1970s I was recuperating from a coronary infarction that I experienced in Riyadh and a subsequent bypass operation in London. Arthur and I were accustomed to walk in Hyde Park as part of my regime to return to approximate normality and on one such walk he called my attention to a very striking golden hound galloping across the Park, tail up and ears pricked. This was my first meeting with a Pharaoh Hound and from that encounter the interest that sparked this book evolved. Her cruel and melancholy fate is recorded in the Preface.

My other debts are many. I am especially grateful to Dr Juliet Clutton-Brock, the doyenne of archaeo-zoologists and an incomparable authority on the origins and history of the domesticated dog. She kindly read an earlier draft and gave me valuable advice, not only on the zoological and biological aspects of the text but also on the presentation of what was inevitably an often complex thesis, in the scientific aspects of which I was wholly a novice. If any errors or incompetences remain they are entirely my own, unaided effort.

Andrew Wheatcroft, of the University of Stirling, a prince of editors, gave me, as always, excellent editorial advice. Likewise Jonathan McDonnell of I.B.Tauris, whose company has seen the book through to publication.

I am indebted to the following institutions and individuals for permission to reproduce images of material in their collections or to quote passages from publications for the copyright of which they are responsible. The Ashmolean Museum, Oxford, for the details of the Scorpion mace head and the Flute Player from the 'Two Dogs' palette. The Museum of Fine Arts, Boston for the stelae of the Nubian soldier Senu, his family and his hounds. The Oriental Institute Museum, Chicago, for permitting me to reproduce Fig. 58 from B. Williams, *Excavations between Abu Simbel and the Sudan Frontier*, Chicago, 1986. The Committee of the Egypt Exploration Society for most generously permitting me to use a number of illustrations from the Society's publications. These are acknowledged in the List of Sources. The Petrie Museum of Egyptian Archaeology, University College London, for permission to reproduce images from M.A. Murray, *Saqqara Mastabas Part I*, London, 1905. The British Museum Press for permission to publish the drawing of the Inyotef stelae and to cite the transliterations of the dogs' names inscribed on it, from Parkinson 1991, and the reproduction of the sealing from Abydos, from Spencer 1993, with Khentiamentiu leading the names of the First Dynasty kings. The Department of Coins and Medals of the British Museum, for their help in finding coins of the Sicilian cities of the first millennium BC depicting hounds. My old friend John Ross, whose historic colour photograph of the Emery excavations in the 1950s must be unique. Profesor G. Dryer, Deutsches Archäologisches Institut Kairo, for permission to cite the Abydos labels excavated by him. Kathryn Piquette of the Institute of Archaeology, University College London, for advice and help with the Abydos labels. Terence Duquesne for access to his published work on the significance of the hound in Egyptian mysticism. Dr Jeanne Druce, breeder of the Merymut Pharaoh Hounds, for her advice and help. Mrs Jane Moore for the illustration of the Cirneco. Mr and Mrs Simm for the illustrations of the Pharaoh Hound and the Ibizan Hound. Stephen Meade for valiantly attempting to explain my computer to me.

If I have omitted any institution or individual whose help I should have acknowlededged, I beg forgiveness.

We are alone, absolutely alone on this chance planet and,
amid all the forms of life that surround us, not one excepting
the dog has made an alliance with us.

MAURICE MAETERLINCK

All knowledge, the totality of all questions and all answers, is
contained in the dog.

FRANZ KAFKA

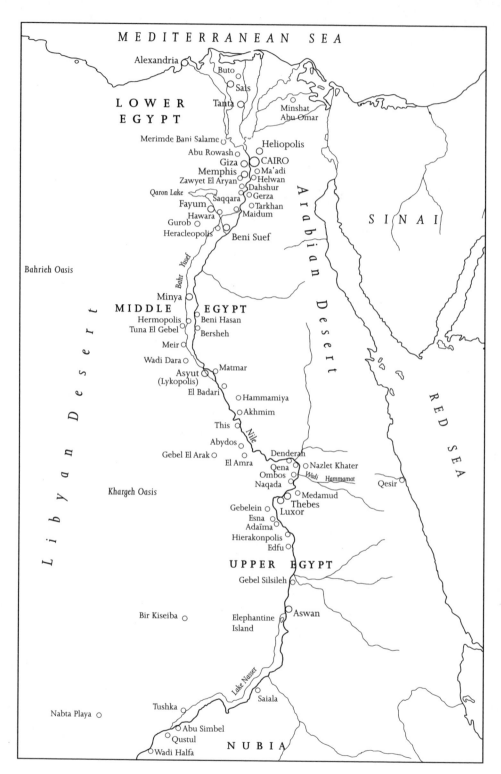

Map Sites mentioned in the text

PREFACE

Canines and Ancient Egypt

There are two integrated themes explored in this book. The first is the quite exceptional place in their society allotted by the people of ancient Egypt to the golden-coated, slender, elegant hunting hounds that they called tjesm. The Egyptians' profound attachment to their hounds made them the first nation to bring the dog into a close, familiar and declared friendship. The second theme considers the belief that the ancient Egyptian Hunting Hound survives in a modern breed recognised by the Kennel Clubs of the United Kingdom, the United States and others, as the Pharaoh Hound and to the people of the Maltese islands as Kelb tal-Fenek. There are communities of hounds, too, apparently indigenous to other of the Mediterranean islands, that seem to replicate the appearance and behaviour (so far as it can be assessed) of the ancient hounds. Enthusiasts for all the breeds have insisted that these dogs are directly descended from the Egyptian hounds of antiquity. This book is less certain that this is so, but the exploration of the history of these most distinctive dogs and their putative relationship with the ancient world is rewarding and remarkable, as remarkable indeed as was the survival of the Egyptian hound in its homeland for more than two thousand years.

Sprung from a family that has always lived with dogs, I have nourished these two enthusiasms, for dogs and Egypt, which were combined in the person of a slender, elegant, golden hound with large pointed ears and eyes as golden as her coat. She was one of the breed called Pharaoh Hound; she was my devoted companion for nine years. I loved her dearly.

Pharaoh Hounds are strange, rather mysterious dogs, quite unlike any other that I have encountered. They are reserved, confident and strong-willed. They have a tranquil but nonetheless rather disconcerting, steady gaze, as if evaluating their companion, not altogether flatteringly; sometimes they seem to smile, rather eerily. They are tireless hunters, ranging over a wide territory across which their clear belling cry will sound, calling their companions to the quarry as do their handsome tails, carried high with a white fleck at the extremity. They are gaze- or sight-hounds, hunting by sight, and once locked on to their prey cannot be deflected; they will also track their quarry by scent. To any rabbit or hare caught in their gaze, they represent inevitable doom; yet in the household they are gentle, well-mannered and deeply affectionate.

Wandering about the Nile Valley, as I was able to do during a particularly well-favoured period of my life, I became interested especially in the origins of the ancient Egyptian kingdoms and in the character and lives of its people. I responded happily to the myriad representations in their tombs of the natural world and of the animals that filled it, which brought so much delight to the Egyptians that they were determined to extend their enjoyment of such god-given bounty into the Afterlife, of which they were a good deal more confident than I am.

That my hound united Egypt and dog for me was especially apt, for the Egyptians were the world's first nation of dog-lovers to be recorded in history. This observation is the dominating message of this book; it chimes with the fact that Egypt was the first nation-state in the history of the world. Hence, *Swifter than the Arrow* is as much about the nature of the ancient Egyptians, and the origins of a complex society in its pristine form, as it is about their hounds; indeed I believe that the hounds played a not insignificant part in the develop-ment of that society and its mores. At the outset of their mutual history the Egyptians bred the dogs for the chase, in the process transforming them into hounds, but later they took them into their homes and every aspect of their lives. For several thousand years dogs played an altogether exceptional part in the life of the people of the Nile Valley. The Egyptians never tired of recording their lives with hounds in the multitude of works of art that they bequeathed to succeeding generations with such prodigality, the products of the most powerful and enduring of all artistic traditions from the ancient world.

The Egyptian experience of living in affectionate companionship with dogs is part of the larger history of the interrelationship between canines and humans, but it is the first documented example of such a collaboration between two disparate species. The relationship between dogs and humans has not, I believe, been altogether adequately examined; it seems often to have been taken for granted, perhaps because it is so close and so mutually supportive. I do not attempt to relate all of it here, rather concentrating on one episode in what I believe to have been an immensely long and mutually profitable relationship. Humans and dogs, in an almost mystical way, supplement each other to a remarkable degree and, in a truly wondrous fashion, nourish each other's needs: their coming together is one of the more fortunate and happy events in the record of human social evolution and in the interrelationship of species.

Although this book is principally about the hunting hound, it takes account of the happy fact that the Egyptians kept all manner of dogs, not only the aristocratic hound they called tjesm (a word which, rather disappointingly, probably simply meant 'hound'), but also big dogs, small dogs, tall dogs and some very short dogs. Nonetheless, it is the tjesm that reveals the most arresting evidence of the Egyptians' concern for and interest in canines and their management. Their commitment to these animals was the consequence of the beauty and intelligence of the hunting hound and its value in the hunt, an occupation for the people of ancient Egypt that was more important and more resonant than the simple provision of protein. The Egyptians' enthusiasm for their hounds was demonstrated by their careful training and management of them for the hunt and by the honour that they paid to them when they recognised canines as some of the most ancient of divinities. By representing the canine as one of the dominant manifestations of the divine principles that powered the cosmos they revealed much both about their understanding of social imperatives and of the place of man in nature. These considerations also suggests that, as many have long suspected, the Egyptians of antiquity were a very agreeable people, with whom modern dog-lovers would be happy to be acquainted.

There is a still broader question that is prompted by the relationship of the Egyptians with their hounds. The values that informed the emergence of the ancient Egyptian state and the social attitudes that underlay those values provide a lesson which it would be well for us to learn today. We are striving to reconcile our involvement with the natural world and our responsibility to it and to the other animals with which we share it; we are generally failing to achieve any sort of meaningful resolution to that dilemma. The society that we have created becomes ever more materialistic, more frenetic and more grossly overpopulated by our wildly proliferating species. It is one of the wonders of their extraordinary culture that the Egyptians seem to have apprehended the inherent relationship between the community of living forms and to have striven to produce a balance between them.

An abiding testimony to what might have been achieved in the sustaining of an environment which is appropriate for our planet is contained in the mutuality of the bond that exists between dogs and humans. The virtual universality and immense antiquity of the companionship of these two, otherwise disparate species which we see around us in all supposedly advanced societies and in those few that still retain their connection with the natural world indicates the importance that the human–dog bond represents. It is certainly more complex and more disparate, I believe, than the simple affection that both partners display towards each other, though this is undoubtedly one of its most pleasing, profound attributes and compensations.

At the outset of the historical period the Egyptians took dogs into their hearts and their homes, into every aspect of their lives. To be understood to its full extent, the association between the Egyptians and their dogs needs to be set against the larger study of the nature of that which persists between the two species virtually universally. It has generally been assumed that the beginnings of the bond between canines and our species came about at the time of the domestication of various other species at the end of the last Ice Age, approximately 12,000 years ago. This assumption has been based essentially on archaeological evidence. It has recently been proposed that the association is in fact considerably more ancient.[1] *Swifter than the Arrow* considers the strong probability that from very soon after the appearance of our particular subspecies of fully modern humans, dogs (at the beginning of the association the term 'canids' is more apt as they were obviously still wolves, which were drawn to human habitations) were there, sharing in the hunt and its spoils and, in all probability, lying by the fires lit in the entrance of sheltering caves. It is most likely that canids participated in the hunt and their presence may have indeed stimulated the refinement of *Homo sapiens'* hunting techniques and modern humans' most significant physical and social characteristic, the power of intelligible speech. This was perhaps the most important contribution that the dog made to the fashioning of our species and its eventual dominance of the natural world, though it occurred long before the historic population of Egypt seeded itself along the banks of the River Nile.

The relationship between canines and humans has, in recent years, come to be the subject of increased scientific interest; indeed, it might be said that until comparatively recent times there was little real scientific investigation of the dog and its history. But in more recent times numerous scientific and academic publications and conferences have examined the nature and implications of the process of domestication, and a steady stream of scientific reports has flowed from such sources, substantially augmenting the evidence previously available. Such studies are beginning to throw new light on the relationship between dogs and humans and on the origins of that relationship, as much as they throw on the richness of the life of canines.

One of the reports referred to in the text was published under the title 'Genetic Structures of the Purebred Domestic Dog';[2] it is particularly germane to the subject of this book. It was presented by scientists from the Fred Hutchinson Cancer Center in Seattle at the Annual Meeting of the American Association for the Advancement of Science and subsequently published in the journal *Science*. This research was supported by related studies produced by the Canine Studies Institute, located in Aurora, Ohio.

The various scientific researches into the descent of the domesticated dog that have been published in recent years all clearly support a wolf ancestry for all dogs living today. This issue has been one that, over the years, has occupied the scientific community to an extent greater than most observers might have expected, for the presumption of a wolfish descent must be strongly in the mind of anyone who has paused to consider the matter. There is an alternative theory, however, which, though it is not now widely supported, does merit consideration, as it is hoped will become apparent as this study unfolds. All scholars recognise that dogs possess extreme genetic diversity.[3]

The second principal theme of this that represents a less assured dimension to the story of the Egyptian hunting hound and its place in the catalogue of canine strains. This is the possibility that breeds of dogs living today are *directly* descended from the tjesm of antiquity; my Pharaoh Hound was said to be one of these. There are certainly singular and highly suggestive similarities, in morphology, pelage (the colour and nature of the coat or pelt) and behaviour between the Pharaoh Hound and the Egyptian hound; more than this, there seem to be similarities in the behaviour of the tjesm and the several strains of hounds in the Mediterranean islands that have been popularly claimed to be the tjesm's descendants or close relatives. The possibility that there may have been an infusion of canine genes other than the wolf in very early domesticated dogs (or of tamed wolves on the way to domestication) is also considered.

The authors of the report cited above were, naturally enough, primarily interested in the diagnosis and treatment of cancer in humans. Apparently human and canine forms of cancer are similar and the study of the genetic structure of dogs, given the frequency of their reproduction rates compared with those of humans, make feasible the study of the genes that may give rise to carcinomas. Such genes may also determine certain significant behavioural characteristics. In studying the dogs' genetic structures the authors of the report examined the descent of the domesticated dog from the grey wolf. They placed the dogs examined, representing 60 living breeds, into ten basic groups and plotted the closeness of each group's descent from the ancestral wolf, thus determining the relative 'age' of each breed and its separation from the pure wolf strain. The oldest, those closest to the wolf, appear to be the domesticated breeds established in the Far East, suggesting that it was in this region that domestication was first achieved. Other breeds diffused westwards from this original stock.

Parker et al. included the Pharaoh Hound and the Ibizan Hound in their research into living breeds; they were not included in Vilà et al. The findings that they drew from the inclusion of these breeds will be examined in Chapter 4.

Nowhere is the early evidence that the bonding of canine and humans is a virtually unique experience in the history of species more extensive and cogent than in Egypt.

Those familiar with the sequence of Egyptian history and its chronology will recognise that this book does not follow any strict chronological pattern. But although it takes proper account of the long historical sequences that determined human life in the Valley, the prehistoric period (or predynastic, as Egyptologists call it) and the succession of the dynasties that provided more than three hundred sovereigns who ruled the Two Lands it is governed principally by the issues relating to the Egyptians' experience with their dogs overall, rather than any more directly focused historical process. It is the dogs that are in charge here, rather than the historians, but in the nature of anything to do with Ancient Egypt an excursion into the records of the distant past is inevitable.

When I wrote *Egypt's Making*,[4] a study of the influences that led to the formation of the Egyptian kingdoms, my own Pharaoh Hound sat with me. One day she vanished. Though I was deeply saddened, I like to think that the Great God, himself a canid, had called her home. She went away soon after the great storm of 1987; she was terrified of thunder, which in the minds of the Egyptians themselves was a manifestation of the equivocal divinity Set, and would hide whenever a storm approached. Set, too, has his place in this narrative and perhaps he also sought her presence. I have no doubt that she was a dog that could walk with gods. Many years later I learned that she had been shot, wantonly, by a malignant farmer who now, I trust, has learned what price must be paid by those who harm the god's creatures.

I dedicate this book to her memory, who gave me love and, I believe, a particular insight into this aspect of the ancient Egyptian experience, one of the most compelling of the inheritances of antiquity.

In memoriam
Neferneferruaten Tasheri, a hound,
born 24 August 1978, murdered 12 November 1987,
that she might be honoured before the Great God Anubis

Michael Rice,
Odsey, Cambridgeshire

CHAPTER I

Wolf to Dog to Hunting Hound

The point at which wolves transmuted into dogs clearly occurred long before the Nile Valley was permanently occupied. We do not know when there first emerged a transitional creature, a wolf evolving into a dog, its morphology changing as its social life and behaviour changed. The first archaeological evidence for evolved canines that can with some confidence be described as dogs, comes from the end of the last Ice Age, about 12,000 years ago, in the Near East. But the transition from wolf to demi-wolf and certainly the contact between canines and humans must have happened long before. Archaeological evidence has indicated some form of association between wolves and premodern humans at Zhoukoudian in North China, *circa* 300,000 years BP.[1] At a cave site at Lazaret near Nice in southern France there is similar evidence, in the form of a wolf skull found in the entrance to the cave, dated to *circa* 150,000 years BP,[2] perhaps placed there in some ritual or for a placatory purpose. What may be evidence of human–wolf contact has been reported from a site even earlier than these, at Boxgrove in Kent, *circa* 400,000 BP,[3] thus providing a suitably ancient origin for the British enthusiasm for canines.

Such evidence as these early examples does not imply the domestication of the wolf, either attempted or achieved. The wolf's pelt will always have been valued and sought by hunters, particularly in times of extreme cold, but the presence of the wolf even on the perimeter of these early communities does suggest that at least the observation of the ways of canids must have had a very long ancestry, long before (by the present reckoning) the appearance of modern humans.

It is likely that the end of the last Ice Age witnessed not the beginnings of the process of domestication but rather the final, full and irrevocable establishment of the partnership between humans and canines. This was the time when modern humans changed their ecological relationship with the world around them and became sedentary, and the dogs (for by this time the ancestral wolf strains will certainly have evolved into dogs, probably with distinct characteristics, though perhaps not yet permitting the use of the term 'breeds') would have settled with them. Domestication and the evolution of different types of dog, selected for different purposes – for hunting, as guardians, herders or companions – would obviously have served to confirm the viability of the partnership and to have given it a quite distinct, more rewarding, significance.

If the bond that links humans and canines is so profound and so very ancient, it must have been of crucial importance in formulating the characters of both species, as they are today. The dog's natural environment, it has been remarked, is the human family. Dogs are interested in the emotional and intentional content of their human companions' minds and are quick to learn and to maintain the rules of the human group. Such a degree of empathy which the bond demonstrates can only have been the product of mutual experience over a protracted timescale.

The ancestral wolf was a powerful animal, much like its modern descendant; it was highly evolved, a cunning and skilful predator, with an immensely widespread distribution. But, although the belief that all domesticated dogs descend from the wolf is strong and widely supported by the most competent authorities and those specialists whose opinions demand respect, it is at best a presumption: there is no absolute, scientific proof of an exclusively wolfish descent. However, the strongest argument advanced for a lupoid ancestry of dogs is the wolf-like behaviour of modern strains of dog.

Wherever and whenever the first steps in the formation of the human–dog bond were taken there would clearly have been ample opportunity for the progeny of wolves to have evolved into dogs, from the earliest times. The transitional stage, from wolf to dog, would probably have occurred in isolation. In the wild state, packs of wolves would have tended to keep away from the camp sites of humans and the wolf progeny which did come in contact with humans would probably have been rejected by the pure-bred wolves and would have avoided them. These populations of 'tamed' wolves, often the result of the adoption of abandoned or orphaned wolf pups, would have become accustomed to the presence of humans and, similarly in isolation from their own pack, would doubtless have begun to breed from the other 'half-wolves' and to display distinct characteristics of physique, the colour of their coats and their size. Eventually and by purely empirical processes these characteristics would have been selected and then enhanced by their human companions.

The differentiations in physical structure, size and coloration that can be sustained over many generations by selection are unlikely to emerge in nature and therefore there must have been a degree of human intervention early in their management over an extended timescale. The two species, canid and human, will have known each other since man's earliest days as a hunter, if in no other way as competitors for the same, smaller or more vulnerable prey; when such prey was not readily available, both would have competed for the same carrion. Even if the human–canine contact was relatively light initially, over time the more aggressive wolfish characteristics would have begun to fade into the tractable behavioural patterns of the domesticated dog, if only because the humans involved in the exchange would have favoured less aggressive and more tractable animals.

With domestication came morphological change among the canids.[4] While changes in body size and structure, as well as in the development of secondary characteristics, can take many hundreds of generations to evolve in nature, in domesticated species the changes can be effected in a relatively short time. Such changes can indeed be brought about in no more than perhaps a few centuries, and even more rapidly when careful selection is introduced into the breeding cycle. This can be seen to be the case when breeds of dogs living today are compared with paintings and even photographs of their predecessors. Breeds such as spaniels, mastiffs, wolfhounds, bassets and bulldogs have all changed their appearance in the last hundred years. Breeds have been developed exhibiting particularly admired characteristics of behaviour, colour or build, not always to the benefit of the dogs concerned. The extreme foreshortening of the bulldog's muzzle is a case in point, resulting in many of the dogs experiencing chronic breathing difficulties; another is the uniformly smoke-grey (with a hint of pink) pelage of the Weimaraner hound, selected in the early nineteenth century by a fashion-conscious Grand Duke of Weimar, who wanted all his gun dogs to sport the same elegant, even exquisite, coloration. The Weimaraner, in contrast to the bulldog, seems not to have suffered any ill-effects by this example of canine redesigning. But the dachshund and the basset are two breeds that, like the bulldog, have not benefited unreservedly from human intervention.

It may be incorrect to speak of domestication before the time when humans could be said to possess a *domus*. Wolves and their progeny may well have been tamed and have experienced centuries of casual or transient integration in human habitations; living on the edge of human hunting bands will have accustomed them to a human presence. When our ancestors began to live in settled communities, remaining for long periods in one location, the canids would have adjusted seamlessly to this new way of life. In Upper Palaeolithic times (Late Old Stone Age, c. 24,000–10,000 BP), the final phase of the last (or latest) great European Ice Age, the interaction of the two species began, no doubt as a matter of gradual toleration on the part of the humans and gradual trust on the part of the canids, of the observation of each other, of the sharing of resources and the gradual growth of a bond. Such contact between them must have led to the hunter's recognition of the canines' propensities and abilities that would soon have made it apparent that the canine could considerably facilitate and augment human hunting skills. This may have originated in so obvious a circumstance as the humans recognising that the canines had an advantage in reaching the prey, by virtue of their greater speed, and their realisation that from time to time humans were useful in bringing down large prey which they could not themselves have tackled unaided.

Hunting has been an important component in human history, not least in furthering a sense of community and developing techniques of cooperation and leadership. It has been remarked that the success of humans in establishing themselves as the dominant animal species across the world owes much to their partnership with the dog and its help in securing a regular supply of protein in the form of the wildlife in whose hunting it cooperated enthusiastically, and that 'for the last 10,000 years dogs have been an indispensable adjunct to the well-being of humanity'.[5] This observation neatly expresses the extent and significance of the bond between dogs, their forerunners and humans; it demonstrates the natural character of the relationship between them, with both partners benefiting from it.

Both canines and primates, the family to which humans belong, are intensely social animals in their natural habitats. In short-hand terms both dogs and humans could be described as 'pack animals', though humans largely surrendered this characteristic as they became more fixed on living in large, agglomerative communities. Nonetheless, one of the reasons for the success of the human–dog symbiosis is precisely because of this similarity in social behaviour. Whilst perhaps not too much should be read into the point, it is nonetheless possible that the human 'packs' also quickly adopted their canine counterparts. It has been observed that in living hunter–gatherer communities the women will 'adopt' a motherless or abandoned puppy and suckle it, in the same way as in the raising of an abandoned or orphaned human infant. It is not difficult to imagine the workings of the maternal instinct in such circumstances conditioning the ready acceptance of a canine into the human group.[6]

Contrary to popular belief, it is possible to tame, if not entirely to domesticate, a wolf in captivity.[7] The essentially tractable nature of the canine, its inherent and boundless optimism and its capacity (and apparent need) for affection, would have, over generations, conditioned its behaviour so that it gradually surrendered its more wolf-like characteristics. Many of these, however, are still visible in modern dogs, in the way for example that puppies and young dogs play, where play is an important part of the process of learning social skills and becoming part of the pack.[8]

The modern wolf, *Canis lupus*, is a much older evolved species than modern man. The wolf was an established, highly successful member of north European and Asian ecosystems for nearly a million years, far longer than the duration of man's presence in the same ecological context, which represents, at the most, little more than a tenth of the period during which wolves have been around. The association of humans and wolves was, in essence, an association of near equals; both represent the most intelligent and resourceful predators extant and both species have spread over most of the world's surface. Admittedly, humans have penetrated some regions where wolves have not deigned to go, but these are relatively few.

The wolf is one of the most successful of all mammalian species. The intelligence, pertinacity and powers of endurance of wolves are legendary qualities that their domesticated descendants have in large part inherited. Wolves are found from Ireland to Spain, throughout Europe, their domain extending from Siberia to Japan. The wolf is established in India, in company with the other principal canid with which this book is concerned, the golden jackal that is native to North and Central America.[9]

From the wolf's standpoint the relationship between the wolf and man, the agriculturalist and domesticator of animals, has not been uniformly happy. The wolf is a determined predator and as such is the enemy of the shepherd and the goatherd. He has been ruthlessly hunted and the wolf's survival is now severely threatened. It is now estimated that there may be no more than 100,000 wolves living in the wild today.

An extended ancestry for domesticated canids, as suggested by some researchers,[10] has not been unequivocally accepted by other specialists, especially those concerned with archaeozoology, who point to the absence of supporting archaeological evidence. Given the general lack of permanent settlement sites before the Epi-Palaeolithic period (10,000–7000 BP), this absence of evidence may not be wholly conclusive; the absence of evidence is, as is often observed, not necessarily evidence of absence. A more puzzling omission is that canids seem never to be represented in those early compendia of the relationship between humans and animals, the marvellous painted caves of south-western Europe; nor have the remains of any canid which might be regarded as domesticated (or even tamed, a slightly different status) been found in or near the caves. The absence of such evidence gives some support to the idea of a later date for what might be described as the institutionalisation of domestication after the end of the last Ice Age and of the late Upper Palaeolithic period. Perhaps there was some inhibition about portraying canids in these contexts, just as there seems to have been a similar constraint about representing humans in the company of the splendid animals depicted on the walls, ceilings and niches of the caves.

The lack of any representations of canids in the caves of south-western Europe may simply be evidence that canid domestication was not achieved by those particular early modern humans who manifested such extraordinary artistic skills though they are generally recognised as the first fully modern humans yet identified. The earliest *archaeological* evidence of the domestication of the dog comes not from the Near East but from central Europe. The remains of a tamed wolf were identified at Oberkassel in Germany,[11] dated to the late Magdalenian phase of the Upper Palaeolithic, circa 14,000 years before the present. This predates the evidence of canid domestication from the Near East by some 2000 years, though this is contextually more significant in the comment which it provides on the relations between dogs and humans living in permanent or semi-permanent settlements. Other canid remains from Magdalenian sites have been recorded from Spain and Switzerland.[12]

The Oberkassel discovery is intriguing for another reason. Germany and eastern central Europe have provided a number of revelations about the development of advanced societies that are substantially earlier than those of other regions. Perhaps the most remarkable is that of the 'Lion-Man' of Hohlenstein-Stadel,[13] one of a group of extraordinary carvings in ivory of a human figure with a lion (or lioness) head. It is a compelling and powerful artefact, some ten inches tall, by far the earliest three-dimensional statue ever recorded in Europe. It is also the earliest example of one of the most puzzling yet enduring projections of the human psyche, the human–animal conflation, the therianthrope, which was to become so pronounced a phenomenon in Egypt, thousands of years later. It is dated to the Aurignacian period (c. 40,000–28,000 BC), the time of the earliest cave paintings of south-western Europe, 32,000 years before the present; curiously the figure's stance anticipates that of many of the statues of animal-headed divinities, including, strikingly, the lion- or lioness-headed examples from Egypt like Sekhmet and Mefnut. If a community existed in this earliest phase of the Upper Palaeolithic capable of producing so advanced a work of art in concept and execution, then it is surely possible that its members would have been sufficiently aware to have recognised the potential of the tamed wolf/domesticated dog, if such a creature already existed. Other examples of similar, exceptionally early works in ivory in three dimensions have been found in the same region of Germany.[14]

By the time of the Epipalaeolithic period, 20,000 years after the carving of the Aurignacian 'Lion-Man', archaeological sites in the Near East reveal the presence of dogs that would have been recognisable today, their present morphology fully developed. One of the earliest examples of archaeologically attested canid remains in the context of those of humans comes from Ain Mallaha, in what is today northern Israel; the burial is that of a woman who appears to have been interred with a puppy.[15] The human inhabitant of the grave has her hand resting on the puppy, as though holding it, clearly suggesting that the bond between dog and human was already deep and affectionate, at least 12,000 years before the present day. The subsequent discovery of another Natufian burial, at the Hayonim cave in Israel, was of a male buried with two adult canines.[16] The Natufian was a late Upper Palaeolithic culture (c. 10,000 BC) that was particularly influential in the development of the complex societies which were to rise throughout the Near East a few millennia later. It is from this time that, in the present state of knowledge, it is possible to apply the term 'dog' with some accuracy when referring to the domesticated canines.

Canid remains have been excavated from early sites at Jericho in Palestine and at Palegawra in northern Iraq.[17] At another Iraqi site, somewhat later in date, from the south of the country where the Sumerians were later to establish themselves with such momentous consequences for the history of the world, there is a burial of a dog which is peculiarly touching. At Eridu, one of the oldest 'city' settlements in Mesopotamia, consecrated to the Sumerian god Enki, a dog was buried with a young boy and, thoughtfully, a bone has been provided for his sustenance in the afterlife. The dog was described by its excavator as a Saluqi, a reasonable enough presumption in a Mesopotamian context.[18]

The bond between dogs and humans was certainly formed and secure when the first settled communities in the Nile Valley began to appear. The dogs would have adjusted – for they are a most accommodating species – to their human companions' change of fortune, the advantages far outweighing any sense of loss of the intimacy of the primeval band, which would, in any case, have quite rapidly been replaced by the family group, into which the dog would fit cheerfully. Living in permanent settlements may have represented a profound alteration in the lifestyle of humans but it would have attracted little notice among the dogs, accustomed by this time to the presence of humans. In any case, it may be assumed they would have welcomed their new situation as a development of the pack principle, with the addition of comfort, warmth and the regular supply of food. To these would, in the fullness of time, have been added the pleasures of companionship with a species which, as the dog developed, it would have found to be particularly susceptible to canines' manipulative skills.

Gradually a compendium of traditional lore and empirical knowledge must have been built up among the communities and clans that managed domesticated animals concerning their treatment and fostering, to the extent at least of protecting and improving an increasingly important investment in the stock which the animals represented. The dog would have shared in this process and further selection would have added to the catalogue of morpho-logical changes and adaptations which similarly it would have undergone. Skill in the hunt, though probably considered secondary in its repertoire of desirable qualities to its role of giving warning of approaching danger, was a technique to be learned; however, the settlement, seasonal or permanent, would need to be warned of and protected from marauders, animal and human. The dog was the obvious candidate for this responsibility, and large and aggressive breeds began to evolve as guards, and others as shepherds.

The early stages of the domestication of the tamed wolf or other wild canid must also have brought about changes in the animals' temperament, much as later domestication and selection brought about major physiological changes. The selection of the more tractable animals obviously resulted in the encouragement of those which were more trusting and less aggressive. From those so chosen must have come the demonstrations of loyalty and affection which have remained the dog's most enduring and appealing characteristics.

The dog, always an amiable opportunist, would soon have realised that the creation of a bond of affection with its human companions would produce an immediate return in food and shelter. Dogs would rapidly have learned that the adoption of behaviour that pleased their human companions produced rewards which were much to be desired and which far outweighed the effort involved in obtaining them. To the useful qualities of service and adaptability that the dog displayed would have been added its capacity for companionship, affection and trust, which over time must have provoked a response in even the most dour hunter or carefree incipient shepherd or herdsman.

Dogs have always been considered primarily as part of the human domain, an accessory to our way of life, as an adjunct to our pastimes, or, if the human partner is a hunter or pastoralist, to his avocation. Now the dogs' own world is beginning itself to come more into focus; one of the reasons for this is the growth of the science of archaeozoology, the study of the relationship of animals to human history and their reaction with the social order which is dominated by humans. In the twentieth century the dog began, however tentatively, to become the subject of scientific study and to bound into the annals of archaeological excavation and research. The dog achieved serious academic, particularly archaeological, interest in an article by a German scholar, Dr Max Hilzheimer, published in an English translation in the archaeological journal *Antiquity*,[19] which has obtained widespread currency; though many of Hilzheimer's conclusions have been overtaken by subsequent research, his work is recognised as pioneering and is particularly relevant to the study of the tjesm, the principal subject of this book, for he devoted much of his article to considering the significance of the hunting hound in ancient Egyptian society. We shall return to some of Hilzheimer's observations, and those of other scientists, later in this study. A subsidiary consideration that Hilzheimer also considered briefly is the possibility that domestication may have produced a situation in which the genes of domesticated canines may have been influenced by the genes of a canid other than the ancestral wolf exclusively.

The possibility cannot be entirely dismissed that the Egyptian hunting hound, whilst unquestionably wolf-born, enjoyed another contribution to its genes; this is a view which has, from time to time, been held by zoologists, though most have now discarded it. The canid candidate for this genetic infusion is the golden jackal (*Canis aureus*), also known as the common jackal. Characteristics shared by the dogs of the Mediterranean islands and the other canines which are thought by some to be the living relatives of the tjesm could suggest a genetic relationship with the golden jackal. These characteristics include physiology and coloration and, in the case of the modern Pharaoh Hound, are most notably indicated by its ability to communicate with its own kind by vocalisation, the consistent and purposeful modulation of sound, to a degree greater than that which is found in other living breeds of dogs today. Hound and jackal also share other attributes and behavioural patterns, which will be further examined in Chapter 5.

The golden jackal occupies a territory more circumscribed than the wolf. Its domain embraces the eastern Mediterranean coastal desert regions, the Nile Valley and the North African deserts. It is found in central Africa, in the Sudan, Ethiopia, Somalia, Kenya, to the north in Libya and Morocco and to the west in Senegal. It has been identified in northern Saudi Arabia, in south-eastern Europe, parts of Asia minor and as far away as India and western Russia.[20] The wolf and the golden jackal share territories in Greece, Turkey, the Levant, the Arabian peninsula, Iraq, Iran, Afghanistan and down into India. The wolf is not indigenous to Africa, whilst the golden jackal certainly is. There is also the possibility that the Pharaoh Hound and the other modern strains that mimic the physiological appearance of the tjesm replicate the golden jackal's morphological and behavioural characteristics, if they do not share its genetic inheritance. This question, too, will also be considered further in Chapter 5. At the same time some of the latest scientific opinion related to the descent of the domesticated dog will be examined.

The emergence of the hunting hound as a specific canine strain in the fauna of ancient Egypt, its origins and the manner in which it became a familiar and acknowledged adjunct of the people's lives, must be set in the context of the phenomenon of complex societies (of which Egypt is one of the most potent examples) and the domestication of species, including the canines. In the first place here it is important to recognise that the Nile Valley was not one of the regions of the Near East in the van of the radical changes that came over the conditions of people living in Iran, Mesopotamia and the Levant at the end of the last Ice Age. At the time of the establishment of sedentary communities in the Northern Tier of the Near East and the development of agriculture and the domestication of livestock there, the Nile Valley appears to have been almost empty of anything like permanent settlements, its principal if transient inhabitants being the hunters who followed the herds of wild cattle into the lush pastures of the Valley, especially from the south. There were temporary communities established in the deserts on the periphery of the Nile Valley in the far south as early as the ninth and eighth millennia BC; few of them were long-lasting. There are, however, anomalies in the evidence, with large gaps that may in time be filled, though it is unlikely that anything like the evidence from the Northern Tier will be replicated.

Clearly, therefore, the social integration of the two species, *Canis familiaris* and *Homo sapiens*, must have antedated by millennia the establishment of permanent settlements in the Valley, the earliest of which date from approximately 5000 BC. The evidence shows that domesticated dogs were present when the Nile Valley began to be permanently settled by migrants who, it must be presumed, brought their dogs with them. These migrants moved towards the Valley as the climate of the surrounding areas desiccated; some came from the Central Sahara, others from the Levant, others still from Western Arabia and others from the south, all seeking a new and more benign environment.

The earliest archaeological evidence from an Egyptian site of the presence of dogs comes from the north, at Merimde Bani Salame, and is dated archaeologically to *circa* 4800 BC; this suggests that the first dogs would have been brought into the Valley by the immigrants who came from the north or west. That the dogs were already present implies an involvement in other, earlier human contexts and it is evident that the dog was fully domesticated by the time the first viable communities were established in the Valley.

The Egyptian experience of the human–canine relationship is particularly apt as it is by far the most ancient of which we have a documented record and the earliest in which the dog was consciously brought into membership of the human family in a settled context. It is probable that, even in times far earlier than the foundation of the Egyptian kingdoms, at the end of the fourth millennium BC, the experience that early domesticated dogs and humans had gained together contributed significantly to particular aspects of human psychology which otherwise might have atrophied. Among the most important of these was the caring for another species and the resultant conditioning of the humans' view of the world and their place in it.

Five thousand years ago, when recorded history began, Egypt was the foremost, indeed virtually the only advanced society in the world; only the Sumerians of Southern Mesopotamia bore comparison with them. The Nile Valley was not the first place in which humans and dogs came into a close and intimate association, for there were probably many instances in the world of the Stone Age hunters where the connection began, however tentatively. Egypt's distinction in this respect is that it was the location for the development of a culture of mutual regard, affection and trust. On the dogs' part the relationship with this quite other, rather bizarre, bifurcated creature, with whom they shared a world vastly more complex than the hunting field, shaded into love and dependence, love being, as all dog-lovers know, the dominant characteristic of the domesticated canine's existence.

There is a paradox here, however. We may affirm that the Egyptians represent the most mysterious of ancient cultures by the evidence of their stupendous and often inexplicable achievements, yet that they are the most humane of ancient peoples, the most accessible as individuals. We know more of their lives than of any other community of comparable antiquity, though indeed in that respect they have few competitors. They were a cheerful people, secure in their Valley, protected by desert and sea, delighting in the natural world, proud of their children, keen to record the triumphs, great or small, of their lives and so ensure the extension of those lives into eternity. As far as we can judge, most of the people of early Egypt were, with it all, essentially placid by temperament, confident in the security that nature and the kingship, when it came to rule their lives, had conferred upon them. They were lovers of gardens and inspired observers of the natural world, ready always to celebrate the abundant pleasures of life and living.

An exceptionally close relationship between the people of ancient Egypt and the animals around them is one of the fundamental marks of their civilisation, especially in the early centuries. It was their perception of the natural world that did much, if not all, to shape their world-view. In the early centuries of the development of their culture the Egyptians saw themselves at one with the natural world around them, where all living things – and even perhaps those that seemed to be inanimate – were part of the same cosmic totality, coterminous and, to an exceptional degree, coeval. They seem not to have assumed that they were necessarily different in essential being from or superior to the other forms of life with which they passed their lives. Their sense of identity with all the other aspects of the world that they shared shows them in their most engaging mood, revealing an extent of commitment to what they considered the proper order that might surprise and delight the most ardent environmentalist today.

This integration with the natural world is demonstrated by the attitude of the Egyptians to those forces that they apprehended as beyond nature but that yet remained part of it, those supposed supranatural powers that, for convenience sake, we define as 'gods'. The Egyptian communities of gods are particularly difficult for us to comprehend, for our understanding of what passes for divinity has been moulded by several thousand years of anthropomorphic god-making. This has resulted in the promotion of congresses of vicious, deceitful and libidinous beings, whose behaviour mirrors only too exactly the worst of human failings, raised to a suprahuman dimension. The Egyptian gods, certainly the most ancient of them, are an entirely different order of entities.

In the earliest periods of their existence as a nation the Egyptians' concept of divinity was quite other than that of the later periods of their history, as different as it was from the attitude to the possibility of divine involvement in human affairs that prevailed in other Near Eastern societies. In later times this included their own understanding of the transcendental when the original pristine quality of their culture and the beliefs which arose from it became infected by influences from beyond their frontiers, as non-Egyptians came increasingly to infiltrate the Valley. It is in the earliest centuries as a nation-state that the Egyptians' particular – and, to our eyes, peculiar – understanding of the numinous was first and most precisely articulated. In their first thousand years as a nation, which roughly bracketed the third millennium before our era, the Egyptians saw the divine as the empowering dynamic of the cosmos, which might be recognised and acknowledged in an infinite multiplicity of forms. The king, whose office was first defined by the people of the Valley long before kingship was, in the Sumerian phrase, 'handed down' to other peoples represented the most powerful and immediately identifiable manifestation of the divine in nature. The king was the god reincarnate, not merely an incarnate god but the supreme living form of the highest suprahuman principle. But the effulgence which indicated the presence of powers deemed to be far beyond the merely human dimension could be recognised everywhere in nature.

Egypt was, in the most literal sense, a theocracy since it was ruled by an eternally incarnate divinity Horus, the reincarnated heir of the leader of the founding spirits who had brought Egypt and its civilisation into being. This had nothing to do with religious observance in the sense that later cultures would understand the term. Religious practice, as a discrete function, was irrelevant since every action, every incident, every creature, every hour of the day and night proclaimed the immutable connection between Egypt and the immense principles which underlay the governance of the cosmos. In later times the people were spoken of as 'the cattle of God', existing for the king's sustenance but also entirely in his care. Even the animals were protected by the concept of right-doing, for, in the Pyramid Texts, the most ancient corpus of religious writings in the world, we learn that animals, on a par with humans, could accuse the king if he mistreated them. But religion, in the sense of a 'rule', requiring the adherents' obedience to its tenets, simply did not exist in early Egypt.

The institution of the kingship was fundamental to the development of the Egyptian state and was one of the most decisive political developments of human history. The creation of a hierarchic state, with its centre focused on the person of one man, had immense and truly long-lasting consequences. From this concept, one of the first and most daring of all political decisions undertaken by any people in antiquity, an entire system of government was devised based on a sophisticated and pervasive state bureaucracy, from which the control of the nation and its generally benign development became for the first time feasible, binding together many diverse and disparate components. Egypt's power and the brilliance of its early flowering are directly attributable to the elevation of one living man to supreme and unquestionable status in the society and the creation of a sophisticated, hierarchic structure to support him, focusing the entire productivity of the state on the personality of the ruler.

In the earliest years of the existence of the Egyptian state the king of Egypt assumed the role of the archetypal Great Individual, to borrow a term from analytical psychology[21] – indeed it might be said that he personified it, for in him the entire personality of the state was subsumed and expressed. But even here an analogy with the animal world is revealing: *Homo sapiens* is an ape with a particular chain of developed characteristics, of which consciousness and its communicable expression, speech, are perhaps the most significant. The king as Great Individual is a relic, perhaps more correctly the heir, of the dominant male who is found in primate societies, notably among the higher apes. It may confidently be asserted that Homo sapiens is one of the more exotically evolved of these higher apes, as baroque in its own way as the mandrill or some of the more colourful inhabitants of the South American rainforests. But behind the king, even behind the expression of him as god, stands the mist-shrouded figure of a gigantic Alpha male, the dominant member of the primate community.

The office of the king also recalled the leaders of the Neolithic hunting and foraging bands from which much of the Egyptian population in historic times directly descended and who inherited many of the attributes and prerogatives of the primate Alpha male. But the invention of all the paraphernalia of a state structure and the rapid growth in population to which the central organisation of the society was one of the most important contributors, had in the long run the paradoxical effect of alienating even the Egyptians from their proper place in nature. The nation-state leads inevitably to agglomerations of dependants even in such near-ideal circumstances as existed in early Egypt.

The close identification between the kingship, the state, the people and the animals with which they shared the world is asserted by the Egyptians' concern for their hounds, an expression of their more generalised appreciation of animals and their vision of them as their companions in the world they inhabited together. This is graphically demonstrated from the records of their lives, which range from rough engravings left by the herders and hunters on the rocks and rock walls of the deserts, to the elegant reliefs and paintings in a noble's tomb. Certainly, their affection did not prevent them from hunting animals (though not the dog) both for sport and as a food resource, in the latter case behaving much as the animals behaved to each other; the scenes of the butchering of bulls, for example, are distressing to a sensitive nature and contrast sharply with the honour otherwise paid to the bull, one of the avatars of the kingship. But their affection is shown by the myriad scenes of the tender care of young animals, for, as Herodotus, the Greek historian who visited Egypt in the fifth century BC and wrote the first considered foreigner's view of the country's history and its people, reported with wonder, the Egyptians were the only people who had their animals to live with them in their houses and who mourned the death of dogs (and cats) with great intensity.

On the death of a dog, Herodotus records, all the members of the household shaved the whole of their bodies and heads. Any food or drink in the house was forbidden for use. The dog was entombed and buried in its own 'sacred vault' in a canine cemetery amidst demonstrations of great grief. Herodotus was no doubt referring to the dog graves at Saqqara and at other sacred locations such as Abydos and Asyut, where, for reasons which will be considered later, there were extensive canine necropoleis. The dogs of the most distinguished Egyptians, including those who were the companions of kings, would merit even more grandiose sepulchres.[22]

The Egyptians delighted in portraying animals in their vibrant, subtle art with exceptional anatomical and zoological precision. This was the case even in predynastic times, very early in the emergence of a distinctive Egyptian culture in the deserts where the richest treasuries of rock art are located. Such representations did not, however, prevent them from depicting them also with affection and humour and sometimes with a cheerful disregard for literal accuracy, a circumstance that has sometimes an exasperating relevance to this study. The representations of canids seem frequently to ignore deliberately the differences between species, to the extent that there is often little agreement about which particular species it is the artist's intention to depict. Jackals, all manner of dogs and even foxes and hyenas are jumbled together in one glorious community, though hyenas belong to the family *Hyaenidae*. It may be that modern eyes expect too exact and accurate a depiction of the differences between the various species, when what mattered to the Egyptians was that all the animals concerned were of one kind, all of them carnivores, a fact that they seem certainly to have recognised.

It is clear that in many of the instances in which canids are represented, with the exception of the hunt and when participating in state occasions, the issue of whether the animal is a dog, a jackal, a wolf or even a fox is not especially material.[23] The qualities for which canids were recognised were acknowledged and in their representations came to stand for something very much more elevated than a simple pictorial record. Thus, the wild dog or jackal stalking through a graveyard on the edge of a Neolithic or late predynastic settlement could in another dimension of existence become the divine entity which led the justified dead to the Afterlife or, by extension, vigilantly guarded the place of communal burial.

Many other cultures, including the ancient Mexicans, Native Americans and the Japanese, have held the dog in special regard, attributing to it qualities that seem to link the worlds of the seen and the unseen. Sometimes dogs have been victims, sacrificed and sent to the other world as messengers; as we may see, this even happened in Egypt, notably in predynastic times. But in such cases and those in which the dog fulfils a purely utilitarian function – herding, guarding sheep or cattle and the like – or merely being tolerated and otherwise ignored, there is no evidence of so deep an affection as the Egyptians reveal. Nor in later times, when other cultures had as many means of communicating with succeeding generations as did the Egyptians, do we find comparable traditions recorded among other peoples of the ancient world until the arrival of the Greeks in the middle centuries of the first millennium BC.

The Egyptian enthusiasm for dogs and their integration into society was the first example of a community advancing the process of the domestication of a species to the point where its members became as much companions and friends as they might serve a more prosaic or practical function, as it might be as guards or adjuncts to the hunt. The archaeological evidence of the process of integration is sparse and often inferential until the period of Egyptian history known as the Old Kingdom (c. 2686–c. 2181 BC) is reached. From that point on, however, the evidence from archaeology and the built heritage of Egypt is extensive.

Although Egypt did not play a significant part in the original domestication of the principal species, as early as the Old Kingdom in the third millennium BC the people of the Valley experimented with the taming of several exotic species, including antelope, gazelle, ibex and hyena; the last-named may have been used in hunting. There are reliefs of hyena on a leash, walking placidly behind a keeper, in a late Old Kingdom tomb, for example.[24] That they did conduct such experiments, unsuccessful though they may have been, demonstrates their deep-rooted interest in the management of animals and assumes the long-term observation of them and their ways, an interest that they retained throughout most of their long history.

Egypt's economy in historic times was essentially pastoral and agricultural, a fact that determined its character when the communities strung out along the River Nile coalesced into the first nation-state. Before the sixth millennium BC the human presence in the Valley was quite sparse, though two exceptionally early modern human remains have been recovered from the south of Egypt.

One is of a male at Nazlet Khater at the site of Boulder Hill, situated between Asyut and Nag Hammadi, 20 kilometres north-west of Tahta, dated to 30,000 BC;[25] the site is the location of an exceptionally early mining experiment. The oldest human remains in all Egypt thus far discovered are of a child at Taramsa Hill, near Dendera, dated to 55,000 BC;[26] this burial represents the earliest evidence of anatomically modern humans in the Valley.

Lower and Middle Stone Age sites (c. 700,000–250,000 BP; 70,000–25,000 BP) have been recorded in the Valley, but whilst these revealed the presence of hunter–gatherer–scavengers they also indicated the absence of permanent human occupation on any significant scale; at this time the Valley was a paradise for animals, including large mammals such as elephant, hippopotamus and giraffe, which inhabited the river margins and the lush regions fertilised by the Nile's annual inundation. The human component in the Valley's population was confined to occasional, particularly valiant or determined groups of hunters such as those who followed the herds of wild cattle, the massive aurochs, Bos primigenius, which later were particularly well established in the northern reaches of the Valley, but which were also known from sites in the south. The wild bull was to become one of the most enduring animal archetypes in Egypt in historic times, particularly associated with the kingship.

The pursuit of the herds by African hunters appears to have precipitated an extraordinarily precocious, if ultimately unsuccessful, attempt at the cultivation of cereals and possibly also of cattle husbandry. Burials at Tushka[27] in Lower Nubia, dated to the twelfth millennium before the present, were marked by the skulls of Bos primigenius bulls, the earliest evidence of the presence of the bull as a powerful element of funerary cults in Egypt. The burials at Tushka anticipate by many millennia the time to come, especially from the late fifth/early fourth millennia onwards, when the wild bull would become the most important of all the manifestations of the divine in animal form, not only in Egypt but throughout the ancient world.[28]

The very significant changes in climate which affected much of the Old World in the aftermath of the end of the last Ice Age continued long after the withdrawal of the ice sheets. Thus conditions in much of what are today the desert regions of North Africa, the Sahara, the Egyptian deserts and the arid lands of the Arabian peninsula, all of which escaped the incursion of the ice flows, were considerably more benign with a savanna environment prevailing over much of the area. This environment developed as the response to periods of increased precipitation and the creation of bodies of standing

water, which in turn were the result of rises in the water table. More arid
conditions eventually supervened and the hunters who continued to follow
the herds from East Africa met and, as far as we can tell, merged with the
pastoralists and hunters who moved eastwards from the Sahara towards the
Valley. Their migration was necessitated by the increasing desiccation of
the rich grasslands of the western Sahara and its consequent assumption
of the desert character which typifies so much of North Africa today. This
merging of the several Neolithic populations that came together in the Nile
Valley has been studied only in comparatively recent times but it is from
this phenomenon that the historic Egyptian population, culture and state
developed. The discovery of an advanced Neolithic culture flourishing in the
Sudan as early as the fifth millennium BC, for example, has brought about
the modification of many previously held beliefs about the conditions which
applied over the ancient Near East in the Neolithic period.[29]

The two groups, from the south and west, coalesced and by the beginning of the sixth millennium a sizeable population, augmented by speakers
of a proto-Semitic language from beyond the north-eastern reaches of the
Valley (though their influence at this time was not great), was enjoying the
exceptional abundance that the Nile's annual inundation brought to the land.
The hunters from East Africa and their successors, together with the inheritors
of the Sudanese Neolithic, brought with them much of the African influence
which was always a most important component in the historic Egyptian
personality. It is possible that a fourth group, the ancestors of the Badarian
culture, which was the first to be identified in southern Egypt (see below
p. 31), also came into the Valley at this time, perhaps approaching it through
the wadi systems of the eastern desert.

The presence of the North African pastoralists and hunters in the savanna of
the central and western Sahara over many centuries is known by the treasury
of rock art that they also left in much of what is now inhospitable desert.[30]
In the aftermath of the last Ice Age, with the consequent changes in climate
resulting in increased levels of precipitation, this region was a comparatively
lush and verdant pasture land on which herds of wild cattle flourished. Wild
cattle required large and regular supplies of water to survive, and it is known
that in prehistoric times there were reserves of standing water in many parts
of the North African savanna, a situation that was duplicated in northern
Arabia. Before the onset of the hyper-arid conditions that have prevailed for
the past four to five thousand years in all of these areas, local variations of

climate and precipitation, brought about by the agency of storms and sustained periods of humidity, produced marked local differences of conditions between one region and another. The paintings and engravings that the North Africans left on every available and appropriate surface, in caves, on rocky overhangs, standing boulders and outcrops, depict with immediacy and wonderful skill the cattle and the hunters who, aided by their dogs, preyed on them. The later onset of pastoralism is signalled by the appearance of domesticated cattle, recognisable by their mottled or speckled pelage and the herders rather than hunters who managed them, again accompanied by dogs.

Egypt's immensely rich resource of the rock art of the Neolithic period provides insights, in the same way as do the works of the Saharan people, into the way of life of the inhabitants of the Valley, in times long before literacy. The scenes that are engraved, pecked or hammered on to the surfaces of standing rocks, overhangs and shelters in the southern deserts comprise an encyclopaedia of information on the life, beliefs and occupations of the early Egyptians, before the rise of the kingship and the Egyptian state. The scenes depicted reveal the elements of continuity that link this segment of the Valley's history with the long sequence of kings who ruled the Two Lands for the next three thousand years, from the last quarter of the fourth millennium. Egypt was still essentially a Neolithic community, little different from all such communities across the ancient world; there was little to indicate the extraordinary flowering of so high a culture that would sweep through the Valley in the first half of the fourth millennium and throughout the third millennium BC.

The scenes depicted on the rock surfaces are striking in the immediacy of the impact that they make – almost as if they were drawings, quickly sketched – and often for their enigmatic quality, depicting situations and personages whose nature is entirely obscure. Many, naturally enough, record the hunt and the immemorial interplay between the people and the animals with which the river banks and the desert teemed. Inevitably, dogs were there, working with the hunters, as they were to do for centuries to come.

The physical appearance of the dogs at this time, as exemplified in the rock art, is particularly interesting. In the early engravings, in the late fifth and early fourth millennia, the most frequently represented dog looks more like a modern terrier, one of the larger strains, stocky and notably deep-chested, with fairly short legs and a flowing tail. The slender, elegant prick-eared hound of the tjesm strain does occasionally appear but it is not as ubiquitous as it will become. It may be that already natural selection is at work, favouring the taller, more slender and lighter-built dog evolving in the desert conditions, which would have encouraged what was to become the normal physiology of the tjesm, whereas the stockier dog may have evolved in the savanna. Some of the dogs show the elements of both the sturdier build of the dog that is usually called a pariah and the longer, lighter frame of the tjesm. The dogs in the rock carvings are also sometimes shown leashed, indicating that even at this time and in the relatively primitive conditions of the early desert hunt hounds are already managed and controlled.

The rock-art of ancient Egypt is so extensive a phenomenon in the southern deserts that it was soon identified by early Egyptologists as demanding study. Flinders Petrie, often considered the father of British Egyptology and one of the most important influences in the development of the discipline in the first half of the twentieth century, compiled records of the principal themes of the rock art that he found in his early explorations of the southern Valley. Similarly, Arthur Weigall, a tireless populariser of ancient Egypt at the beginning of the twentieth century, wrote of many rock art sites and published some of the first photographs of the rock surfaces which bore the engravings. In Travels in the Upper Egyptian Deserts,[31] published in 1909, he illustrated many engravings and inscriptions, though the animals of the hunt were not a principal interest for him.

There are several more recent and comprehensive published collections of the rock art of the predynastic southern Valley which followed the work of pioneers like Petrie and Weigall. The most extensive and the best known is that compiled by Hans Winkler in the 1930s and published immediately before the Second World War in two handsome volumes.[32] The sites which he described, illustrated by many excellent photographs, are situated between Qena and Aswan, a region which is particularly rich in the art.

One of the incursive peoples whom Winkler categorised as the creators of the various artistic styles that he defined and to which he gave a name was the 'Eastern Invaders', whom he considered to be immigrants into the Valley and whom he identified especially by the representations of boats of a type that he classified as 'Mesopotamian'. Winkler's work drew attention to the frequency with which large sailing and rowing craft were depicted, in remote desert locations. Because many of the boats do seem to be of typical Mesopotamian form their presence has fuelled the debate on whether the Mesopotamian influences which have long been detected in the late

Figure 1   The Eastern Desert of Upper Egypt is a rich resource of petroglyphs, rock drawings and engravings created over many centuries by hunters following the game and, later, by herdsmen.

1a   A typically enigmatic scene: a commanding, perhaps divine figure stands in a boat with a high prow and stern, accompanied by a quadruped. In front of the boat two horned animals are confronted by a small hound whilst two 'warriors' with tall plumes in their hair stand nearby; the smaller of the pair appears to be handing a bow to his companion.

1b   The hound attending another warrior/ hunter appears to be threatening an ostrich, as the warrior shoots at it with bow and arrow.

1c   Attributed by Winkler to the work of the 'Earliest Hunters' this scene shows a group of men, the principal of whom has strangely exaggerated physical features. One of the men leads a hound on a leash.

predynastic cultures of the southern part of the Valley were introduced by seaborne 'invaders'. In his commentary Winkler noted that 'occasionally the greyhound occurs in drawings of these invaders'.[33] A number of the boats contain animals and it has been suggested that they may have been intended for sacrifice. It does not appear that the dog was among them; rather, the dog was already the hunter's partner.

It is probable that some of the scenes depicted in the rock art may have a ritual or cultic significance. In many cases large, generally male figures with high, plumed headdresses stand in boats or in the midst of a hunting scene and have been interpreted as divine beings (Figure 1a). It is likely that there were rituals connected with the hunt and there is some evidence of what look to be sacrificial acts in the course of the hunt or in preparation for it. Examples are known of hunters with bow and arrow apparently shooting a tethered bovine or sometimes a captive ostrich (Figures 1b, 1c).

What is certain is that many of the most frequent themes of historic Egyptian sacred and funerary decoration – the hunt, the divine and other figures carried on boats and the celebration of the beauty, dignity and integrity of the natural world – had their beginnings in the myriad rock drawings and engravings from the Egyptian deserts. It seems likely that the concept underlying the origin of the Egyptian animal cults, as was indeed the case in other ancient hunting cultures, is that of honouring the animal which is the object of the hunt and, by paying reverence to it, deflecting its anger or ill-will from the community that hunts it. Though such an attitude may seem bizarre to the modern mind, there have been plenty of parallels among surviving hunter–gatherer communities to make the likelihood of the predynastic Egyptians following the same process very probable at the least. In the case of the Egyptian examples, the killing of the animals is made especially portentous by the fact that each could be the manifestation or 'herald' of a divinity.

Soon after the publication of the results of Winkler's explorations a British scholar, J.H. Dunbar, published a survey of rock inscriptions in northern Nubia[34] (Figure 2). This presented material obtained in a series of explorations in the deserts of Northern Nubia, to the south of Winkler's territory, which were carried out between 1929 and 1939. Like Winkler, Dunbar illustrates a range of rock carvings and engravings and many themes similar to those from Winkler's journeys. Dogs feature more frequently in his photographs, including a hound or jackal in the company of a herd of giraffe, a hound with long-horned cattle, two hounds on leashes,[35] a handsome running hound,[36]

Figure 2   Petroglyphs, showing a variety of hounds,
carved on the rocks of the Nubian desert.

four hounds together and a pack of hounds harrying a quarry. One dog is represented according to Dunbar, 'without ears'; it may be that a drop-eared dog of the Saluqi type is intended, rather than the tjesm that appears in the majority of the illustrations.

Dunbar writes extensively on the dogs pictured in the rock-art tradition with which he is concerned. Among the observations that he makes is the absence of the dog in scenes in which elephant appear; this, he suggests, is because the elephant had already withdrawn from this part of the Valley before the dog arrived.[37] Recent excavations in the desert around Hierakonpolis, just north of the area surveyed by Dunbar, have revealed what may be burials of elephants which have been ritually slain and of some of the hunters who pursued them.[38] By the time of the engravings that Winkler and Dunbar recorded, most of the large game had migrated further to the south, deep into Nubia, driven there by the forays of hunters and their dogs in the Egyptian part of the Valley. Dunbar proposed that the arrival of the hound coincided with the introduction of the bow and arrow; whilst the employment of hounds undoubtedly represents a refinement of hunting techniques, the use of the bow and arrow had long preceded the likely date of the Nubian engravings, which come from the late predynastic period in the second half of the fourth millennium BC. Rock carvings from Bir Hima in Western Arabia, dated to the seventh millennium BC, already show warriors armed with bows.[39]

At least two of the pictures that Dunbar illustrates show dogs with tightly curled tails, a characteristic of the tjesm that was much favoured in later, Old Kingdom times. He compares these to the dogs on the Hemaka disc, a product of the later First Dynasty, which will be further described below, and makes the interesting comment that 'the nearest modern approach I know to the Old Kingdom dog is the Nyem-Nyem of Southern Sudan'.[40] He describes a bitch of the breed that he once owned which, 'though small, was of greyhound build and had a greyhound's coat, whilst her ears and tail were exactly like those of the Old Kingdom dog'.[41] He remarks that 'the most peculiar characteristic of the Nyem-Nyem dog is that it cannot bark',[42] an observation that prompts the speculation that the dog is in fact more closely related to the Basenji than the tjesm, which, to judge by its modern counterparts, must have been an enthusiastic vocalist. It is doubtful if the Nyem-Nyem is in any way related to the tjesm.

In the 1970s Gerald Fuchs carried out an important investigation of the engravings on the rock surfaces of the Wadi el-Barramiyya, in the south-eastern desert, close to a major trading route that in ancient times led to the gold mines that supplied much of that precious metal for the temples and palaces.[43] His was one of the most productive surveys since Winkler's. Like Winkler he recorded many of the 'Mesopotamian-style' boats that are widely depicted in this region, though it lies far away from the river. He reproduces a scene of a dog following an ibex and trying to separate its kid, a fine and rather affecting piece of observation.[44] In one very extensive sequence he shows a mêlée of dogs, ibexes, antelopes and men with bows and what appear to be whips or lassoes,[45] a scene also recorded by Winkler.

Another, well-equipped and well-focused series of expeditions in the Eastern Desert under the style 'The Followers of Horus', led by David Rohl,

Figure 3 Hounds are also present at predynastic desert sites recorded by a more recent survey conducted in the same region as that surveyed by Winkler.

3a   From the Wadi Barramiya, a quite complex scene of a pack of hounds harassing an antelope, attended by two huntsmen with whips or, possibly, lassoes or bolases.

3b   From Wadi Umm Hajali. A horned quadruped seems to be chasing a hound attacking an ostrich, which flees in evident alarm.

have revisited Winkler's sites and reviewed his work.[46] Many of the sites have been lost over the intervening 60 years and more; the 'Followers of Horus' expeditions have also identified others, several of which are of particular importance. The region in which the rock art is located was climatically somewhat more benign in the predynastic period and would have supported more life, both animal and human. It was good hunting country, hence the concentration of rock-art in what is now a particularly desolate region.

Many of the sites pictured high-prowed 'Mesopotamian' boats and the mysterious standing figures, generally represented as of superhuman scale, sometimes nude, sometimes wearing what look to be short tunics, or long, caftan-like robes. In one scene in the Wadi Barramiya, which was also recorded by Fuchs, two of these enigmatic figures wearing double plumes stand beside a high-prowed boat, a horned animal and two hunting dogs, both deep-chested, attended by a smaller hunter, with a single plume or feather in his hair. In the same location another scene shows a pack of hounds harrying antelope and asses, attended by hunters, two of whom frame the scene, almost heraldically. They too are carrying long bolases or, possibly, whips[47] (Figure 3a).

In the Wadi Mineh (South) is a scene in which a group of hounds, their prick-ears indicating that they are *tjesm*, are among a mixed herd of antelope and ibex. A huntsman with a single plume is gesturing, and, as in the earlier examples cited, the hounds appear to be attempting to separate a young ibex from the rest of the group.

Another lively scene is to be found in the Wadi Abu Markab-el-nes. A hound, in a flying leap, pursues an ostrich that hurries away, its small wings raised in an almost comic expression of alarm[48] (Figure 3b). In another scene hunters with dogs are lassoing or tethering animals. It is notable that in all these episodes of the hunt the hounds and many of the other animals are represented more literally than their human companions. The hounds' enjoyment of their tasks is also very evident.

When the paintings of the Central Sahara were first discovered and recorded, what appeared to be stylistic similarities with Egyptian art were immediately recognised; this led to the conclusion that the artists of the Sahara had been influenced by the Egyptians.[49] In fact the Saharan paintings date from long before the first flowering of Egypt's historic culture. There may be little doubt that it was the Saharan artists who influenced the Egyptians, as a result of their migration to the Valley after conditions in the Sahara deteriorated and could not sustain the herds of cattle and other large game animals on which the people depended.

The Saharan paintings are greatly different in execution from the Egyptian rock-art though they deal with very much the same material and situations. There are very few examples of paintings in the Egyptian deserts, but it is the work of the artists who produced this Saharan resource of the highest quality, dating from the end of the fifth millennium BC onwards, that must have inspired some at least of the later Egyptian genius for painting and the carving of the reliefs which make the walls of the tombs of the magnates of the Old Kingdom so unique a record of life in the Valley.

One of the animals attending both the hunters and the herders which is encountered in the Saharan rock engravings and paintings is a hound with notably pricked ears, a feature that gives the dog a particularly lively, alert appearance like that of the tjesm, one which is sometimes expressed, in terminologies applied to the characteristics of breeds of dogs, as 'tulip ears'. As with dogs portrayed in the Egyptian engravings, in the earliest examples the hound is quite powerfully built; later, again as in Egypt, a more slender dog comes to predominate, which, as we have seen, is most probably the result of selection for speed and in response to the hot, increasingly desert conditions in which it was living. This dog is similar in build to the Egyptian hunting hound and is possibly one of its ancestors.

Similar, if generally less skilfully executed, petroglyphs of hunters, their prey and their dogs, with the same slender, prick-eared hounds very like their Saharan cousins, are found on many rock-faces in Western Arabia. There, in conditions similar to those which persisted in the Sahara, large brackish lakes provided the water necessary for the sustenance of the wild cattle which roamed the savanna-like lands. The desiccation of Arabia, which occurred at the same time and under similar conditions as the increase of aridity in the Sahara, can be traced in the petroglyphs left by the Arabian hunters as conditions forced the cattle – and hence the hunters – to move southwards down the length of the peninsula. Their journey began around 6000 BC. Then *circa* 2000 BC, having reached the edge of the Empty Quarter, Ar-Rub al-Khali, where once had been brackish lakes supporting exotic game such as hippopotamus, they could go no further.[50]

The tall, slender hounds that appear on the rock carvings of North Africa, Egypt, Nubia and Arabia all belong to the family of greyhounds. They were all bred for the chase and are an exclusive though geographically widely distributed group. They are also very ancient, indicating that their selection for speed, stamina and the ability to thrive in hot climates, which made them the companions of the early hunters, began a very long time ago. The Egyptian hunting hound is one of these, as is the Saluqi, which is associated more with Mesopotamia, Persian lands and Arabia, though it does appear later in Egypt, in the Middle Kingdom (2055–1650 BC) and especially in New Kingdom times (1550–1069 BC). These dogs are sometimes confused and are difficult to distinguish by skeletal evidence, but they are quite distinct. The probable evolution of the greyhound has been expressed thus:

> The greyhound group, of which the saluqi is the most elegant, probably evolved out of the aboriginal dogs of Egypt and Western Asia very early on, for long-legged, narrow headed dogs [appear] in the Egyptian tomb paintings from around 2000 BC. That these early greyhounds were owned and valued is shown by the wide collars and leashes pictured on some of the wall paintings of dogs.[51]

It should be noted in passing that representations of the Egyptian Hound appear long before 2000 BC and more generally in reliefs on the walls of the tombs, rather than in paintings.

Figure 4 The Golenishchef dish is a
survival from the early Naqada period that
indicates that the management of hounds was
already practised at the very commencement
of Egypt's development as a state.

One of the likely routes of entry into Egypt for many of the founder
stocks of the domesticates was through the north-eastern approaches, skirt-
ing the eastern Delta and coming into the northern Sinai. In historic times
this was known as 'The Way of Horus', the route that, according to legend,
was taken by the 'Followers of Horus'; Horus was the divine ruler who was
forever reincarnated in the person of the king. The arrival of the Followers
of Horus, who provided one of the fabulous semi-divine dynasties of Egypt
in legendary times supposedly long before the creation of the Egyptian state,
was celebrated throughout the Pharaonic period. The knowledge that the
early inhabitants of Egypt were not indigenous but migrated to the Valley
from outside was evidently thus preserved over many thousands of years,
throughout the entire sweep of Egyptian history.

At the point when the migrations into Egypt had seeded the historic
population and the first, relatively sophisticated cultures appear we find
evidence of the presence of dogs and of their evident domestication arising from what must have been generations of selection. The most ancient
depiction of Egyptian hunting hounds is to be found on a pottery dish, once
held in a pre-revolutionary Russian collection, the Golenishchef dish[52] (Figure
4), on the base of which a man, presumably a huntsman or a warrior for
he carries a bow, stands with four hounds held on leashes. The dish dates

from the Naqada I period (c. 3800–3600 BC), more than half a millennium
before the accepted date for the Unification of Egypt and the creation of the
First Dynasty. That four dogs are held in this way may have had a symbolic
significance, as four leashed hounds are often represented in later reliefs and
paintings (for example, drawing the sun-god's solar boat across the sky) and
in representations of the mysterious 'Souls of Nekhen', reputedly the spirits
of the kings of Upper Egypt of predynastic times, where they appear as four
black hounds or jackals. Nekhen was the ancient name for the town called
Hierakonpolis ('Hawk City') by the Greeks. It was the most important political
centre in the southern Nile Valley during the late predynastic period and was
of great significance in the development of the archaic kingship. The 'Souls of
Nekhen' and the Souls of other places, which were manifestations of canines
as divinities or sacred creatures, will be further considered in Chapter 5. In
any event, hounds were evidently a familiar and acknowledged part of the
Egyptian scene very early in the fourth millennium.

The figure holding the hounds is also himself interesting. He stands in an
almost balletic pose, as if leaping. He appears to be naked and has a feather
in his hair. He holds the leashes in his right hand, the bow in his left. This
weapon and the way in which he holds it are identical to the representations
of the hunter/warrior on the rock carving at Bir Hima in Western Arabia,[53]
which may be even earlier than that of the hunter on the Golenishchef dish;
the Bir Hima warrior, in turn, is almost precisely paralleled by the men on
the 'Hunters' Palette', an important late-predynastic Egyptian artefact, which
is discussed below. The timescale which these portraits of predynastic hunters
represent spans nearly three thousand years.

That the hounds are constrained in the way indicated on the Golenishchef
dish at so early a period, and that they are shown as morphologically distinct,
indicates that they were already prized and protected and it must be assumed
that their selection, breeding and care had been in place for many canine
generations. Writing of the Golenishchef dish the distinguished Egyptological
prehistorian, Elise J. Baumgartel, observed that the leashed dogs had been
described as 'Libyan greyhounds, a species still nowadays used as hunting dogs
by Hamitic tribes of Central Africa'. Whilst it may be questioned whether the
African dogs are actually of the same race as the dogs pictured on the dish,
the association with Libya is pertinent, given the probability that migrants
from North Africa and their dogs had moved eastwards towards the Valley
in Neolithic times.[54]

Throughout the Old Kingdom the hounds are sometimes shown as leashed and restrained by a huntsman but more frequently running free; hence it must be that they were trained to return to their handler or to wait by the prey until the handler came. It is this element of evident training that clearly indicates that they must also have been accustomed to obey a repertory of commands or signals. The ancestors of the Egyptian hound of historic times would have been carefully selected to maintain the qualities and appearance that the early Egyptians evidently admired – elegance, lithe strength, stamina, alertness; the process of selection must therefore have begun long before the time when the settled population began to establish itself in the Valley. By the time that the dogs had become fully integrated into the society, the hunting hound was evidently distinct and the 'breed', if such a term, however anachronistic, may be used, was securely established.

Hilzheimer commented on this aspect of the hunting hound in his 1932 article:

> much care must have been taken to keep them pure-bred. They are always depicted with long, pointed, fine heads, ears stiff and sharply erect, and a tightly-curled tail like that of a pug. According to Egyptian ideas this curly tail must have formed a sign of good breeding for it is always carefully represented in all works of art, often to an exaggerated degree. Obviously the Egyptians were especially proud of this characteristic, quite unnatural in a greyhound, who needs a long tail to guide himself; it must therefore have been extremely difficult to achieve by breeding.[55]

He questions whether the other dogs associated with the tjesm, the dogs from the Mediterranean islands, for example, which appear to share many of the Egyptian hound's characteristics (and which are further described in Chapter 4) are of the same or a related breed. Hilzheimer remarks that he has 'proved' that the skull formation which is characteristic of the 'Eurasiatic greyhound' exists in the

> early Egyptian mummified dogs. On the other hand these mummified skulls correspond very closely to one of the three Egyptian types of jackal, the Canis lupaster.... I believe therefore that the Tesem represents a very ancient Egyptian breed. My opinion is strengthened by the fact that the ancient Egyptians were complete masters of the art of domestication, and tamed a large number of animals which were not so elsewhere.[56]

The earliest culture to be identified in the south of the Valley is the Badarian (c. 5000–4000 BC), which flourished even before the period from which the dish with the four leashed hounds is dated. It was from the south that the dynamic that powered Egyptian culture and society always came, and the Badarian was one of the cultures seminal to the development of the Egypt of historic times.

The Badarians were agriculturists and the makers of a particularly fine pottery, of an exceptionally thin, hard fabric. They maintained connections with the Red Sea, at least to the extent of using shells from that region for decoration. They also seem to have been aware of the influences from Western Asia which were already percolating into the Valley. It used to be said that there was no archaeological evidence for the domestication of the dog in the Badarian period, whilst there was ample evidence for the domestication of sheep and goats, showing that these animals had already been brought into the Valley from abroad. However, it is now known that the skulls of dogs, as well as those of sheep, goats, antelope, cats and jackals, were regularly placed alongside the deceased in graves of the period;[57] the assumption that the dogs at least, and probably the sheep and goats and, less certainly, the cat, were domesticated is reasonable. At Maadi, animals were also laid in their own graves among the human burials: the species represented there were antelope, sheep and dog. Like their human counterparts they were wrapped in skins, though they were buried without grave goods. Clearly the animals were prized, and, with the likely exception of the antelope, were already domesticated.[58]

The remains of the dog excavated from Merimde Beni Salame in the Northwestern Delta in the northern reaches of the country are dated to circa 4800 BC,[59] thus very early in the equivalent Badarian times in the south. Merimde is a large site, covering over 50 acres of occupation, one of the earliest settlements in Egypt. It provides evidence of the oldest fully developed Neolithic culture in Egypt and its pottery is directly related to that of the early Neolithic of south-west Asia, particularly of the Levant. The people of Merimde were hunters and preyed on gazelle, antelope and ostriches; in all probability the dog whose remains were found in the earliest settlement levels was already their partner in the hunt, as these quarries would certainly demand pursuit in open country. The evidence of occupation at Merimde occurs early in the time of the migrations that first populated Egypt, the northern location of the burial perhaps implying that the dog (or its ancestors) came from one of the North African migrations which were set in train as the Sahara became increasingly arid. The dog is found with other domestic species from the earliest stratum of settlement onwards, with cattle, pigs and a few goats.

It is not unlikely that when the hunters from East Africa began to settle in the Valley they brought dogs with them and that the dogs merely followed the cattle migrations and the hunters, opportunistically. It may be relevant to this proposition that the Basenji and the Rhodesian Ridgeback (though the latter is a comparatively recent introduction to the catalogue of recognised breeds) have a number of characteristics in common with the Egyptian hound; in particular the Basenji's coloration and its tightly curled tail are strikingly like some of the representations of Egyptian dogs, especially those depicted on the rock drawings of predynastic times. The Basenji is most likely descended from an ancient Congolese dog whilst the Ridgeback seems to have been developed by European settlers, crossing imported dogs with native Africanis.[60] There are other similarities too, which will be discussed later.

Diverse places of origin for Egypt's founder stocks of domesticated dogs have been suggested, though there is little hard evidence for any of them, other than the notable iconographic evidence left by the Saharan hunters. Another possible location is the land of Punt (Pwene). This quasi-legendary region, the source of Egypt's supplies of incense and spices, monkeys and all manner of exotic importations in later times, may have been located in Eritrea in Somalia; another location for Punt which is not infrequently proposed is southern Arabia. Throughout Egyptian history Punt was regarded as a magical land, full of wonders.

In historic times Punt was a source for the exporting of dogs to Egypt and there is a tradition that tjesm were imported from there.[61] This may be a significant pointer at least to one of the dogs' places of origin; East Africa, the most likely location of Punt, is also part of the domain of the golden jackal. As the Badarians are known to have maintained contact with the Red Sea coast, this putative connection with Punt may be significant, though, at so early a date, any contact is likely to have been by land, travelling up the coastal strip, rather than by sea. The Naqada I people, whose culture succeeded that of the Badarians, seem to have had close links with the Badarians and may be their descendants; the Naqada period, which Egyptology divides into three principal phases, was one of intense and rapid development in Egypt, which would lead, in a few hundred years, to the formation of the world's first nation-state – and, it will be said again, of the world's first nation of dog-lovers.

One of the animals that was brought into Egypt during the period when Western Asiatic influences were permeating the Valley was a massive, heavily built dog of the mastiff type. This dog seems to have been one of the contributions made to the fauna of ancient Egypt by the travellers from south-west Asia who, it must be presumed, actually entered Egypt, for there are many strong south-west Asian influences apparent in southern Upper Egypt at this time. It is probable that there were immigrants, or perhaps more occasional visitors, in Egypt from Sumer (southern Mesopotamia) and Elam (south-western Iran) during this period, the late fourth millennium BC.

In the years that immediately precede the foundation of the Dual Kingship the mastiff seems to have been popular, and models of it have been recovered from important predynastic sites such as Hierakonpolis. A well-known example of this type of dog in the art of the late predynastic period is to be found in the decoration of a ceremonial knife from Gebel el-Arak, on the ivory hilt of which a pair of heavily built dogs attend a powerful male figure[62] who is shown dominating or subduing two lions, a familiar Western Asiatic theme motif. He has been identified as a very early manifestation of the god Anhur, the patron of This, one of the cities which was of great importance in the establishment of the kingship and which was particularly associated with the kings of the First Dynasty. He is dressed in what looks suspiciously like Sumerian clothing, a long coat or caftan and a round turban, a head-dress typical of the statues and reliefs of Sumerian divinities in the early third millennium.[63] The lions are heavily maned and have been described as belonging to the Asiatic subspecies, rather than being African lions, as they might have been expected to be in such a context. The knife would seem to display a number of distinctly Western Asiatian elements, including mythical animals more at home in a Western Asiatic context than in Egypt and boats that, more arguably, have been described as Mesopotamian.

The two dogs stand with their ears pricked alertly; their necks seem to be longer than would be appropriate for examples of the mastiff-type, which their heavy build has been taken to suggest, and their muzzles are also longer than would be with the mastiff. They are shown as wearing collars of the sort that the tjesm in later times often wears. That they are undoubtedly more substantially built than the tjesm of historic times may suggest that they are examples of a transitional form between the rather squat dog of the early predynastic period, to be found in the earliest rock art for example, and the more finely boned tjesm, and they may be a variant of the Mesopotamian mastiff.

5a Hound with plant.

5b Hound and falcon.

5c Hound and tree.

5d Canine with plant.

Figure 5 The excavation of what proved to be the largest elite tomb in the Nile Valley at Abydos, which was attributed to a ruler probably named Scorpion (some two centuries earlier than the king of the same name commemorated on the great mace head from Hierakonpolis), produced a group of ivory labels that have been described as early examples of hieroglyphs. Their discovery and this interpretation of them have pushed back the origins of writing in Egypt by at least two hundred years. A number of the labels bear representations of canines, though it is not yet evident whether these are intended to be recognised as hounds or as more generalised expressions of the manifestations of divinities.

Intriguing depictions of canids appear in one of the most important
Egyptological discoveries of recent times, the excavation of Tomb Uj at
Abydos[64] (Figure 5). This, described by its excavators as the largest predynastic
tomb in the Valley, was evidently built for one of the rulers of Upper Egypt,
circa 3300 BC. It is a substantial construction and testifies to a high degree
both of building technique and of prosperity in one of the principal centres
of emerging political power in the Valley, centuries before the process leading
to the Unification was fulfilled. It is thought that the tomb was the resting
place of a King Scorpion, his status revealed by an ivory sceptre which was
found in the tomb. This was not the Scorpion long known from the great
ceremonial mace head showing him opening a canal that was recovered
from Hierakonpolis, but another, earlier, prince of the same name, ruling
from Abydos.

Although the tomb had long ago been robbed, the German excavators
recovered from it important and wholly unexpected evidence of the origins
of Egyptian hieroglyphs, in the form of a quantity of small ivory labels,
probably used to identify merchandise or tax receipts sent to Abydos from
outlying districts. The labels represent signs that are phonetic, conveying
word meanings: many of them are of animals and one is an unmistakeable
tjesm hound. The German excavators suggest that some of the animals may
represent chieftains or members of a royal dynasty; another of the animals
is the elephant, and the discovery of what appear to be ritual burials of
elephants at Hierakonpolis has supported the same possibility.

One of the engravings on an Abydos label is particularly arresting for it
shows the animal in the unmistakeable form of the tjesm which is typical of
later, Old Kingdom representations of a tall hound with powerful shoulders
and the characteristic, upstanding pointed ears. This is significant, given the
early date at which the labels were made, when the hounds shown on the
contemporary rock engravings (and the painting from Tomb 100, which will
be described below) are still the stocky, heavy-chested dog from which it
has been proposed the more elegant tjesm was bred. The Abydos label would
seem to call this into question and to advance the possibility at least that the
classic form of the tjesm was already present in the Valley as early as 3300 BC,
perhaps already being associated with the ruling elite. The discovery of these
early hieroglyphic labels at Abydos extends the invention of writing in Egypt
significantly further back than hitherto was accepted, putting it into the range
of the invention of writing in Sumer and possibly anticipating it.

The well-published painting found in Tomb 100 at Hierakonpolis is a unique survival from the third quarter of the fourth millennium. Like Tomb Uj at Abydos, Tomb 100 was probably the burial place of one of the 'kings' of the time immediately before the foundation of the Dual Kingdom, a momentous event that is described below. The tomb is dated circa 3300 BC,[65] considerably earlier than the date ascribed to the Gebel el-Arak knife but conforming precisely to the date ascribed to Tomb Uj. The scenes the painting depicts are complex: a hunt, sailing ships, ritual dances, the slaughter of prisoners; cattle are present, and with them prick-eared hounds. The paintings in Tomb 100 were unfortunately lost, as was the whereabouts of the tomb itself; they are known only from photographs and copies made at the time of their discovery in 1898.[66] The dogs shown herding or harrying the animals in what is presumably a hunting scene are the first to appear in the decoration of a tomb, though the Abydos labels are now to be added to the repertory of hound images from this early time.

That dogs were already loved and valued companions when Hierakonpolis was first a flourishing metropolis, and an important centre of the burgeoning 'royal cult', has been revealed by excavations there in recent years. Among the graves excavated were several which were dated to the Naqada I period by examination of the pottery recovered from Tomb 13. The burial in the grave, so far as it could be reconstructed, was of two young males, an adolescent and a young adult, accompanied by the remains of what were described as 'domesticated dogs'. There were at least seven dogs in this tomb and the adjacent Tomb 14. Remarkably, the latter also contained the remains of a wholly unexpected companion (or perhaps the object of the chase) for the grave's inhabitants, a juvenile African elephant, which had been buried intact.[67]

The evidence of the rock-drawings and engravings of southern Upper Egypt suggests that the elephant was only present in those regions of the Valley in which the Egyptians had established themselves early in the fourth millennium. The young elephant at Hierakonpolis, and others whose remains have been found at the site, were presumably amongst the later survivals of the herds before they and the other large animals withdrew to the extreme southern reaches of the Valley.

The skeletal remains of dogs are frequently found in graves of the pre-historic period. Baumgartel instances several in the second volume of her *Cultures of Prehistoric Egypt*, published in 1960. At Matmar a dog was buried in its own wooden coffin, in the grave of a man; pots were placed over the burial.[68] At Badari dogs were buried wrapped in mats, in the same manner as the human dead and like the dog at Adaïma described below.[69]

In predynastic times in Upper Egypt there seems to have been something of a cult that involved the sacrifice of dogs. They were not the only animals to be treated in this way though they do seem to have been a notable category of sacrifices, among the assembly of bovines, birds and caprids.[70]

The belief underlying such sacrifices was probably the retuning of the animal to its protecting divinity, of which it was considered to be an emanation or to whose presence it gave witness. In the case of the dogs the deep-seated belief that canines, uniquely, could move at will between the two worlds, of the living and the dead, must have been a powerful motivation in sending the dogs back to represent their human companions in the presence of the divine entity.

Dogs were, as we have already seen, often associated with human burials, a practice that has a very long history in Egypt. Sometimes the dog would share the same grave, as with Queen Herneith and her hound, as will be seen to be the case. These may be simply the evidence of the arguably logical outcome of the loving companionship between canine and human. But other, more enigmatic instances are known from predynastic times. Thus, at Risqalla in Nubia, dogs were buried surrounded by a cluster of human burials, dated to the early A-Group in Nubian chronology, the equivalent of early Naqada times in Egypt. Also in Lower Nubia burials of sacrificed dogs are known from Shellal and Khor Bahan; altogether 33 dogs were exhumed.[71]

The burial of dogs at Hierakonpolis has already been recorded, associated with high-status human burials. Further north, at the point where Upper and Lower Egypt march, a particular type of burial has been found: at Helwan, the burial together of a dog and a bird, possibly a falcon, each in its own coffin. In the forecourt of the great mastaba tomb of Hemaka, from which came the remarkable disk of hounds and gazelles, three birds and seven dogs, all buried in a row, were interred close to a human burial.

An important predynastic site is Adaïma, which lies a few kilometres to the south of Esna, on the edge of the cultivable land on the west bank of the Nile. It is under excavation by French archaeologists. Like Hierakonpolis, with which it is approximately contemporary, Adaïma was a substantial settlement, which flourished in the late Naqada I–early Naqada II period, in the middle of the fourth millennium, and then again a little later, in Naqada III, immediately prior to the establishment of the kingship, at the end of the millennium. It has a number of features that distinguish it from other excavated sites of the period. Some of the graves, many of them intact, revealed what appeared to be evidence of human sacrifice. Some of the dead had had their throats cut, others had been mutilated and one had been decapitated.

The main area excavated (Group 1001) produced a number of burial pits, some of which contained animals, including four dogs. One dog had been carefully wrapped in a mat before being laid in the ground, a procedure which was also employed for human burials at the time. The dog's skeleton is virtually intact and from the excellent photograph that accompanies the report it is clear that the dog is one of the greyhound type and in all probability is a tjesm.[72] It is virtually identical to the dog whose skeleton was also intact recovered from the tomb of Queen Herneith, who lived early in the early First Dynasty, a century or two after the burial of the dog at Adaïma.

At Cemetery T at Naqada 20 dogs were buried in the same pit and at Hammamiya at least 15 dogs were laid together in one grave.[73] Whether these burials represented the outcome of some form of sacrifice or whether there was some other reason for such collective interments is unknown. Equally, though it is tempting to see the burial of individual dogs with a human as an anticipation of the canine's role of the guide for the dead, it may simply be that a favoured pet was obliged to accompany its human companion on the last journey. The two earlier examples cited here may indicate that even in predynastic times dogs were accorded the dignity of a formal burial.

The majority of the dogs so buried appear to be of the greyhound, hunting dog strain. Unlike the mastiff-type dog there is no suggestion that the Egyptian hound came from Western Asia; indeed the antiquity of the representations in the rock engravings indicate that the breed was indigenous to Egypt, probably at least from the time of the first migrations. The Saluqi (Saluki or Sloughi) is the typical hunting dog of Mesopotamia, Iran and, later, Arabia and like the Egyptian Hound is related to the greyhound group, which 'probably evolved out of the aboriginal dogs of Egypt and Western Asia very early on'.[74] The Saluqi is less common in Egypt in the early periods, though not unknown; skeletons and depictions of Egyptian Hounds have often been described as being of Saluqis, in most cases probably mistakenly.

Whatever may have been the extent of late predynastic Egypt's relations with south-western Asia, there was another region with which it did maintain the closest of connections throughout its history. This was the land of Nubia, called by the Egyptians Ta-Seti, the region immediately to the south of Egypt's traditional frontiers, occupying much of what is today Sudan. The earliest references to 'Nubia' are said to date from the third century BC.[75] It has been suggested that Nubia derives its name from the Egyptian word for 'gold', of which it was a most important producer; gold was both the source of its prosperity and the reason for its constant harrying by successive, acquisitive kings of Egypt.

Egypt's relationship with Nubia was close and sometimes cordial but by no means always so; a significant percentage of Egypt's relatively infrequent military adventures in the early periods were directed to the policing of the frontier with Nubia, though mercenaries were also customarily recruited from the Nubian tribes to serve in the Egyptian forces. The frontier, in fact, was reasonably secure as a result of its topography, for the existence of the First Cataract, south of the modern city of Aswan, meant that any marauders coming up from the south could generally be swiftly detected and contained.

In late predynastic times Lower (northern) Nubia was the location of an important, highly prosperous political entity based on Qustul, to the south of Abu Simbel. It displayed many of the characteristics that came to be associated with the royal administration of Egypt, to such an extent that it was suggested that tombs in the very rich cemetery at Qustul were the burial places of kings who were actually ancestral to the Egyptian tradition and that they antedated the evidence of the kingship in Egypt.[76] This view is no longer supported, but Qustul was evidently a rich and sophisticated society, developing on lines very similar to that which was evolving at the same time in Egypt. For whatever reason, the kings of the First Dynasty in Egypt saw their Nubian contemporaries as a threat and destroyed them.

The people of Nubia always identified with the animals of the river banks and the desert, not always in a wholly benign fashion. The evidence of the existence of an exceptionally early funerary cult in northern Nubia, at Tushka, involving wild bulls has been mentioned. A seal impression from Siali, published in 1910[77] (Figure 6), demonstrates a number of the design elements associated with the Nubian state: a personage sits on an elaborate chair, before a recessed and panelled 'palace façade', an architectural motif which is probably of south-west Asian origin and which is strongly identified with the early kingship in Egypt. With one hand he reaches behind him, apparently to grasp or otherwise touch the throat of a horned animal, perhaps a bull. Behind the horned animal are two hounds with raised tails; their ears are blunted but there is little doubt that they are of the same strain as or

Figure 6 An early (c. 3000 BC) sealing from the Royal Cemetery at Siali in Nubia shows a presumably chieftainly or royal figure seated in front of a serekh surmounted by the Divine Falcon, gesturing towards a horned animal (a bull?) with two alert hounds standing behind it.

closely related to the hunting hounds of Egypt. They are robust in build, like many of the hounds portrayed on the rock carvings of the late predynastic period found both in Egypt and in Nubia, before the breed seems to have slimmed down, presenting the familiar slender, elegant profile of the 'classic' hunting hound, which came to be the more favoured.

The Nubians shared the Egyptian enthusiasm for dogs. Burials of dogs have been reported from Neolithic contexts; on a more sombre note, dogs were buried, probably alive, in what was effectively a shambles at Kerma, far to the south, where in the mid-second millennium the rulers of that part of Nubia were buried with a holocaust of retainers and animals, who were cast living into the immense grave dug for the potentate whose tomb it was.[78] Not long after the time of the Kerma burials a young man, probably a Nubian noble, was buried in the Valley of the Kings at Thebes with a rich treasure that included two finely made collars for his dogs (see below, p. 72).

Nubia continued to be both a threat to Egypt and an incitement for its kings, hungry for its gold; relations between the two were rarely easy. Eventually, some 2000 years after what appears to have been a period of confrontation between the two emergent kingdoms, Nubia provided one of the great dynasties of Egypt in the Late Period, when the kings of the

Twenty-Fifth Dynasty, drawn from the princes of a family from Kush, restored what they believed to be the pristine culture of Egypt and the proper worship of the gods, which they considered to have become degenerate. The Kushite kings were particularly devoted to their horses and were customarily buried with some of their favourite mounts. The founder of the conquering dynasty upbraided one of the petty kings ruling in Egypt at the time for his neglect of his horses, a lack of concern which greatly shocked the Kushite. We do not know if they favoured dogs also; possibly not, though horse-lovers have generally tended also to be admirers of dogs.

Yet whatever may have been the attitude of the Kushite kings, more than 2000 years later, the history of the period that culminates in the declared unification of the Valley and the creation of the Egyptian state everywhere reveals the presence of the dog, closely integrated into the society that was emerging along the Nile's banks. For the next 2000 years the dog, specifically the golden hunting hound, is part of the immemorially unchanging Egyptian landscape and of the monumental civilisation of the Nile kingdoms.

CHAPTER 2

The Beloved Companion

The Egyptians were the first people known in history not only to take dogs into their community on terms of affection and mutual dependence but also to record the names, often affectionate and sometimes engagingly silly, that they conferred on them. Kings, queens, great princes, modest officials, farmers and all manner of private persons gave their dogs names and perpetuated them in monuments, inscriptions and their own tombs.

That we know the names of some of the dogs, as we do many more of their human companions in the long course of Egypt's history, though inevitably fewer in number, is the consequence both of 200 years of archaeological activity and research and of the Egyptians' own overwhelming concern to record, and hence to preserve, the evidence of their lives. By so doing, they ensured a beautiful eternity; with them would go their dogs also, similarly protected by their engraved, sculpted or painted images, their mummified remains and the preservation of their names. Because so much effort was expended by the Egyptians at all periods on the building and decoration of their tombs, which were intended as an insurance for themselves and for all that they treasured, we know much about their concern for their dogs. These were the 'mansions of millions of years', as they optimistically – and, sadly, mistakenly – called their tombs.

The creation of the Egyptian state, an event of quite extraordinary significance and enduring resonance, occurred in the last quarter of the fourth millennium, circa 3200 BC. It signalled the formalisation of the process to

Figure 7 By convention from the earliest times of the kingship the king was represented as a duality, Lord of the Two Lands, Upper and Lower Egypt. This concept is brilliantly captured in this First Dynasty seal cómmemorating King Den, the fourth of the dynasty, enthroned twice and wearing the crowns of the Two Kingdoms. Before the figures of the king stands the ancient canine divinity Wepwawet, mounted on his standard with which he led the king into battle and the gods in procession. In front of the god is an object that has been identified as the king's placenta, which was considered to be of particular sanctity and which was under Wepwawet's protection.

bring about the Unification of the Valley, a process which had been developing for several centuries before this time. The initiative for this momentous change in the political structure of the Valley came from the south, from Upper Egypt, whence all creative advances in politics and social organisation in Egypt seemed always to come.

The Unification is a term which at first reflects an aspiration rather than an immediate reality, since it probably took several generations before the political control of the Valley, the rule of which was previously fragmented into a number of small, competing 'principalities', was actually brought into a unified whole. The Unification was immediately preceded by the emergence of three particularly active centres of political power, at Naqada, This/Abydos and Hierakonpolis. Much of the second half of the fourth millennium was taken up with the manoeuvrings of these three statelets, with the paramountcy slipping from one to another. Finally, the prize went to the princes of This/Abydos, though both Naqada and Hierakonpolis remained as honoured centres, especially revered for their involvement in the origins of the kingship, and as such were always considered essentially worthy of veneration.[1]

The victorious princes of This/Abydos and their supporters rapidly imposed a sophisticated and effective system of government over Upper Egypt, gradually exercising more and more direct control and extending their domain to the north and south. A hereditary kingship (again, the world's first) was inaugurated, the king being identified as the living incarnation of the god Horus, who became the patron of the royal house; each king bore the name 'Horus' as a title before his own throne name, thus emphasising his right to the two crowns. These symbolised the dual nature of the Egyptian polity, south and north, Upper and Lower, which the First Dynasty of kings was believed to have brought into a unified entity.

Egypt, even in its earliest united form, was always a duality: it was the Two Lands, notionally therefore two kingdoms. The king himself was the Dual King, who wore the crowns of Upper and Lower Egypt (Figure 7). The First Dynasty of kings, who ruled circa 3180–2981 BC, were the founders of a state system which was to survive in all essential details for 3000 years. During this time, more than 300 kings ruled Egypt.

In a very short space of time all the panoply of a royal state was invented and was brought into place, with a bureaucracy of high officials, a hierarchy of nobility, the beginnings of regional or provincial administration and the ceremony and paraphernalia of court and temple life. Hunting became not merely the quest for the next meal but a ritual act in which the king and his close associates were engaged. At this point, the dogs that were part of the royal entourage acquire names, which, when perpetuated, ensured their eternal companionship with the king in the Afterlife.

It is fitting to record, when celebrating the respect and affection which the Egyptian hunting hounds earned for themselves, that the first dog identified with a named Egyptian should have been the evidently beloved companion of a great queen. The dog that was thus honoured was buried, lying across the entrance of the great mastaba tomb of Queen Herneith of the early First Dynasty, circa 3000 BC, at Saqqara[2] (Figure 8). Although there are other early representations of hounds (some of which, as we shall see, were named) any serious study of the Egyptian Hound should begin with Queen Herneith's dog, for its relationship with its mistress indicates that even in the very earliest days of the kingship the hound had achieved a status and a regard far removed from the more workaday attitude that might be expected to be extended to the companion of the hunters. Queen Herneith was one of the first women whose name is known to history and one of the first of Egypt's

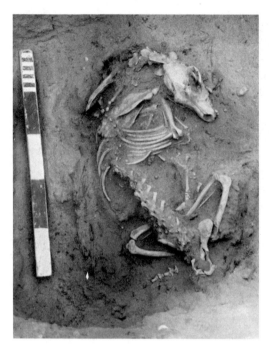

Figure 8   In one of the great mastaba tombs of the First Dynasty, excavated by W.B. Emery at Saqqara and attributed to Herneith, an early queen of Egypt, the skeleton of her hound was found lying across the entrance to the tomb, guarding the queen in perpetuity. The hound survived but of the queen herself there was no sign.

queens; she was also the first identifiable dog-lover in the history of the world. Women in Egypt were highly regarded and exercised considerable influence, particularly in the earliest periods, sometimes indeed holding the royal power itself. Herneith was the wife of a king of Egypt and possibly the mother of a king; in her first capacity her title was ' She Who Sees Horus and Set', the duality of gods particularly associated with the early kingship.

Herneith's hound was presumably sacrificed at the Queen's burial and laid across the threshold of the tomb to guard her. It may seem to us a harsh fate for a beloved animal, but to be selected to join one of the Great Ones of Egypt in death was regarded – or, perhaps, was promoted – as a singular privilege, for it guaranteed the individual concerned eternal life in the service of the owner of the tomb in which they were laid together. In the First Dynasty, the formative period of the Egyptian monarchy which lasted for some two hundred years, it was the custom for the kings, royal persons and the great officers of state, the nobles of the Two Lands, to be buried with large numbers of the members of their households. The hecatombs of retainers, often numbering several hundred individuals, were killed to join

Figure 9 A burial similar to that of Herneith's hound was found in a grave at Al-Hajjar, Bahrain, dated to approximately a millennium later.

their master or mistress in the Afterlife and so ensure that they could maintain a state proper to their exalted rank; their ritual killing was also believed to have ensured their own eternal survival.[3]

It is all the more remarkable therefore that Queen Herneith, a very Great One indeed, chose to go into her tomb accompanied only by what we must assume to have been her favourite hound. The fact that she was not joined by phalanxes of servitors and attendants is strange and there may be some explanation other than that her sensibilities prevented her from bringing about the deaths of those who served her – on balance, an improbable suggestion for the time. What is clear, however, is that even at this early date the hound was already domesticated and respected to the extent of being selected as the sole companion of a great queen.

Dogs were not infrequently immured in the entrances of important buildings in many ancient societies, to guard them from harm. An early example of the practice in Egypt is in the late predynastic gateway that gave access to the temple area in Nekhen, the city known to the Greeks as Hierakonpolis.[4] A similar dog-guardian was found in the east entrance of Maiden Castle in Dorset, England.[5] Another canine burial which recalls that of Queen Herneith's dog was also far away from Egypt, hundreds of years later, in a grave *circa* 2000 BC, at the site of Al-Hajjar on the island of Bahrain in the Arabian Gulf;[6] there, the dog had been laid on its side, as if sleeping, in a niche at the head of the grave, as if guarding it, just as the Queen's dog was guarding her (Figure 9). When the Egyptians mummified their dogs, as they did frequently, they often laid them out, as though sleeping.

In the earliest periods of Egyptian history the sacrifice of companions for the illustrious dead was not confined to dogs, nor indeed to animals. Human sacrifice is a custom that seems particularly un-Egyptian, for the people of the Valley valued life above all other considerations that the world had to offer. The practice was discontinued after the end of the First Dynasty. Subsequently, all the pleasant and agreeable aspects of life associated with the Valley that the deceased wished to perpetuate and to continue to enjoy forever were pictured on the walls of the tombs, the simulacrum serving for the reality. It is perhaps significant – it certainly is not a little sinister – that most of the great tombs of the First Dynasty show evidence of being destroyed by fire, soon after the end of the dynasty, *circa* 2890 BC. Perhaps there was a revulsion against a custom that not only wasted the talents and abilities of craftsmen and artists but that was also manifestly inhuman. Whatever may have been the reason, only in the First Dynasty was the living sacrifice of the companions of the illustrious dead acceptable. The burning of a tomb was a terrible calamity for its owner, an appalling disaster, for by the destruction of the corpse, the owner of the tomb forfeited the Afterlife. It should perhaps be noted that in the case of Queen Herneith's burial, the skeleton of her dog survived, but of the Queen's body there was no sign.

The evidence of the continuation of the practice of human sacrifice in Nubia in the middle of the second millennium was exceptional beyond Egypt's frontiers, and that the dogs were buried alive in the huge tombs erected at Kerma is probably evidence of a local custom, far removed from the more humane rule of the Egyptian kings of the time.[7] At el-Kadara, 200 kilometres north of Khartoum, the presence of a dog in a burial seems to be associated with human sacrifice.[8]

Professor W.B. Emery's excavations at Saqqara uncovered a line of huge First Dynasty mastaba tombs, including Herneith's built on the escarpment looking down on to the first capital of the Dual Kingdom at Memphis, close

Figure 10 The huge, brick-built mastaba tombs on the escarpment at Saqqara, looking down on Memphis, where Queen Herneith was buried, survived despite having been burned in fierce conflagrations after the end of the First Dynasty.

to where the Two Lands notionally met.[9] The tombs were immense brick-built structures. the first in Egypt. They appear to replicate the plans of mid-fourth millennium temples from southern Mesopotamia, which is further evidence of some as yet unexplained connection between the land that was to become Sumer and southern Egypt (Figure 10).

The tombs at Saqqara seem to have been built for the most important officials in the service of the kings of the earliest period of Egypt's history. Their architecture testifies to the extraordinary advances in technique and monumental splendour to which the coming of the kingship gave rise. Not only were the tombs of the nobles significantly more substantial than any buildings known before in Egypt; their contents, though extensively pillaged when many of them were set on fire, were clearly rich and diverse, with skilfully fashioned pottery, fine stoneware frequently of a breathtaking refinement, ivory exquisitely carved, woodwork very sumptuously decorated, and copper vessels of superb quality.

From one of these tombs (No. 3035), attributed to Hemaka, a high official in the reign of King Den,[10] a beautiful carved steatite disc has been recovered

Figure 11   Stelae recording the names of favoured hounds were set up
around the grave of a First Dynasty king at Abydos. c. 3100 BC.

(*Frontispiece*). It is probably a gaming piece, though how it was used is not
known; it is pierced in the centre to allow a spindle to be inserted by which
it might be spun. On the obverse of the disc are two tjesm, each chasing a
gazelle. The coat of one of the hounds is represented as the familiar golden-tan
colour, though the inlay is a pinkish stone; the other, grasping its quarry by
the throat, is black. The present writer knows of no other representation of
a black tjesm, where it is clear that it is the real hound which it depicted and
not one of its divine or mystical surrogates, or a jackal. Anubis, the most
frequently represented of the canid gods, was customarily shown with a black
pelage with embellishments of gold. The pink stone of the inlay of the other
hound shows that already in the early third millennium artistic convention
would portray the acceptable colour by a skilful approximation to the red-gold
pelage, which it may be presumed already typified the tjesm.

The earliest dogs in Egypt whose names have survived may, like Herneith's
hound, have been the victims of the custom of sending a dead king's favourite
companions with him to the Afterlife. A number of funerary stelae survive
from First Dynasty tombs of the early kings at Abydos, which record the
burials of what were presumably sacrificed retainers as well as the kings'
favoured dogs, sent to join their masters[11] (Figure 11). It would, of course, be
entirely logical, if to modern eyes regrettable, to despatch a favoured hound
in such circumstances. King Den, Hemaka's sovereign, was buried at Abydos
and had the name of several of his dogs recorded on funerary stelae. Their
presence so close to the king's tombs almost certainly indicates that the dogs
were intentionally buried beside their master. The name of one was Nub;

another to be granted his own grave and his own commemorative stele was named Sed.[12] He was evidently a contemporary of Nub, his master the same King Den. He is a sprightly animal, his ears pricked and his tail tightly curled. Sed was also a name of an ancient canine divinity, Wepwawet, who was particularly associated with the person and office of the king, who will be discussed further in Chapter 5.

The practice of giving dogs formal burials, in addition to proclaiming the affection of their human companions, may have been a reflection of their role as messengers between the worlds of the living and the dead, a responsibility that the canine gods were considered to discharge. By honouring the dogs in death, their human companions could expect them to reciprocate by communicating their affection and concern for those whom they had left behind, to those powers to whose company they would have been translated.

The similarities that the Egyptians must have detected in the psychology and emotional responses of dogs that so engagingly mirror those of humans were doubtless decisive influences in bringing the dog into their close community. This factor alone may well have made them feel that dogs should be treated not only with affection but also with respect and honour, their passing to be mourned and their remains treated with the same dignity in death that would be accorded to a beloved human. Canines seem always to have had a faintly uncanny significance to the Egyptians, as indeed to many other ancient peoples, their evident absorption in an inner life from which even their most beloved companions were excluded adding to their mystery. This view of canine nature would have been reinforced by the idea that they could move freely between the worlds, to allow them to continue to exercise their benign role as guardians and guides; therefore it was reasonable enough that they should be preserved after death in the same fashion that humans were. After the end of the First Dynasty there seems to be no evidence of dogs having had their lives terminated to join their masters prematurely, except possibly those bred in the temples consecrated to canine divinities. That such was the attitude of the Egyptians to their dogs, given the extent of their concern for them, their determination to prolong life and their evident intention that dogs should share their lives in terms of mutual respect, is only to be expected.

The First and Second Dynasties, whose kings ruled Egypt from circa 3180 to circa 2680 BC, were responsible for the laying down of much of what was to follow in the administrative, social and religious character of the Dual

Kingdom in the centuries to come. The history of the period is only now being pieced together in more detail than has been possible in the past, the consequence of more advanced archaeological technology. Paradoxically, more is known about the First Dynasty than the Second; despite the fact that it survived for some two hundred years, it is only recently that the succession of the kings has been satisfactorily established and even now the tombs of several of the dynasty have not been found. At the end of the Second Dynasty there appears to have been something of an upheaval, which resulted in the identification of the kingship with an incarnation of a divine entity, Set, with notably canine characteristics. This has some relevance to the more mystical role of the hound and will be described in Chapter 5.

The most influential event in the evolution of the early Egyptian state's historic character was the establishment of the Third Dynasty of kings (c. 2686–c. 2613 BC): the succession of the first king of the dynasty marked the beginning of the period that is called the Old Kingdom by Egyptologists. The most celebrated king who ruled Egypt in the Third Dynasty, one of the most important of all those who held the Dual Kingship and whose name was remembered throughout Egyptian history by reason of the great monument which was built for him at Saqqara,[13] was King Netjerykhet, who is also known today, probably anachronistically, as Djoser. He conducted the obsequies for his predecessor, King Khasekhemwy of the Second Dynasty, a fact which suggests that he was his son, though in the king lists another, Sanakht, perhaps Netjerykhet's brother, is credited as the founder of the dynasty. The greatest achievements of Egypt in art and architecture and in the creation of the essential mores of Egypt in antiquity trace their origin to this time. Though the dynasty was not long lasting, surviving probably for less than a century, its influence on what was to come after it was very great and long enduring. Netjerykhet was a builder of great temples and from the ruins of one of them, at Heliopolis, was found a number of representations of the god Set, depicted as a mysterious creature with marked canine attributes, who will be further described in Chapter 5.

King Sneferu was the founder of the succeeding Fourth Dynasty (c. 2613–c. 2494 BC) and one of the most remarkable builders in the history of the world. Sneferu deserves to be remembered for far more extraordinary achievements even than his son, the celebrated Khufu (Cheops in the Greek form of his name), the same who is thought to have been responsible for the building of the Great Pyramid. The Fourth Dynasty of kings is exceptional for the number, scale and quality of the great monuments which were erected during the 120 years of its existence. Sneferu himself built three pyramids, in the process excavating some 9 million tonnes of stone for their construction, making the 2.5 million tonnes of Khufu's pyramid at Giza look quite modest.[14]

Another of Sneferu's sons, Prince Nefermaat, bore the title 'Great Son of the King'. He was a senior member of the royal family and was a partisan of King Khafre, the builder of the Second Pyramid at Giza. Khafre seems originally to have been deprived of the succession to the kingship on the death of his father, Khufu, whose immediate successor was Djedefre, who died after about eight years on the throne; Khafre then became king. One of Nefermaat's sons was Prince Hemiunu, who is credited with the supervision of the building of the Great Pyramid for Khufu, who was probably Nefermaat's brother.[15]

Nefermaat was buried in a mastaba tomb at Meidum, where one of Sneferu's pyramids is located. Nefermaat's tomb and that of his wife, the Princess Atet, are remarkable for several striking features and particularly for the quality of the paintings that decorate them. The most familiar of these is the line of geese from the Princess's tomb, which march solemnly along in the Egyptian Museum, Cairo, their plumage and colouring as bright today as they were when they were painted 45 centuries ago.[16]

The prince was evidently a man of talent. He describes his invention of a new technique for the decoration of the walls of the mastabas in which the great nobles were buried. This involved the infilling of hollowed-out bas-reliefs with coloured pastes. Unfortunately Egypt's exceptionally dry climate meant that the inlays became desiccated and crumbled. Before this unfortunate mishap the effect must have been dramatic, and that a person so exalted was apparently capable of such invention is commendable.

The inlays were used in the bas-reliefs which recorded the scenes of life on Nefermaat's estates. In Princess Atet's tomb these include their young sons playing with their pet animals, monkeys, geese and dogs. A dog also features in another sequence where it is shown hunting foxes, which it seizes, perhaps a little improbably, by their tails.

King Khufu, for whom the Great Pyramid is believed to have been built (or, as some would have it, adapted),[17] also valued and honoured his hounds. One of them, Abutiyuw (it has been suggested that, very aptly for a tjesm, his name meant 'pointed ears'), was given a 'royal' burial in his own tomb, a reward for his service as one of the king's guard dogs. An inscription describes the honour paid to the dog:

The dog which was the guard of this Majesty, Abutiyuw is his name. His
Majesty ordered that he be buried ceremonially, that he be given a coffin
from the royal treasury, fine linen in great quantity and incense. His Majesty
also gave perfumed ointment and ordered that a tomb be built for him by
the gangs of masons. His Majesty did this for him that he [the dog] might
be honoured before the great god, Anubis.[18]

The rubric 'Honoured before the great god, Anubis', appears frequently in
the memorials of Egyptian dogs; Abutiyuw's inscription is possibly the oldest
to survive, though, as we have seen, in the First Dynasty dogs were given
commemorative stelae, recording their names.

At the height of the Old Kingdom, in the Fifth Dynasty, circa 2400 BC, life
at the royal court was highly civilised, sumptuous and elegant, for centuries
of peaceful development had made Egypt both rich and tranquil. Not only
those close to the king enjoyed the fruits of this happy time – and assuredly
they benefited greatly – but life seems generally to have been agreeable, and
even the workers on the land and the fisher folk and sailors on the river are
represented as living fulfilled and enjoyable lives. It was one of the singular
characteristics of Ancient Egyptian society and its political and social economy
that, outside the circle of the king and his immediate family, progress up
through society was always open to a young man of enterprise and talent.
Many of the tombs of this period record a multitude of scenes and incidents
from life in Egypt at this singularly fortunate time. The hound is included
in the company of the nobles who bred and cared for them. One of the
greatest of the Fifth Dynasty nobles, Mereruka, has a pair of his hounds with
a pet monkey displayed on the walls of his tomb at Saqqara, with their own
attendant[19] (Figure 12a). Also at Saqqara, Ptahhetep (Figure 24) sits in state with
his hounds and a monkey (Figure 12b).

A fortunate courtier was Ka-Hay, a singer in the royal court who, by the
quality of his voice, attracted the notice and interest of the king. He was
favoured and promoted to the higher ranks of the court bureaucracy. His
son Nefer was especially fortunate, for the king had him educated with the
princes, a circumstance which guaranteed his future prosperity, as nothing
else could conceivably have done.[20] Nefer grew up to become one of the
principal officials at the court, a holder of a number of important appoint-
ments in the royal service and an intimate of the king. As a special mark of
the royal favour the king, probably King Niuserre (2445–2421 BC), granted
him a tomb, 'when he is grown very beautifully old'.[21]

Figure 12a   *Tjesm* are often shown leashed, even from the earliest times. In dynastic times the royal court and the courts of the great magnates included men who were evidently charged with the handling and management of the hounds, and no doubt of their training also. Not infrequently they are shown in the company of another popular household pet, a tamed monkey, as here from the Old Kingdom tomb of Mereruka at Saqqara. Sometimes the monkey leads the dogs.

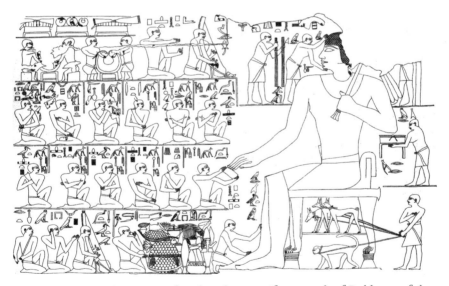

Figure 12b   A similar scene is found in the magnificent tomb of Ptahhetep of the Fifth Dynasty, also at Saqqara. Ptahhetep sits, enthroned, attended by battalions of retainers and even a small orchestra and chorus. Behind his chair of state a senior servant hold three *tjesm* and, on another leash, a monkey. This time, their relative positions are reversed to those in Mereruka's tomb.

Figure 13 An important official in the Fifth Dynasty was Nefer, son of Ka-Hay. He, his wife and sundry relations were buried in a small tomb at Saqqara that was buried during the excavations of the Causeway of King Wenis' pyramid. The Nefers' tomb thus remained largely intact until the late twentieth century. The family were evidently animal lovers and in this scene Nefer, a lady who is probably his wife Khensuw and their small tjesm (perhaps a puppy?) watch the loading of one of their ships, about to take them to their estates in Upper Egypt.

The tomb was built at Saqqara. It is quite small, most engagingly decorated, in a slightly naive or provincial style, and was still in a remarkable state of preservation when it was discovered in the 1960s. This was the consequence of a chance which might at first have seemed to be a misfortune. A century or so after Nefer's death, when he was sealed in the tomb with his father and a number of his relations, all tucked away in their respective burial niches, King Wenis, the last king of the Fifth Dynasty, had his pyramid raised on the escarpment above the line of tombs built for high officials of the Fifth Dynasty, in this part of the Saqqara necropolis. Wenis commanded a handsome causeway to be built leading up to his pyramid, along which his sarcophagus would be drawn at his funeral. The construction of the causeway resulted in the tombs of the Fifth Dynasty officials, since they were not persons of the first rank, being buried by the rubble of the excavations, thus preserving them virtually intact until the late twentieth century.

The reliefs in Nefer's tomb, when it was first excavated still bright with the colours that were originally applied to them, depict the familiar scenes of daily life as it was lived by a highly favoured official and his family in Egypt in the late third millennium BC. Nefer and his wife, Khensuw, are always attended by their dog, a young Egyptian hound, which is clearly part of the family and stands alert between Nefer's legs[22] (Figure 13), surveying with them the work on their estates and the produce which the workers garner. One sequence shows the unloading of ships bringing supplies from the estates in the south. Directing the work of the sailors is another favoured pet of the Nefer household, a handsome cynocephalus baboon, which is also an important participant in the pressing of the grapes in Nefer's vineyards, where the baboon himself turns the press from which the juice pours, eventually to be made into wine.[23] The Nefers' baboon was evidently versatile; he is also shown supervising the sailors as they launch a ship, bound for Nerfer's estates in Upper Egypt;[24] in another relief he appears to be commanding the vessel. Hounds and monkeys were often shown together in Old Kingdom contexts, the monkeys holding the dogs' leashes. Nefer's dog, however, was evidently above being led by monkeys and is shown standing obediently beside Nefer and his wife, unleashed.

Nefer and Khensuw were clearly animal-lovers. But, as befitted a family descended from a distinguished musician, they also maintained a small orchestra which entertained them as they went about their affairs – and, according to Egyptian belief, must continue to do so in the Afterlife where

Nefer, his wife and family, their baboon and their dog now live in contentment for ever.

Two of the Nefers' neighbours in the small necropolis of important Fifth
Dynasty courtiers at Saqqara were Khnumhotep and Niankhkhnum, who shared
a nearby tomb. That the two men were buried together and are shown in
scenes in which they display considerable affection for each other, untouched
by the presence of any members of either of their families, has inevitably
prompted speculation about their relationship, perhaps also fuelled by the
fact that they were the chief royal manicurist and the chief royal wigmaker
respectively. That they were rewarded with a tomb provided by the king in
so favoured a place is a tribute to their rank as priests, for only properly

Figure 14 The Egyptian hound quickly became an established and much-loved family companion. Here, from reliefs in the tomb of Sekhemka at Saqqara, the family hound, Peshesh, has an important place in the design, ensuring that, by the repetition of his name, he too will be granted eternal life.

initiated members of one of the orders of priesthood would be permitted to touch the body of a living god. In one of the scenes of their domestic intimacy Khnumhotep and Niankhkhnum (who, it has been suggested, may in fact have been brothers) are shown in the company of their dog.[25]

The Egyptians of the Old Kingdom carried a preoccupation with the balance of dualities – a characteristic of the Egyptian psyche that was fundamental to their understanding of the universe – into their art, particularly that which dealt with their concern with the Afterlife and with the eternal verities that governed their lives as they did the cosmos. Figures of deities and men are frequently shown in pairs, and in funerary inscriptions two representations of the deceased – sometimes identical, sometimes differentiated by dress or accoutrements – would be carved in relief on the same wall in the tomb. An example of this practice is to be found in the mastaba tomb of Sekhemka at Saqqara; he was an official also living in the Fifth Dynasty (2494–2345 BC). On one of the walls Sekhemka is shown twice seated in a chair with high sides, in one case with his wife crouching on the floor before him, her arm embracing his legs, and in the other seated before a table piled high with offerings of food and drink to sustain him in the Afterlife.[26]

In several instances Sekhemka's dog is shown lying under his chair (Figure 14). With Sekhemka's wife the dog is lying stretched out, his head on his paws, doubtless in that state of half-sleep in the way of dogs when they have nothing in particular to do or when there is nothing of interest to attract their attention. In the other scene he is wide awake and alert, perhaps encouraged by the presence of the ample supply of eatables, which no doubt he expects Sekhemka to share with him. According to the scholar who published Sekhemka's tomb, the dog's name is Peshesh.[27]

The Old Kingdom saw the frequent introduction of hounds into tomb reliefs, in everyday contexts and preoccupations, very much part of the family. Like Peshesh they were often accommodated under the tomb owner's chair. One such, in a particularly appealing scene, shows a handsome tjesm bitch suckling her puppies. Another has the hound lying quietly, intently observing the antics of a pair of monkeys, evidently also the pets of the tomb owner. In yet another scene the hound is to be seen, again beneath the chair, demolishing a goose.

The Pyramid Texts, the earliest surviving version of which was inscribed on the interior walls of the chambers in King Wenis' pyramid, are ancient literary inventions of extraordinary power, though much of their language is still obscure and their allusions often fugitive.[28] They are carved in exquisite hieroglyphs. These once were infilled with a wonderful, brilliant blue paste, which, unlike Prince Nefermaat's invention, survived well into the twentieth century, until it was destroyed by the breath and sweat of legions of tourists. The superstructure of Wenis' pyramid was entirely ruined in antiquity and the existence of its interior chambers unknown until late in the nineteenth century.

King Wenis' decision to have the Pyramid Texts inscribed on the walls of his tomb's chambers has relevance in this record, though the episode that it relates is perhaps an apocryphal one. An oft-repeated story attends the discovery of the Pyramid Texts, after they had lain in darkness for 4000 years, entirely forgotten. In the 1880s a man, a worker employed in the excavations of the area, one of the richest archaeologically in all Egypt, was strolling in the pyramid field at Saqqara in the evening. As the brief Egyptian dusk fell, he saw a hound or a jackal walking among the debris of a collapsed pyramid. He was intrigued, for it was unusual to see animals of this sort alone in this part of Saqqara, the more so since it seemed not to be apprehensive of a human presence, indeed rather to invite observation. The animal disappeared suddenly: the man guessed that it must have entered, or perhaps had fallen into, a cavity in the ground, with which the surface in that part of the pyramid field was pitted. He followed it; he never saw it again but it had led him straight to the hidden chambers of Wenis' pyramid and to the immeasurable treasure of the Pyramid Texts.

Romantics have always insisted that the animal must have been Wepwawet, the 'Opener of the Ways'. His earthly domain was graveyards; he led the gods in procession before the king in great public ceremonies and on campaign against his enemies. In this event in the Saqqara necropolis it was the living man whom he led, to make the discovery of one of the greatest products of the human mind in antiquity – or indeed of the human spirit at any epoch.

The royal authority disintegrated at the end of the Old Kingdom and the rulers of the nomes (the administrative districts into which Egypt was divided) increased their power greatly. The governors of the nomes were called 'nomarchs' in Greek-dominated Ptolemaic times, a term which has stuck, replacing the Egyptian word *sepat*. The power of the provincial governors waxed exceedingly in the terminal stages of the Old Kingdom, to the extent that they created what amounted to independent fiefdoms that paid only the most notional allegiance to the nominal king of Egypt, indeed if on some occasions there was a person who could be thus identified. A succession of weak claimants to the royal authority came and went; one of the more enduring lines was established at Heracleopolis, which survived for about a century.

A family of nobles, long seated in Thebes, then a quite unimportant provincial centre, opposed the Heracleopolitans and gradually assumed power over more and more of the south. The founder of the family's ultimate fortune was named Inyotef. The second of the name, Inyotef II Wahankh, was acknowledged as an authentic king of Egypt, and with his father, the first Inyotef, was recognised as the founder of the Eleventh Dynasty of kings, who were eventually to consolidate their rule over the Two Lands.[29]

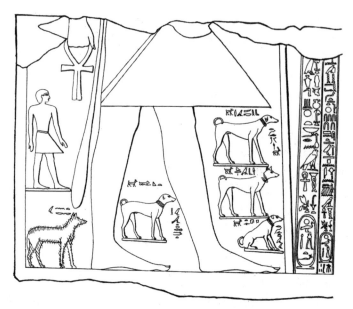

Figure 15 A family of nobles from the region of Thebes, long before it became
the capital of the Egyptian Empire and the greatest city in the world of the day,
were the ancestors of the kings who founded the Eleventh Dynasty. They were
responsible for the eventual reunification of the Valley and one of their number,
Nebhetepre Montuhotep II, was celebrated as a unifier of the Egyptian state on a
par with Narmer and Aha. This dynasty was the first of the Middle Kingdom, a
period of particular splendour in the history of Egypt. Several of the early members
of the family bore the name Inyotef. Inyotef II was a particularly notable dog-lover
and had himself portrayed on his stelae with several of his hounds; the names of
most of them are also recorded, transliterations of which will be found in the text.

Inyotef II Wahankh seems to have been especially fond of dogs. Like many
Egyptians in antiquity he evidently enjoyed giving his dogs elaborate, often
rather declamatory names. In the Old Kingdom, for example, we know of a
favoured dog who was called 'One who is fashioned like an arrow', a tribute,
no doubt, to his speed and precision in the chase,[30] an adaptation of which
provides the title for this book. On a stele in Inyotef's funerary shrine at el
Tarif, Western Thebes, he is shown with five of his dogs grouped around
him (Figure 15). One of them, Behkai, a name of Libyan origin, is obviously
much favoured for she is sitting between the king's legs. Her name is glossed
as 'Gazelle'.[31] The other dogs, too, all have their names recorded: Abaqer,
an Old Berber word meaning 'hound', like tjesm in Egyptian; Pehtes, 'Black

Figure 16 In the First Intermediate Period, during the time of civil unrest and the breakdown of the royal authority that followed the end of the Old Kingdom, Nubian soldiers were employed to provide a security force, particularly in the southern desert regions. One of these mercenaries was Senu, seen here with his wife, two sons and two attentive hounds, from his tomb at Gebelein. c. 2150 BC.

One' (or, perhaps more familiarly, 'Blackie'); Tegra, 'Kettle' (*sic*); and Tekenru, whose name is not translated. Three of Inyotef's dogs are Saluqi, including Behkai. Abaqer is a *tjesm*, as is Tekenru, though somewhat heavier in build. It seems that at this time Libyan and North African names were popular choices for the owners of Egyptian Hounds. It is possible that this reflects some traditions of their origin in the once-upon-a-time hunting lands of the Saharan savanna. One of Intef II Wahankh's dogs was buried with him, in a wooden coffin, decorated in black and red.[32]

Dogs were particularly favoured during the First Intermediate Period (2181–2055 BC), as the two centuries or so after the end of the Sixth Dynasty are called by historians, when the central royal administration fell apart. At this time Nubian mercenaries were recruited into the militias of the various principalities, particularly to police the frontiers between them. One such a mercenary was Senu, who lived during the Ninth/Tenth Dynasties, *circa* 2160–2125 BC. He was stationed at Gebelein, where a contingent of Nubian troops had been long established; there he married a local woman and lived in some comfort. On his funeral stele, in addition to the presence of his wife and sons who are making offerings to him, Senu is attended by his two dogs, which sit obediently before him, their ears pricked alertly[33] (*Figure* 16). Dogs were recruited to serve with militiamen such as Senu to track fugitives and to warn of interlopers. Recently an inscription cut on the rocks of Gebel Tjauti, outside Thebes, has been published that shows a Nubian police official with his leashed dog, which is snarling fiercely.[34]

The First Intermediate Period, from which this inscription dates, is often represented as a time of unrest, even of anarchy and nationwide disorder, following the end of the Old Kingdom. It certainly does not seem to have been an unfavourable time for Egyptian dogs, whatever it may have been like for some of their human companions, who in the past had enjoyed one of the most secure and prosperous of existences. It embraces the ephemeral Seventh and Eighth Dynasties, the Ninth and Tenth Dynasty Heracleopolitan kings and the princes ruling from Thebes who formed the early Eleventh Dynasty, before their rule extended over the whole Valley.

The impression that this was a time of national catastrophe for Egypt has been gained from what may be rather overexcited literary productions of a somewhat later date which portrayed a state of mayhem and social chaos across the Dual Kingdom during this interregnum between the Old and Middle Kingdoms. It is true that Egypt fragmented into numerous competing statelets, but the texts from which the impression of a period of considerable unrest and social upheaval has been derived were probably written either simply as literary exercises after the supposed events that they describe or by a propagandist employed to paint a lurid picture of the disasters attendant upon the collapse of the royal authority, after the restoration of the kingship by the victorious Eleventh Dynasty, *circa* 2000 BC. In fact the times were probably only hard for the little kings and their followers, who tried to assume some semblance of royal authority, often ruling over very small territories indeed. For the bulk of the population, life probably continued much as it had always done, though a succession of low Niles in the closing years of the Sixth Dynasty may have brought hardship to the countryside.

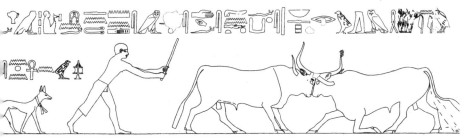

Figure 17   Senbi, the son of Ukhhotep, was a member of a dynasty of nobles that provided the rulers of one of the important nomes of Middle Egypt in the Twelfth Dynasty. His attachment to his hounds is indicated by the name of this one, 'Breath of life to Senbi'.

The near-century-long reign of King Pepi II at the end of the Sixth Dynasty did not help either the political or the administrative condition of the Two Lands, as the power of the king attenuated and eventually more or less totally vanished in Pepi's successors' reigns.

Yet dogs became still more closely integrated into the families not only of the kings and great officers but also of lesser folk, like Senu. Many funerary monuments and inscriptions now contain references to dogs, a custom which will continue throughout the succeeding Middle Kingdom. Though, perhaps inevitably, we know more of the lives of the great nobles and high officials and hence more of the fortunes of their dogs, the Middle Kingdom was a time when the individual increasingly came to the fore. As a result we have the funerary records of the families and lives of less exalted Egyptians available for study. Such records also ensured that the dogs acquired the benefits and delights of immortality.

When the kings of the Eleventh Dynasty (2125–1985 BC), particularly the great Nebhetepre Montuhotep II (c. 2055–2004 BC), set out to consolidate once more royal rule over the entire Valley, the nomarchs who had in the intervening period become especially powerful sought to stay in office and some of them prospered, especially those who acknowledged the reinstated royal authority when Nebhetepre Montuhotep II unified the country once more. In the Fourteenth Upper Egyptian nome with its capital at Meir a family of princes ruled, several of whom were called Ukhhotep. Ukhhotep I was probably the son of Senbi (Sonebi) and named his own son and successor in his father's honour. Senbi II was nomarch in the reigns of King

Amememhat I, the founder of the Twelfth Dynasty, and his son, Senwosret I. He was buried at Meir, in a rich and well-appointed tomb. His dog, a *tjesm*, is represented in the tomb with his master (Figure 17): he bears the sort of extravagant name 'Breath of life to Senbi', which could only be the invention of a truly besotted dog-lover.[35]

Another great prince, Serenput, the ruler of the First Upper Egyptian nome, centred on Elephantine Island in the far south during the Twelfth Dynasty (1985–1795 BC), commanded the vital southern approaches to the Valley. He was buried in a magnificent tomb on the escarpment at Elephantine, looking out across the river to Aswan. On the façade of his tomb Serenput sits magisterially on his chair of state, with an air of great assurance, with his dog, a handsome Egyptian Hound, though more like a Saluqi than a *tjesm*, which looks as confident of his position as does his master, seated alertly beneath Serenput's chair. The prince is also depicted walking in a stately measure by the entrance to his tomb, followed by his hound, who in turn is followed by a small bitch, her size relative to the dog's perhaps reflecting the Egyptian convention of representing females on a smaller scale than their male companions. The powerful magnates who ruled the Oryx nome during the Middle Kingdom, and who were buried at Beni Hasan, also had their dogs frequently represented in the paintings in their tombs, wearing handsome collars.[36]

The exalted status enjoyed by at least some of the canine population of Egypt in the Middle Kingdom (2055–1655 BC) is well attested in the tomb of the great prince of the Hare nome, Djehutyhetep, who ruled his province in the Twelfth Dynasty, one of the most prosperous and sophisticated periods in Egyptian history. He was buried in a magnificently decorated tomb at Bersheh, north of Asyut. The decoration is rich and finely executed; one famous scene shows a huge statue of the nomarch being dragged by an army of workers from the quarries at Hatnub, where the limestone for Djehutyhetep's statue was mined. Another sequence of painted reliefs represents Djehutyhetep's sedan chair, a sort of *sedia gestatoria*, being carried in procession on the shoulders of his men; the procession is attended by a retinue of soldiers and retainers. Walking beneath his master's chair is Djehutyhetep's dog, one of a curious, long-bodied, short-limbed breed, somewhat resembling a prick-eared basset hound,[37] probably an achondroplastic dwarf (Figure 18). Whatever he was did not diminish the affection in which Prince Djehutyhopep held him. His name is Ankhu, whose place in the heart of the prince is demonstrated by

Figure 18 A great noble of the Middle Kingdom, Djehutyhetep, was Lord of the Oryx nome during the Twelfth Dynasty. A famous scene from his tomb at Meir shows him being carried in procession, borne on a palanquin. In another scene from the same sequence his favourite hound, a strange-looking animal rather like a large basset hound, is shown walking sedately beneath the palanquin, though Djehutyhetep is not present.

his being portrayed on nearly the same scale as the female members of the prince's family. These included his sisters, who are shown in a nearby register of the reliefs as comparable in size to Ankhu.

One of the greatest of the Middle Kingdom provincial princes was Hepzifa (alternatively Hapidjefa) who was nomarch of the XII Upper Egyptian nome, centred on Asyut (Lykopolis, 'Wolf City', in Greek) during the reign of King Senwosret I. He had built for himself and his wife, the Lady Sennuwy, a magnificent tomb there, in which a number of mummified dogs were also found. Lykopolis was a centre of the cults of the most important of the canine divinities, Anubis.

For a long time it was believed that Hepzifa and Sennuwy were the original occupants of the huge tomb at Kerma, in Upper Nubia, which was the site of a holocaust of retainers and dogs, described earlier. For some reason statues of Hepzifa and Sennuwy had been sent to Kerma, but it is not known what connection, if any, the couple had with the settlement. It is now believed that they were buried at Asyut, presumably with their dogs.[38] As prince of the Lykopolite nome, Hepzifa would have been especially concerned with the rites of Anubis, who was the patron divinity of the city, to the extent of being the high priest of the cult. He would certainly have ensured that he was attended by canine supporters, though, as far as is known, they would not have been sacrificed for the privilege.

During the Middle Kingdom a recension of the spells and incantations intended to guide the deceased to judgement and eternal life was painted

Figure 19   In the Middle Kingdom the benefits of an elaborate and costly burial began to be extended beyond the royal court and its immediate associates. Khui was an official at Lykopolis (Asyut) and he commissioned a handsome coffin, richly decorated, which was well supplied with texts ensuring his admission to the Afterlife. On one side of the coffin Khui is shown walking with his dog, Iupu, which he leads on a long leash. Though Iupu is not of the classic strain of golden-tan tjesm, he and Khui typify the Egyptian and his dog, walking together for all eternity in the Islands of the Blest.

in the interiors and on the exteriors of wooden coffins, which became very elaborate and sometimes very beautifully executed. The inscriptions are derived from the Pyramid Texts of the Old Kingdom and are known as the Coffin Texts; they, in turn, are ancestral to the various documents and inscriptions known as the Books of the Dead of later times, each of which has its own title.

A typical, though certainly a particularly handsome, example of an elaborately inscribed coffin was made for an official, Khui, who lived in Asyut in Middle Egypt, the centre of the Anubis cult. Though the coffin is fine its decoration is not particularly remarkable except in one respect: beside two large eyes on the side of the coffin, placed there to allow the occupant to observe what was going on in the world he had left, Khui had himself painted, walking with his dog Iupu, which he holds on a leash (*Figure* 19). Iupu is a tall hound, with a speckled black and white coat; he is not therefore strictly

Figure 20 From the earliest times hounds had been associated with games of chance, much favoured by the Egyptians throughout their history. This small ivory hound is from the predynastic period, c. 3200 BC.

a tjesm, of the tan or golden coloration generally considered here, but one of the other strains of dog favoured by the Egyptians. Khui and Iupu well exemplify the Egyptian man and his dog, enjoying their walks together, for all eternity.[39]

Another Middle Kingdom coffin, of the late XI Dynasty, from Beni Hasan in Middle Egypt, was described by its excavator as containing the skeleton of a jackal.[40] The skeleton was lost (or possibly discarded as unimportant) but later study of the excavator's reports suggested that the remains were probably those of a tjesm. Sometimes Middle Kingdom dog burials had dishes placed on the coffin, presumably to provide sustenance for the dog on his journey to the Afterlife, to join or to await his human companion.

The Egyptians recognised that while the prospect of a well-appointed Afterlife was much to be desired, eternity could have its longueurs. One way of whiling away the absence of time was to take into the tomb the sort of games of chance or skill which they seem particularly to have enjoyed; representations of the owner of the tomb with his wife, other members of his family or a friend, playing one or other of the games are frequent. One of the most popular of these games is known as 'Hounds and Jackals', though it has been suggested that the pieces, which bear the heads of canines, in fact represent two types of domestic dog: a larger hound, certainly the tjesm, and a lighter-built, lop-eared dog.[41]

The rules for playing the game are not known for certain but each complete kit, usually preserved in its own, often decorated, box, contained two sets of five pieces, representing the two animals. The board had two sets of 29 holes, leading by a complex route to the 'goal', a hieroglyphic sign on top of a palm tree. Moves were determined by throws of knuckle-bones, with some of the holes on which a player might land bearing penalties whilst others returned a bonus move. 'Hounds and Jackals' seems to have become popular in the Middle Kingdom, another example of the importance given to the dog at that period, although evidence of it, or of a game very similar to it, is known from the late predynastic period, where small ivory figurines of dogs lying on their bellies, their paws stretched out like miniature lions, are known (Figure 20).

In the New Kingdom, in the middle of the second millennium BC, Egypt entered a period of unequalled prosperity and international influence. Gone were the days of the Valley's isolation and seemingly unchanging security; Egypt now became an imperial power, her kings mighty emperors, ruling lands far beyond Egypt's frontiers. The kings, queens and great nobles now were buried in magnificent tombs, hidden away in the enfolding rocks of the Valley of the Kings, on the west bank of the Nile at Thebes, which was a small town when the dog-loving King Intef II Wahankh was buried there but now was the capital of a great empire, the largest, richest and most powerful city in the world.

Among the kings and senior princes who were the owners of tombs in the Valley was the burial of a most intriguing individual, a young man named Maiherperi, who was given the tomb now designated KV36.[42] Maiherperi bore the high rank of 'Fan-Bearer on the Right Hand of the King', which identified him as among the most important courtiers. His status was confirmed by his burial in the Valley, in the company of the kings, for only the most favoured nobles and members of the court were so honoured – and there were few enough of them.

Maiherperi was very young, to judge by his mummy, which is much less grotesque than many of the time; he was probably in his early twenties. He was certainly young to bear the title which had been awarded to him, one of the most prestigious in the king's gift. His tomb was largely intact when it was discovered in 1898, though robbers had penetrated it and much of the jewellery with which Maiherperi would have been buried was gone; although the wrappings of the mummy had been torn open by the thieves looking for the jewels, the mummy itself had survived.

He was buried with a rich assemblage of valuables to take with him to the Afterlife. These included anthropoid coffins, quivers, a bracer and arrows, pottery, including a beautiful blue faience dish and many other vessels. A fine canopic chest, on runners, contained the canopic jars in which Maiherperi's internal organs would have been preserved. These were separately mummified, to allow them to be reunited with his body after the completion of the rituals to restore life to the mummified corpse.

One of the most precious of Maiherperi's possessions was an exceptionally beautiful copy of the Book of the Dead, an essential guidebook to direct the deceased on his journey to judgement and the Afterlife. It is magnificently illustrated and finely written, in an elegant cursive script. Rather in the manner of a Book of Hours made for a medieval nobleman, it was custom-made for Maiherperi and he himself appears in the papyrus, in several episodes. His funeral procession is depicted, his sarcophagus borne on a sledge, drawn by men and oxen and guarded by attendant goddesses. He appears before Osiris, Lord of the Dead, when his heart is weighed under the supervision of the god Thoth; Maiherperi is declared to be 'justified' and one aspect of his spirit, the ba, is now free to fly from the tomb in the form of a human-headed bird. In his human form, Maiherperi worships the seven cows and a bull that will magically supply the catering needs of the dead for ever.

This episode in his copy of the Book of the Dead shows that Maiherperi was dark-skinned, as indeed his mummy confirms. He is slender and elegant, wearing a diaphanous robe, with a short kilt beneath it. Maiherperi was 'a child of the kap', educated in the academy in which boys of the royal family were taught, together with the sons of nobles drawn both from Egypt and from notabilities of Egypt's colonies.

It is likely, therefore, that Maiherperi was the son of a Nubian chieftain and brought to Thebes, where he became the close companion of one of the Thutmosid kings of the Eighteenth Dynasty. The name of the king concerned

Figure 21   The rich burial of the courtier Maiherperi in the Valley of the Kings, in the company of some of Egypt's greatest sovereigns, contained two richly ornamented collars, evidently made for his hounds.

is not recorded but it is possible that it was King Thutmosis IV (1401–1391 BC). It has also been suggested that Maiherperi might have been the son of a king of Egypt by a Nubian woman, but in this case it might be expected that his royal parentage would have been recorded. Whoever he was, he was clearly greatly loved and honoured.

On the evidence of the quivers and the 75 arrows that he took with him, Maiherperi intended to engage in hunting in the Afterlife and he would clearly want to have his dogs with him. He also had two dog collars buried with him, made of leather dyed in pink, green and white, decorated with metal studs and finely set with prancing horses[43] (Figure 21). It appears that he did not take his dogs with him, perhaps preferring that they should follow him in the normal course of nature.

The Valley of the Kings had tombs specially reserved for favoured occupants, other than the kings themselves and their close family; these were the family pets of the kings. Three of the tombs have been described as comprising 'a pet cemetery, of the animal-loving king', Amenhotep II, whose own tomb is nearby and who was renowned as a sportsman as a young man. Each animal was mummified and wrapped in cloth, supplied with jewellery and provided with a sarcophagus. One of the animals so favoured was 'a yellow dog', which, to judge by the painting of it produced by the Egyptologist G. Harcourt Jones, was a tjesm, though it has drop ears like a Saluqi (Figure 22). This may, however, be the consequence of the difficulty in ensuring that the tjesm's pricked ears remained upstanding when mummified.[44]

Figure 22 A remarkable survival from the New Kingdom of 3500 years ago, this mummified tjesm, recovered from one of the tombs (KV50) in the Valley of the Kings, may be associated with King Amenhotep II (c. 1427–1400). The hound shared the tomb with a similarly mummified monkey.

One of the lesser-known achievements of the Ancient Egyptians was the invention of landscape gardening and the painting of pastoral themes. From the early Old Kingdom the kings and nobles delighted in modelled landscapes and the making of gardens. In the Middle Kingdom, King Nebhetepre Montuhotep II built an entire artificial landscape under which his tomb was concealed at Deir al-Bahari. The New Kingdom saw the introduction, on a generous scale, of landscape painting, in which natural environments and pastoral scenes were represented with considerable skill.

In the New Kingdom the rituals and techniques for preserving the bodies of the dead, a procedure essential if they were to be returned to life, advanced considerably, though surprisingly the appearance of the finished mummies of the New Kingdom and later were not nearly as naturalistic as in the Old Kingdom. This may well have been because something like a full-scale funerary industry grew up where once only the very great could hope for the services of the priests of Anubis; in later times the rites designed to secure the perpetuation of life beyond death became available to all who merited such a privilege or who were able to afford the not inconsiderable cost of a well-appointed and decorated tomb and the attentions of the priests of Anubis, the Lord of the Necropolis. Anubis' priests were responsible for the mummification of the corpse and for the despatching of the deceased to the next world.

During the long reign of King Rameses II of the Nineteenth Dynasty (1297–1213 BC) a sculptor named Ipy (or Ipuy) was buried at Deir el-Medina. It was there that all the craftsmen, artists and builders who worked on the royal and other tombs lived. They were known, collectively, as 'The Servants of Truth'. Ipy's tomb (Theban Tomb 217) lies in the necropolis of the workers engaged in the building, equipping or decoration of the tombs in the Valleys of the Kings, Queens and nobles. In addition to his work as a sculptor, Ipy was also a furniture designer and provided furniture for the chapel of King Amenhotep I.[45]

His tomb is decorated with scenes in the pleasant garden in which his funerary chapel was built and in which the ceremonies at his entombment were conducted. A man, perhaps Ipy himself, is working in the garden with his dog sitting placidly by his side. An even more pastoral note is struck by the presence of shepherd boys with their goats; one of the boys is playing a flute, a distinctly Arcadian touch. Ipy was also a lover of cats: in another scene he nurses a kitten on his lap whilst the mother cat, a silver ring in her ear suggesting that she was a temple animal, watches him narrowly.

Rameses II seems to have been fond of animals, which may have provided him with some distraction from his perpetual erecting of great monuments recording himself, his achievements and the begetting of sons, at which he was prolific. In his immense inscription claiming a victory over the King of the Hittites at the battle of Qadesh (a claim disputed vigorously by the Hittite sovereign, who left his own description of the battle, also claiming victory, an early example of competing diplomatic versions of the same incident), Rameses names two of his brave horses, which, he insists, saved his life when all around him, with the exception of his charioteer, had fled. He also liked to be attended by his pet lion, 'Slayer of his Foes'.

In one of his temples, at Bait el-Wali, Rameses is shown in the immemorial royal posture, smiting a Libyan. He holds a curved scimitar with which he appears to be cutting off the Libyan's topknot, anticipating no doubt doing the same with his head. A small tjesm bitch, wearing a collar with a tie to which a leash could be attached, is sinking its teeth into the hapless Libyan's buttocks. The dog's name is 'Anath is a defender'. Anath was a goddess, originally of Asiatic origin, popular in the New Kingdom.[46] She was introduced to Egypt from the Levant, where she was one of the aspects of the Great Mother god-dess, who was not generally accorded the same degree of worship in Egypt as she was in lands to the north. She was associated with Set, the equivocal god of thunder and the desert, and Rameses' naming of his daughter echoes his family's known adherence to the cults of Set. The kings of the XIX and XX Dynasties particularly honoured him; several of the kings adopted his

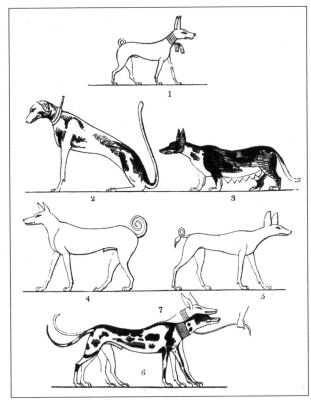

Figure 23   Sir J. Gardner Wilkinson, a distinguished Egyptologist of the mid-nineteenth century, illustrated a rather eclectic collection of hounds and other canines that he recorded in the tombs in his celebrated work *The Manners and Customs of the Ancient Egyptians*.

name in their royal nomenclature. Rameses named his favourite daughter, Bint-Anath, 'Daughter of Anath'. His dog's name also honours the goddess, suggesting that dog and daughter could, without offence or mockery to the goddess or the princess, both share a dedication to the goddess.

The Egyptian concern for dogs did not only extend to the tjesm. The variety of dog types or breeds evident in tomb decorations caught the attention of scholars from the earliest days of the European discovery of the Nile civilisation. Thus, Sir John Gardner Wilkinson, in his immensely influential work *Manners and Customs of the Ancient Egyptians*,[47] first published in 1836, described and illustrated a number of rather strange-looking canines, 'various kinds of dogs, from the sculptures'[48] (Figure 23). He wrote

The Egyptians had several breeds of dogs, some solely used for the chase, others admitted into the parlour or as companions of their walks; and some, as at the present day, were chosen for their particular ugliness. The most common kinds were a sort of fox-dog, and a hound; they also had a short-legged dog, not unlike our turn-spit, which was a great favourite, especially in the reigns of the Osirtasens; and, as in later days, the choice of a king or some noted personage brought a particular breed into fashion.

Mummies of the fox-dog are common in Upper Egypt; and this was doubtless the parent stock of the modern red wild dog of Egypt, so common in Cairo and in other parts of the lower country.[49]

Gardner Wilkinson's is a very nineteenth-century view of these aspects of ancient Egyptian customs, as clearly he believed they affected the people's relationship with their dogs. It is unlikely that the Egyptians acknowledged the existence of parlours; that they chose dogs for their ugliness seems, on the generality of the evidence, improbable; nor did fashion play so important a part in their management as he seems to suggest. Despite Gardner Wilkinson's formidable reputation as a philologist and his translation of many important hieroglyphic inscriptions, the reference to 'the Osirtasens' is presumably a misreading of the name of the Montuhotep kings who reigned in the Eleventh Dynasty, though there appears to be no surviving evidence of their having sustained a particular affection for these seemingly rather ungainly dogs, mentioned by him. The 'fox-dog' in the quotation above is presumably the tjesm.

Later in the nineteenth century the great English Egyptologist William Matthew Flinders Petrie, whose work at Abydos was particularly influential in recording the earliest phases of the kingship in Egypt, recorded the measurements of the crania of a number of mummified dogs, including specimens of the hunting hound. These were taken from dog cemeteries at Qau, Dendereh and Hawara;[50] he also recorded the memorial stelae of royal dogs in the First Dynasty necropolis at Abydos which have already been noted. Several of the dogs from Dendereh are described as 'tesm dog', 'Egyptian greyhound' and 'greyhound'. One dog from Hawara is noted as 'hound', whilst the remainder are simply classified as 'dog'.

Petrie placed his collection of the remains of mummified dogs in the Natural History Museum in London. This is one of the very few such collections available for study. The Vienna Museum of Natural History also has a group of 73 mummified skulls, drawn from two of the principal centres of the cults of canine divinities, Abydos and Asyut, as well as from Thebes.

One of the few accessible modern studies that describes the skeletal remains of ancient Egyptian dogs is based on material recovered from Tomb 34 in Ein Tirghi Cemetery, at Balat in the Dakhleh oasis in the Western desert.[51] The remains of 16 canids, including puppies and immature dogs, were found there in a part of the tomb where they had been trapped by the collapse of a section of the tomb's roof, under which they had created a den.

These unfortunate dogs are representative of the period which marks the extreme limit of the history of Ancient Egypt. However, the comparison of their remains with those of other dogs from Balat,[52] including tjesm from an Old Kingdom context, confirms the exceptionally long survival of the hunting hound strain, at least from the third millennium (and, as we have seen, from demonstrably earlier times) until the very end of the first millennium BC.

The Balat dogs are also among the last examples of the pure tjesm stock to be identified from Egypt. For reasons that will be examined later, the status of the dog seems to have declined after the end of the New Kingdom, at the beginning of the first millennium BC. To judge by the iconographic evidence at least, the Egyptians no longer cosseted their dogs as once they had done.

It becomes clear that, as seemingly immemorial Egypt moved towards its third millennium of existence, the dynamic which had powered the majestic achievements of the Old Kingdom, the forceful state-building of the Middle Kingdom kings and the imperial splendours of the New Kingdom, had begun to attenuate. After the end of the Twentieth Dynasty, Egypt was rarely ruled by a native Egyptian king.

For another thousand years Egypt would be a wonder to the nations, would still be a byword for wealth, mystery and magic. But, in truth, the glory had gone and, strangely, the millennia-old affection for dogs seems to have declined with its passing.

CHAPTER 3

The Hound in the Hunt

Even when the Unification of the Two Lands had finally been achieved, many of Egypt's social mechanisms were still rooted in the Neolithic, a condition that would have applied to the lives of the vast majority of her population for most of the Early Dynastic period. It was only when the state – in the person of the king and his attendant nobles, many of whom were territorial magnates – touched their lives that the condition of the people appreciably changed, for better or worse.

A major preoccupation for the people of most ancient Egypt, as for all Neolithic peoples, was hunting, to supplement whatever edible plants, roots, small animals, and sometimes the scavenging of the kills of larger animals, might be accessible. Although the primary objective of the hunt was the provision of food through the consumption of game animals, a consideration that was particularly telling as the population grew rapidly as a result of the state system that now directed Egyptian life, a system of rituals and cultic observances attending the hunt also developed, as they did in every department of life. The hunt was a sacred act and the experience of its participants reached beyond the world of the senses; the animals of the hunt, too, were touched with its sacred character.

With the approach of a more structured society the nature and practice of the hunt changed, becoming both more ordered and doubtless more efficient, the latter quality in part at least through the engagement and careful management of the tjesm. It also became more ritualised around the person of the king, when the hunt was conceived as an aspect of his suprahuman function, ensuring that order triumphed over chaos. The hound now became an integral part of the hunter's procedures, when in the past it had most likely been simply a companion, invited or otherwise, with little control or direction, though useful in harrying wounded or exhausted prey and ready to take advantage itself of any leavings that it might scavenge. All this was to change and the hound became the hunters' enthusiastic assistant in the excitement and challenge of the hunt. As in what might be thought to be weightier matters, the turning point in the hounds' status was the first appearance of the Dual King, in the closing decades of the fourth millennium, as witnessed by the commemorative stelae raised over the graves of favourite hounds.

The changes in the organisation of the hunt and its increasing ritualisation are relevant in the history of the Egyptian state even when reviewing the relatively modest issue of the part that the hunting hound was to play in the society newly emerging in the Valley. Egypt flourished as a complex nation-state for something like 35 centuries, an immense expanse of time judged by historical reckoning, for it represents approximately seven-tenths of the whole of recorded history. The historiography of the Egyptian state, in the sense of a deliberately conceived and executed recording of what were judged to be significant events, began with the kings of the First Dynasty. They were able to take advantage of the relatively newly invented technique of encoding information relating to the principal events of their reigns by means of a unique writing system, the hieroglyphs, the origins of which must be sought in predynastic times. The hieroglyphs were swiftly to become one of the distinctive marks of Egyptian culture. It is arguable that no more beautiful and certainly no more mysterious epigraphy was ever invented by an ancient people.

Although the origins of the line from which the first kings of Egypt came are shrouded in the obscurity of the latter phases of the predynastic period, it is possible now to construct a reasonably secure sequence of the events which culminated in the introduction of the kingship, and which led on to the political unification of the Valley.[1] The first man to be recognised as the ruler of the Two Lands, the incarnate Horus, was King Aha, in all probability the son of Narmer, who was conventionally credited with the Unification of the Dual Kingdom. The princes of This/Abydos, having emerged as victorious in the struggle which preceded the creation of the Dual Monarchy, moved

northwards and established the capital of the Dual Kingdom in the region of
what was to become the city of Memphis, to the south of present-day Cairo.
This was to be the pivot of the Two Lands, built at the point at which Lower
and Upper Egypt march; with only occasional interruptions Memphis was
to remain one of the most important of Egypt's seats of royal government
for most of her history.

The Egyptians were the first people to leave documentary records of their
lives. Their motivations, as always with the perpetrators of autobiographies,
were mixed: pride in achievement; hope of the recognition of their worth;
and, particularly for the Egyptians, optimism about the life to come, when
they might achieve the status of the justified and enjoy the perpetuation
of life in the Valley to eternity, exalted to perfection. This last was perhaps
the most frequent impulse to which they yielded, for the Egyptians were
obsessed with life and with its prolongation. In later times, when eternal
life became an option for everyone, not only for the kings and their closest
associates, all well-founded Egyptians, provided they could afford a suitably
decorated sarcophagus, mummy case or tomb, could ensure so desirable an
eternity. This they did by recording all that was favourable, agreeable and
meritorious in their earthly life and ensuring that the record was preserved
in their tombs in the form of carved reliefs, as painted decoration, inscribed
on memorial stelae and papyrus, or in the embellishment of a sarcophagus.
By these means they expected to achieve the continuation of life beyond
death, in the pleasant gardens and the super-Nilotic environment reserved
for the justified dead.[2]

An examination of the wall reliefs in the tombs of the nobility of the Old
Kingdom, who were prodigal in the recording of their world and even that
of the lesser folk, suggests a prevailing mood of happiness and contentment.
This is, of course, an entirely subjective judgement but it is the impression
that a familiarity with the scenes depicted invariably invokes. This sense of
contentment and tranquillity is also enhanced by the fact that, despite the
majesty of old Egypt and the undoubted power of her kings, warfare is
virtually entirely absent, with only the very occasional report of a frontier
disturbance or the infiltration of foreigners (never a category of person
affectionately regarded by the Egyptians of antiquity) requiring small-scale,
punitive action. In its first thousand years' existence the land of Egypt could
really have seemed to be the archetypal Peaceable Kingdom, one of the
few occasions that anything approaching so ideal a concept has been even

remotely realised; it was only when influences from the world beyond her frontiers seeped into the Valley that such institutions as armies and the arts of war began to be required.

Yet warfare is only the hunt raised to a political dimension. The Egyptians were great huntsmen and hunting was as carefully organised as any other department of life. It had its own bureaucracy and teams of officials who were responsible for the protection of the game animals and the maintenance of their numbers in the various hunting lands of Egypt. The King's Huntsman, appointed in each principal hunting locality, held an important and respected office. We know much about Egyptian hunting methods from the wall reliefs and paintings in the tombs of the noblemen who practised the sport in the desert and, as an alternative, on the waters and marshes of the Delta. There, hunting water fowl they might be assisted by an enthusiastic cat, which was as much interested in the game as was the huntsman, and sometimes by the mongoose; it seems improbable that either of these animals could be trained to the chase, but they are affectionately represented in hunting scenes on water at various periods of Egypt's history. The hunting hound, by contrast, was a professional: alert and straining at the leash to be away after the quarry.

The hunt as a formal, and sometimes a ceremonial and symbolic, event had a long ancestry in dynastic Egypt. The earliest kings themselves made provision to allow themselves to go hunting in the Afterlife. Aha was buried at Abydos with a phalanx of young men, all between 18 and their early twenties, who were to comprise the king's retinue in the Afterlife. They were in all probability intended to serve as transfigured huntsmen or warriors and to provide Aha with a perpetual hunting round, and also to ensure that he was attended with a proper royal state. With them was buried a group of young lions, who were presumably sent on to the next world to serve as the king's eternal quarry. Lions and young men alike had seemingly been put to death to serve the king.[3]

This somewhat macabre conclusion demonstrates one aspect of the sacred nature of the hunt, to be pursued through all eternity. That it was considered to be a sacred activity is also witnessed by such episodes as that which appears in the Pyramid Texts when, in a particularly powerful invention, the king on reaching the territory of the gods falls upon them, hunting them as he might the animals of the Valley, before he consumes them in a dramatic cannibal rite.[4]

Figure 24 The *tjesm* was the hunting hound par excellence. In many reliefs from the tombs of the nobles of the Old Kingdom the hound is shown in a variety of activities and contexts in the hunting field and in the deserts. This sequence comes from the tomb of Ptahhetep, a great noble of the Fifth Dynasty.

We know that hunting with dogs was practised in Egypt as early as the beginning of the fourth millennium; it probably had been adopted centuries earlier still. Hunting was celebrated not only as a pastime appropriate for great nobles: it was the ritual act also that, in Egyptian eyes, demonstrated the power of order over disorder. Certain animals of the hunt represented the powers of chaos that, on a cosmic scale, were believed always to threaten the prosperity, even the survival, of Egypt itself. Controlling them on the hunting field would stand as a witness to the subjugation of such forces in the cosmos.

A crucial element in the refinement and increasing efficiency of the hunt was the presence of the hound and his participation in the pursuit of game, before the introduction of the horse in the middle of the second millennium (Figure 24). The hunt was originally conducted on foot; its techniques had changed little since the late Stone Age. Hunting techniques in the Ice Age, in Upper Palaeolithic times and even in the later Neolithic period were, as might be expected, distinctly basic. Game was selected generally from the very old or the very young animals, the ailing and the injured. Large prey was speared to death, smaller animals were brained with stone axes. Sometimes herds of animals were driven over cliffs or precipices to die on the rocks below or, if they were injured, to be despatched by the hunters. Hunting, then, was not an elegant pastime.

In Egypt in the third millennium more sophisticated techniques evolved. The hunting of the larger desert game appears to have consisted of driving the quarry into corrals. In this process the hound was vital in herding and corralling the animals, which could then be slaughtered by the huntsmen. If the game was pursued in open country the dog was even more important in harrying the quarry, tracking and running down young or injured beasts and in bringing down vulnerable prey. A pack of hounds would be effective in bringing even a larger animal, an oryx for example, at bay and keeping it immobilised until the hunters came.

The identification between the hunt and warfare as well as its nature as a ritual action are graphically illustrated in the scenes on one of the most important surviving examples of a form of art peculiar to Egypt and to the period immediately before the foundation of the First Dynasty. At this time there appears to have been a disturbed phase preceding the presumed confrontation of the princes of Naqada, This/Abydos and Hierakonpolis, which resulted in the integration of the Valley and ultimately the imposition of the rule of the princes of This over the entire country.[5] As we have seen, the time immediately before the emergence of the kingship was a period of ferment in the Valley. Rival dynasties of the various principalities that made up the Valley's polity seem to have jostled for power, sometimes forming alliances, as often in opposition one with another.

The documents that are taken to indicate the likely course of events in the southern part of the Valley survive in the form of rectangular plates of schist or greywacke and are known as 'palettes'; they were derived from the plates on which the predynastic Egyptians mixed a cosmetic made from ground malachite and bonded with animal fat. This was daubed on the eyelids and upper cheeks to protect the eyes from the sun's glare. Sometimes the palettes take on a form dictated by the scenes carved on them, with animals real and imaginary and scenes of battle. They are of great historical and, even more, of great mythographical value, coming as they do from the time of preliteracy. They also provide glimpses into the complex psychology of the people who were to become the dynastic Egyptians in an early stage of their advance towards nationhood.

In the late predynastic period the palettes became highly stylised, evidently with a votive or dedicatory purpose; many of them have been found in temples and shrines and are too large ever to have been used for their original utilitarian and rather modest function. The scenes which these ceremonial or commemorative palettes now relate have been interpreted as incidents in the struggles of the various regional princes to establish their hegemony over larger areas of the Valley than that represented by their ancestral lands, or to oppose the ambitions of other rulers with similar objectives. The animals that participate in the actions portrayed are taken to be symbolic of the particular prince or a federation of clans, 'hacking-up' the citadel of an opponent. In the case of the wild bull, for example, goring the fortified walls of a town under attack, the animal is intended as a manifestation of one of the ultimately victorious princes, and the bull is trampling the enemy beneath its massive hooves. In the period immediately before the creation of the Dual Monarchy the palettes also acquire a religious dimension in that they show personages who, in historic times, were to be recognised as 'gods', and so appear to record cultic as well as political events. Sometimes, the animals are identified with solar or stellar entities.

One of the most compelling and ornate of the palettes is that which is known as 'The Hunters' Palette' or 'The Lion Hunt'.[6] This palette is an elongated rhomboidal schist plate, narrower at one end than at the other. It survives in three fragments: one in the Musée du Louvre, one in the British Museum and the third in the Ashmolean Museum, Oxford. Along the edges of the palette ranks of warriors or hunters are shown marching in file. They carry weapons which are carefully differentiated: bows, arrows, spears, lassoes, boomerangs and maces. The leader of the most numerous file is followed by a figure carrying a pole on which is mounted the Falcon standard; he is perhaps the prince who is the eponym of the Falcon clan, which ultimately was to be victorious over the whole Valley. The very small scale of the skirmishing that took place during the period preceding the Unification is well suggested by the very few warriors/hunters who are taking part in the events that the palette relates.

Between the two files of warriors/hunters a lion hunt is in progress, hence the palette's alternative name. Two lions are depicted; one, looking distinctly disappointed, as well he might as he is stuck full of arrows, appears to be leaving the field. The other lion, at the extreme end of the palette, is also wounded and is followed by his cub, surely unusual lionine behaviour. Like the lions on the Gebel el-Arak knife, the lions on the palette are said to be Asiatic; they are heavily maned, unlike the generality of African lions that might be expected to feature in such an event, as it is assumed to be occurring in Egypt. In the area in which the lions are being hunted, many other animals are congregated: hartebeest, hare, red fox (?), Dorcas gazelle, ostrich, Dama deer.[7]

It is possible that the palette, whose actual provenance is unknown though it may have come from Hierakonpolis, represents a conflict between the Falcon prince and the Lion prince, the latter being attended on the field by his 'cub'. It has long been recognised that the predynastic divisions of Egypt were ruled by princes who took particular animals as their emblems. These may have included the lion, the bull, the scorpion and possibly the dog, in addition to the ultimately victorious Falcon. Among the other animals represented in the field there is one which has not thus far been mentioned, a slender canid, of which there are two examples, with upstanding ears and long, brush-like tails. The latter feature has been taken to indicate that the animals are red foxes; certainly, their tails are thick and bushy, more like that of a fox than a dog. But this does not explain what foxes are doing in the middle of the hunting field, apparently cooperating with the hunters and harassing the prey. Although it is possible that the animals represented are intended to be desert foxes, it is surely more likely that the animals are dogs, their tails being represented with more imagination than strict zoological observation. They also seem to be notably taller than a fox, more nearly in keeping with the height of a tjesm.

The uncertainty in the matter of these canids' tails highlights a recurring problem, which will also arise when considering the nature of those animals which the Egyptians regarded as manifestations of particular 'divinities'. On occasion, Egyptian artists and craftsman could record their subjects with the most exact accuracy and observation, but they did not always do so. It is not at all unlikely that, for whatever reason, the craftsman who made the Hunter's Palette, though possessed of the highest talent, consistently showed the tjesm with tails more luxurious than those which the animals would naturally have borne in life.

A feature of the Hunters' Palette is that all the warriors/hunters are dressed identically, almost as though in uniform, with feathers or plumes in their hair, like those who appear in the predynastic rock engravings in Egypt and Nubia, in south-western Asia and in Western Arabia. In the last-named example the warriors/hunters are closely paralleled by the figure on the rocks at Bir Hima.[8] The Bir Hima engravings are probably much earlier than the

Hunters' Palette. Their location is due east of Najran in south-west Arabia across the Red Sea and it is tempting to see some connection between the Egyptian and the Arabian shores; the coincidence of the similarity of the two figures, the Egyptian and the Arabian, is certainly very singular. It should be said, however, that Neolithic hunters are depicted in much the same way in other regions, in Iran for example, holding the same distinctive bow and with feathers in their hair. Indeed, the same figure has already been noted from a much earlier time in Egypt, in the hunter holding the four tjesm on leashes on the Naqada I dish from the early fourth millennium.

The Egyptian hunters on the Palette wear short, pleated kilts from the backs of which hang the tails of canids, identical with those of the two hounds that are shown in the hunting field. It may be that a further element of symbolism is intended here, showing perhaps the participation of warriors from a notional dog clan (if such an institution actually existed, which is quite likely) in the Falcon prince's campaign to unify the Valley. It might be that the presence of the dogs and the trappings of the hunters indicate that the dog clan was linked with one of the territories of which canids were the presiding divinity or symbolic animal.

There were several of these in historic times. The Eighth Upper Egyptian nome was known as 'The Wolf'. The wolf proper was never indigenous to Egypt; a rarely observed canid, the Egyptian jackal, *Canis lupaster*, has been described as a wolf, but a genetic link with domesticated dogs is unproven.[9] The capital of the Wolf nome was at Teni, better known as This. The city of This was one of the most influential centres of the archaic kingship and the seat of the most active contenders for the eventual control of the Valley. The site of This has not been found but is thought to have been in the region of Abydos, possibly buried today beneath the town of El Girgeh. The Seventeenth Upper Egyptian nome was 'The Dog' and was presided over by the canine god, Anubis. Its capital was at Z3wty, now Asyut, called by the Greeks Lykopolis, 'Wolf City', a result of their mistaken belief that the city's presiding deity was a wolf. The enigmatic 'Animal of Set', a mysterious, probably largely stylised, canine, was the patron of the Fifth Upper Egyptian nome, 'The Two Gods', centred on Coptos, in Egyptian Gebtiu. The Thirteenth Upper Egyptian nome was where Wepwawet, one of the most ancient canid gods, was the tutelary divinity. He, too, is sometimes mistakenly described as a wolf; again, it is possible that this attribution came about by the association of Wepwawet with *Canis lupaster*. It is also not impossible that the archaic Egyptians may have known of the wolf and may have encountered it, though outside their own land. The possibility of a role for the wolf in these matters will be considered further (pp. 159–60 below), in the context of what appears to be an important ritual that involved royal officers wearing what are described as wolf pelts and caps.

Canids appear on many of the surviving palettes, along with a veritable menagerie of animals, real and imaginary. The 'Hierakonpolis (or 'Two Dogs') Palette', a particularly imposing example of the genre, is double-sided and each side is bounded by a leaping canid; it is likely, however, that hyenas are intended to be portrayed, rather than the domesticated dog or the jackal. But the animals on the Hierakonpolis Palette have also been described as 'hunting dogs', which by no stretch of the imagination could hyenas ever be said to be. As we have seen, very occasionally hyenas are shown leashed, evidently a reflection of the attempts to domesticate them, attempts which ended in failure, though apparently they did serve as a food resource in the Old Kingdom.[9]

On the obverse of the palette, surrounding the circular disc on which the kohl would have been ground (notionally, since these large palettes are obviously dedicatory) there are two fabulous monsters, with short heavy bodies and long serpent necks, known as 'serpo-pards', which are licking what is probably a dead gazelle. The quarrys in the hunting scene below the two long-necked monsters are being harassed by Saluqi, their lop-ears identifying the breed and serving to distinguish them from the prick-eared tjesm.[10] On the reverse of the palette the two large canids frame the hunting scene, the participants in which include another monster, as well as more Asian lions, together with the more familiar animals of an African hunt. These include a giraffe, which, like the elephant and the hippopotamus, was being driven out of the upper reaches of the Valley at this time, the consequence of the depredations of the hunters themselves.

The monsters included on these palettes are Western Asiatic in origin,[11] where both forms are known from seal impressions of the latter part of the fourth millennium; that they are associated with the palettes which seem to be very closely connected with the emergence of the kingship is both significant and, as has already been noted, surprising. The Egyptian elite of early antiquity was deeply conscious of its identity and it is the more surprising therefore that several of their most cherished icons of the kingship should be of Western Asiatic provenance. The idea of an invasion by a master-race,

Figure 25 A singular figure in one of the finest of the surviving predynastic palettes is that of the mysterious 'Flute Player' from the 'Two Dogs' palette. The Flute Player's precise nature is much disputed but the head at least (perhaps a mask) has marked canine characteristics, with the tjesm's long muzzle and pricked ears.

tactfully identified as 'the Dynastic Race' by its more recent protagonists, is now largely discarded, for there is no evidence of any substantial incursion of foreigners in the late predynastic period, certainly not on a scale that would appear in the genetic record.

The reverse of the Hierakonpolis Palette has one other strange, most intriguing, feature: standing at the base of the palette, a little aside from the main action, is a human figure with the head of a canid, probably a tjesm hound, playing a flute (Figure 25). A human–canid therianthrope conflation would, in dynastic times, have been identified as Anubis; he is not known as a flute-player, however. The figure on the Hierakonpolis Palette has been described as an anticipation of the Orpheus archetype or of Pan, a well-known flautist. This figure has also been described as 'wearing a giraffe-headed mask';[12] whatever he may represent the flute-player of Hierakonpolis is one of the most enigmatic and disturbing figures in predynastic Egyptian iconography.

The tjesm remained a popular subject in the repertory of Egyptian artists throughout the Old Kingdom and on into the Middle Kingdom, and is always shown in close association and partnership with its human companions. Indeed, the hound provides one of the few connecting links between the late predynastic repertory of designs and those of the Early Dynastic period and the Old Kingdom, which extends onwards into the New Kingdom, in the second millennium BC. There is a marked hiatus between the art of the late predynastic period and the subsequent First Dynasty. Certain forms and glyphs are carried over but the art of the dynastic period generally contrasts distinctly with that of the period from which it must be presumed that it descends. The most likely explanation for this apparent discontinuity is to be found in the establishment of the kingship. This event, with the attendant raising of the king to the status of the godhead, probably acted as a major stimulus to the artists and craftsmen of the day, who now had a god-king and his state to celebrate.

The hunting hound must have been the companion of the hunters long before any move to consolidate the Valley into a corporate political entity had come about, when the people of the Valley and the adjoining deserts were still closer to primitive wild men, hunting naked with spears and equally primitive bows and arrows; thus they appear in the earliest representations that we have, in the rock engravings of the eastern desert in Egypt and, even earlier, in the paintings and engravings of the North African hunters in the Sahara. He was their companion still when they were elegant, handsomely dressed aristocrats, engaged in what sometimes looks like the wholesale slaughter of animals driven into corrals. The rise of the Egyptian state was not good news for many of the animals which previously had enjoyed the lush resources of the Nile banks largely to themselves for so many millennia, apart from the periodic incursions of the hunting bands.

The tjesm was favoured by the Egyptians because of its ability to sustain powerful bursts of speed over extended distances; in this it was probably able to outrun even the Saluqi, though it could not compete with it over shorter distances. It was also particularly well suited to existence in a desert environment and had probably evolved physiologically to adapt to working in such conditions. The Egyptian Hound (like the Pharaoh Hound/Kelb tal-Fenek of today) was well-muscled at the shoulder and this meant that it could tackle quite large game, worrying it until the hunters came when the quarry was weary, actually bringing it down. In the oldest Egyptian wall-painting, the 'mural' in the now lost Tomb 100 at Hierakonpolis, tjesm are shown attacking oryx; this scene often appears in Old Kingdom reliefs in the mastabas of the nobles, when the dog is shown harrying a supine oryx. If this actually happened in life it could only have been when the animal was on the edge of exhaustion, for the oryx is both formidably built and dangerous, its long, sharply pointed horns capable of eviscerating a dog with little difficulty. There are even reliefs of dogs attacking bulls and lion; in such cases the dogs must have been prepared to harry the bull until the hunters came and despatched it. In many of the instances the symbolic meaning of the struggle between the hound and the animals associated with the god Set (who is further described in Chapter 5), and hence with the forces of disorder and chaos, is probably more important than a literal depiction of a hunt in progress.

When hunting young animals, gazelle for example, the tjesm could probably kill outright, by breaking the quarry's neck, as some modern hounds are able to do. This is suggested on the Hemaka disc, where the black hound has a gazelle by the throat. In pursuit of small game such as hare the tjesm would have been unbeatable, for it doubtless shared the remarkable ability of greyhounds and that of its modern counterparts to 'lock on' to the quarry and instantly to replicate its movements, no matter how energetically the prey attempts to shake off its pursuer. The tjesm, like the Pharaoh Hound, the hounds of the Mediterranean islands, which will be described in the next chapter, as well as the Saluqi, hunted by sight as well as scent. In the arid conditions of the Egyptian desert the latter faculty would be of less value than the dog's keen sight, especially in open country, though it would have been valuable in tracking a wounded animal. The spectacle of a Pharaoh Hound or Kelb tal-Fenek set on a rabbit or hare demonstrates the importance and the efficiency of the powers of sight possessed by hounds of this sort.

The tjesm is rarely depicted other than as an individual, though one or two couple will sometimes be shown leashed. In the mêlée of the hunt several tjesm may be shown working together as a pack, but as often each will be engaged in tackling its own quarry. In the carvings and engravings which appear on the rocks, in both the eastern and western deserts, packs of dogs are sometimes shown working in concert. On these occasions it is probable that the intention is to represent open country, where a pack of hounds would be of greater value in isolating the quarry, than individual hounds working separately. Whilst they have the tjesm's characteristic prick-ears they seem to be more squat than the slender and elegant hounds of the later periods, but it is perhaps unfair to expect the recorders of such scenes, put down upwards of 5000 years and more ago, to have concerned themselves too intently with a literal rendering of the dogs' morphology.

The huntsmen must have had the responsibility of training the hounds to undertake what were obviously quite sophisticated hunting routines. There are reliefs that show the men working with the dogs, holding a couple or sometimes more, the dogs straining to slip their leashes and keen to be away. There are similar scenes of men with very young dogs, their actions suggesting a considerable degree of concern for the animals' welfare.

In addition to the king's huntsman there were less exalted officers who were designated 'custodian of hounds'; in the ways of bureaucracies everywhere there was also a custodian (or supervisor) of such custodians. These officials became particularly important in the Middle Kingdom The huntsman was nu (B.352a). He is provided with the hound as his determinative, signalling the principal object of his concern. The term 'master of the hunt' is expressed in a related word in plural form: (B.352A) again employing the hound determinative. The office of 'chief huntsman', kherp (B.352A) is known from the Middle Kingdom.[13]

The Egyptians were convinced of the virtues of specialisation in crafts, trades and what in the present day would be called professional disciplines. Craftsmen and artists who have left records of their lives have emphasised their technical abilities and the long and careful training they underwent. It is fair to assume that workers on the great estates, those belonging for example to the king or the leading nobles, were similarly specialised in the training, handling and management of animals. The nobles, like the members of the royal family, maintained very large retinues of servants and, like their successors in the European Middle Ages, would have had a multiplicity of crafts and trades represented in their households. Also like European princes in the Middle Ages the kings of Egypt, even in the Old Kingdom, maintained menageries of exotic animals. Bears, which are not indigenous to Egypt, appear on reliefs in the Fifth Dynasty sun-temple of King Sahure; it has even been suggested that a miniature mammoth appears on one of the reliefs.[14] This may more likely be the result of artistic experiment or even fantasy, rather than the portrayal of a living animal, but it may be remembered that miniature versions of species such as rhinoceros and elephant survived, for example, in the island of Cyprus at the end of the Ice Age. It is more likely that a dwarf elephant is depicted in the Sahure relief.[15]

Animals which had a special use or value such as the hunting hounds and guard dogs, but also more challenging species like the fighting bulls which were popular especially among noble households in the provinces, required careful training and handling. Fighting bulls, which were valuable animals and important for stock breeding, were carefully managed to ensure that they did not damage themselves or their opponents too gravely, confining their fighting to a sort of ponderous wrestling.

One of the professions maintained in every royal or noble household of which we have particular knowledge, since the Egyptians placed great importance on it and were the earliest of all peoples to systematise its practice, was that of medicine. Medical practitioners were highly regarded and were retained as members of all the greatest households; we know the names of many of them and of the nature of their practices.[16] It is remarkable how many sophisticated clinical specialisations seem to be represented among the practitioners. There are specialists in diseases of the abdomen and bowels, opthalmics, pharmacology, and bodily fluids, whilst others practised as herbalists. Such a specialised practitioner was Aha-Nakht, a veterinarian, who was employed by the nomarch Djehutyhetep and who probably therefore numbered among his charges the fortunate Ankhu, Djehutyhetep's favourite, who, as we have seen, was accorded by him a status equal to his (Djehutyhetep's) sisters.

Aha-Nakht is mentioned in connection with a more important physician, Hesy-shef-nakht, who, with others, was working in the quarry, concerned with the health of the workers and officials engaged there. Aha-Nakht is specifically described as 'one who knows bulls' and presumably was responsible for maintaining the health of the cattle at the quarry.

Whether Aha-Nahkt was, in modern veterinary parlance, qualified in the treatment of 'small animals', as well as cattle, is not known. It would, however, have been wholly consistent with Egyptian medical organisation for such specialisations to have existed. One of the most important documents to have survived from the Middle Kingdom, the Kahun Papyrus, which deals with medical practice, specifically gynaecology, also details veterinary treatments for conditions of the eyes of a bull and a dog.[17]

It may well be that veterinarians were more common than the few extant texts which mention them suggest. The care of the dogs and their health, as much as the supervision of the huge stocks of living cattle, must have been a matter of concern to their owners. As we know, the death of a dog was regarded by the Egyptians as a calamity and as an occasion for formal mourning by the entire household. Cats, too, were much loved and respected, similarly were mourned at death and given formal burials often, like the dogs, in their own sarcophagi. Sometimes the two animals, presumably household pets, would be mummified together and placed in a double-compartmented sarcophagus or wooden coffin.

The burial of canids fulfilled a ritual purpose also, confirming their status as creatures which could move freely between the worlds of the living and the dead. Mass burials of canids are well known, from sites such as Saqqara and Asyut, the focus of pilgrimage by the people of the Late Period (664–332 BC) in ancient Egypt.

CHAPTER 4

Golden Jackals, Egyptian Hounds and the Hounds of the Mediterranean Islands

There is nothing inherently impossible about the proposition that the living breeds of hounds described here are related to the Egyptian Hound of antiquity. A 4000-year pedigree is a formidable, even if it is not a wholly improbable, lineage; the fact that the Egyptians managed to preserve the tjesm strain over at least 2000 years should give pause to anyone who might be inclined simply to dismiss the claim as insupportable. It must be admitted that many of the statements advanced by breeders and others about the origins of 'their' breeds are based more on optimistic supposition than on science. That situation is clearly about to change. The possibility of such lineages may repay examination, not least because the research published in the United States appears to have demonstrated that it is possible to establish the relative antiquity of the descent of specific breeds from the ancestral wolf,[1] implying a lineage substantially greater than the notional 4000–5000 years of the hounds' putative descent.

Dogs are remarkable creatures – just how remarkable is only now being revealed by writers such as Masson and Sheldrake,[2] who have examined sympathetically the behaviour and psychology of canines. To their work may be added that of the many scholars that fills the published proceedings of the increasing number of seminars dedicated to the study of the descent, behaviour, morphology and psychology of the domesticated dog. The inner life of dogs is very complex and their species' history, very different from that of primates, is only now beginning to be approached analytically.

That the dog's acknowledged ancestry from the wolf is obviously crucial both to the development of much of the species' characteristic behaviour and to its psychology has been frequently and convincingly demonstrated; the wolf is an ancestor about which to boast, for it is assuredly one of the most successful of all mammalian species, having, like *Homo sapiens*, colonised most of the world. The wolf has been described as demonstrating a sense of purpose; this is evident from film records of wolves in the wild, in, for example, their clearly intelligent and purposeful cooperation in separating selected animals from herds during the hunt. The wolf is a vigorous, skilful hunter, careful of its progeny, relatively long-lived. In the wild, wolves will take care of sick, injured or aged members of the pack. The wolf has become shy of humans, with good reason, but this may not always have been so.

The descent of living breeds of dogs and their interaction with humans has been copiously studied by zoologists, palaeozoologists, anthropologists, biologists, archaeologists and many other specialists, at least since the mid-nineteenth century. Indeed, the system of classification applied to canines, as to other species, is a century older still, when Linnaeus in 1758[3] listed the dog as distinct from the wolf and other canids. It is estimated that there are some 400 individual breeds of dog extant today,[4] as well as countless mongrels and feral dogs.

Darwin considered the descent of dogs in his work, *Animals and Plants under Domestication*, published in 1868.[5] Whilst in general he agreed that the wolf accounted for most of the dog's lineage, he proposed that another canid, the golden jackal, *Canis aureus*, might also have contributed to it. This view has few professionally qualified supporters today. But a limited qualification of the exclusively wolfish descent has been voiced, however cautiously, by some distinguished specialists. Thus: 'The justifications for the assumption [the descent of dogs from wolves] are beginning to look convincing but not proven; they are based on dental morphology and more importantly on comparative behaviour.'[6] This last point, relating particularly to behaviour, will be returned to later.

Scholars from the more recent past also voiced reservations about the *exclusively* lupoid descent of dogs from wolves. Hilzheimer in his often quoted article is specific in voicing his reservations the descent of the tjesm, 'I believe that all breeds of dogs, with the single exception of the Egyptian and its derivative the greyhound, have been evolved ultimately from the wolf.'[7] This comment would today be phrased differently, as it is broadly agreed that the tjesm, like the Saluqi, is part of a group of dogs all of which are classified as greyhounds.

Apart from Darwin other scientists, including Konrad Lorenz, also took the view that the golden jackal might, in certain instances, have contributed to the ancestry of the wolf-born progeny that ultimately led to the domesticated dog.[8] Lorenz had the notion that domesticated dogs could be divided into 'aureus dogs', descended from *Canis aureus*, the golden jackal, and 'wolf-dogs', whose descent is self-evident. He further proposed that 'aureus dogs' were more friendly and tractable than the 'wolf-dogs'. He later recanted and accepted the prevailing consensus.

At one time it was believed that the various species of *Canis* could not interbreed; this view is no longer sustained as it is clear that interbreeding between all the sub-species is viable and that fertile progeny can be produced from wolf–dog crosses and from jackal–dog. It is recognised now that all canids have the same chromosome diploid number, $2n = 78$.[9] This is supported by the observation of another authority, Dr Ian Dunbar, who has commented 'It is impossible to say for certain that jackals, coyotes and other wild *Canidae* play no part in the domestication of dogs, especially since it is known that the jackal still breeds freely with pariah, shenzi and dingo-like dogs, in much the same way that some northern breeds, such as Huskies and Malamutes, may be back-crossed with wolves.'[10]

A study of the mammals of ancient Egypt published in recent years, which contains much on the dogs that can be identified in the archaeological record and in the works of art produced by the Egyptians themselves, states: 'The ancestors of Near Eastern, African and Egyptian dogs were bred from tamed wolves (*Canis lupus pallipes*) some 8–10,000 years BC in southwestern Asia.'[11] The emphasis with which this observation is made is misleading, for, despite the authority of professional zoology that occasions it, it is more supposition than certainty.

Whilst it may seem cavalier to fly in the face of so firm a scholarly bias in favour of an exclusively wolf ancestry for the domesticated dog, the possibility remains an infusion of golden jackal genes is not *scientifically* beyond question. Looked at with lay eyes it seems not impossible that, in the movements of populations at the end of the last Ice Age and later, when increasing desiccation forced the large-scale migration of the hunter–gatherers who contributed substantially to the earliest settled populations of the Nile Valley, canids which had developed from wolves also moved into the north-eastern quadrant of Africa, where they met and interbred with the golden jackal, which, as already noted, is indigenous to the region. The possibility of such interbreeding has indeed been acknowledged:

> In summary it may be said that there is no conclusive evidence on either morphological or behavioural grounds to prove that all domestic dogs are descended from a single ancestor. On the other hand, the wolf does appear to have the greatest share in their parentage. It is probable that the small, Western Asiatic wolf, C. lupus arabs, was the progenitor of most European and Southern Asiatic dogs, including the dingo. Perhaps the golden jackal interbred with these dogs from time to time and with dogs that migrated southwards through Africa with humans at a relatively late period.[12]

Judged in terms of probabilities it is surely likely that such cross-breedings occurred, though it must be admitted that there is yet no direct zoological or archaeological evidence to prove it.

The advocates of the theory of the exclusively wolfish descent of the dog raised another objection to the possibility of the golden jackal having been involved in the ancestry of the domesticated dog, an objection that is frequently cited as the most convincing secondary evidence for the dominance of a lupoid ancestry. This was the belief that domesticated dogs bark and wolves vocalise – that is, whimper, howl and bark – in a very similar manner; this observation was thought to dispose of the golden jackal as an ancestor of the domesticated dog since all canine vocalisation, it was said, demonstrably derived from wolves. Nonetheless, based on the observation of the behaviour of living breeds identified, however tenuously, with the ancient hounds and comparing it with what is known of the behaviour of the golden jackal, including the distinctive vocalisation employed by both the golden jackal and the Pharaoh Hound/Kelb tal-Fenek this rejection of the hounds' propensity to vocalise may require modification. Its particular and very distinctive qualities will be described below.

The observations regarding the golden jackal and the hounds of the Mediterranean islands are based on the supposition that the Pharaoh Hound/ Kelb tal-Fenek is, as its protagonists have claimed, either descended from or is a replica of desert hunting hounds of the type which prevailed in Egypt in antiquity; it is certainly virtually identical in form and stance to the hound depicted in so many ancient Egyptian contexts. In the light of the study by Parker et al. – if its findings are accepted by the scientific community – it is the second of these options which appears the more likely: that the living hounds replicate the physiology of the ancient hounds. But even if replication is the preferred option, the precision with which the modern breeds appear to mimic the ancient hound is remarkable.

The characteristic coloration of the Mediterranean island hounds, the Ibizan, the Basenji and the Rhodesian Ridgeback, immediately recalls the coloration of the tjesm where that can be established, either from colour representations or the examination of the pelage of mummified hounds. The modern Rhodesian Ridgeback, as noted earlier, has been bred out of African hunting dogs (now given the breed name 'Africanis'), interbred with European stock.[13]

> It may be speculated that changes in coat colour with related docility of temperament occurred early in the domestication of the dog and that the most favoured mutant form was the all-tan or ochreous body, with white tip to the tail, white on the muzzle and white on the lower limbs. This is the characteristic colouring of the dingo, many pariah dogs and mongrels, and the African Basenji. The skins of mummified dogs from ancient Egypt also appear to have had a uniform coat colour which was probably ochreous-tan.[14]

It is this golden–ochreous–tan coloration, added to the hounds' general physiology, the slender body, long neck, pointed, slightly arched muzzle, that the Kelb tal-Fenek and the other island hounds replicate so convincingly. It does not, however, appear that Parker et al. considered the possibility that the Egyptian hound (nor, just conceivably, the Pharaoh Hound) descended, in part at least, from the golden jackal; nor did they seemingly obtain specimens from the populations of hounds indigenous to the islands from which the modern breeds are derived.

Compared with the Pharaoh Hound/Kelb tal-Fenek another of the island dogs is relatively little known, but it will be suggested here that it is particularly important in establishing the likely extent of these hounds' ancestry. This is the Cirneco dell'Etna, a native of Sicily. That the dog has a recorded ancestry of at least 2500 years is supported by evidence of its presence in Sicily since the middle of the first millennium BC, and it is probable that it became established in the island long before then. The history of this dog and that of the Maltese Hound will be considered further in this chapter.

The golden-tan coat of the tjesm is not the only pelage associated with hunting dogs in ancient Egypt. A tall, rangy hound, very similar in appearance to one of the hounds found in the Mediterranean islands in the last century, the Ibizan Hound, is frequently represented in the art of the Old Kingdom and sometimes in the Middle Kingdom, its coloration suggesting dappling or piebald characteristics. Khui's dog, Iupu, mentioned in Chapter 2, was perhaps one of these. The Ibizan is distinct in its physical characteristics from the other island hounds and this may, in consequence, prompt the question whether it is of the same ancestry as the tjesm and some of the other hounds considered here. It is native to the Balearics, has two distinct strains, which are distinguished by their coats. One, a smooth-coated hound, is closer in appearance to the tjesm; the other, a rough-coated dog, is less so and might be the product of another interbreeding. A dog found in Portugal, the Podorenco Português, is remarkably similar in build to that of the rather squat, terrier-like dogs portrayed on the rock faces of the Egyptian deserts in predynastic times from which, it has been suggested here, the tjesm may have evolved, as the result of selection in Early Dynastic times.

There were other dogs in Egypt in ancient times, too. One is a shorter, more heavily built dog which appears particularly in the early rock carvings; this is the dog that is often, if unflatteringly, called 'pariah'. This dog, with its pricked ears and curled tail has some characteristics which are to be found in the tjesm and it may be that the hounds bred for royal or noble households were selected from these dogs. The Basenji, originating further south in Africa, may also share a similar ancestry, and, allowing for its development in isolation from the other dogs, it shares characteristics common to the tjesm's presumed living counterpart. The Basenji's coat and markings are closer to the tjesm and hence, perhaps, to the golden jackal, though its celebrated reluctance to vocalise argues against any connection. Parker et al. acknowledge the antiquity of the Basenji's descent but there is no evidence of the dog's presence in Egypt and the possibility that it might have contributed its genes to the tjesm may, at this stage at least, be dismissed.

There was also the very short-legged, long-bodied dog, not unlike a large basset hound, that, rather engagingly, was proposed as the ancestor of the dachshund by a German authority many years ago. This proposal, in which the similarity in appearance of the dogs was bolstered by an example of pseudo-etymology that saw the Egyptian name for the hound as being the origin of the word 'dachshund', did not find favour in scholarly opinion. Ankhu, Djehutyhetep's beloved hound, was such a dog; as we have seen, it was probably an achrondoplastic dwarf. There was also a powerfully built dog, known from the reliefs and paintings, which may have been a survival of the similarly built dog which appears in the rock art of the fourth millennium.

An examination of the ways and lifestyle of the golden jackal, *Canis aureus*, is revealing. Jackals are interesting and complex creatures with behavioural patterns that are certainly not typical of all canids. They are an ancient species; their remains have been found in Africa and have been dated to one million years ago, indicating a lineage that is comparable with the wolf's. The golden jackal is complex in its social behaviour, more so than the other species of African jackal, and is strongly familial in its loyalties.[15] The golden jackal family stays together far longer than most other canids, where the young dogs tend to be expelled from the group as soon as they are able to fend for themselves. As with wolves, golden jackal offspring stay together for much more extended periods, sometimes remaining with their parents for as long as two years before setting out on their own, with the young adult siblings from a preceding breeding generation sharing in the care, protection and education of the puppies.

The extent of family bonding among golden jackals is with little doubt the product of one of this canid's most distinctive behavioural traits: monogamy. A golden jackal pair bond for life and demonstrate a concern and affection for each other which is both touching and unmistakeable. The dog and the bitch cooperate in hunting and both bring food to the puppies, which is regurgitated to them. Both parents share in the raising of the puppies, in their feeding and protection; they will also demonstrate a special concern and care for an ailing or weakly pup. Because the puppies and young adults remain in the family for up to two years, golden jackals in the wild have a higher survival rate than other wild canids, the consequence no doubt of the careful strategies of mutual concern and protection.[16]

A strong sense of territory is characteristic of the golden jackal, and it marks and patrols an extensive terrain; the Pharaoh Hound, too, ranges over a wide territory, given the opportunity to do so. The female golden jackal will mark her territory by cocking her leg, rather than by squatting, the 'normal' posture for a bitch when micturating. This practice, too, may be cited in support of the possible connection between the golden jackal and the living hounds. However, this is not unknown in other breeds, but, as a shared characteristic of Pharaoh Hounds and golden jackals, taken with the other characteristics that both animals display, it may be significant.[17]

The golden jackal's family ties are strengthened by a communications system which is unique among wild canids, apart from a similar procedure adopted by their cousins, the silver-back jackals. In the wild each golden jackal family has its own calling repertory, a loud whimpering, modulated cry peculiar to the family, which its members use to contact others, particularly puppies that have strayed dangerously far from the den. It has long been acknowledged that golden jackals have very complicated repertoires of vocalisation. This form of vocalisation is very unlike the howling of wolves and of most dogs. It is these behavioural patterns in the golden jackal community, designed to strengthen and secure familial ties, which suggest that the argument that vocalisation indicated the wolf descent of all canids may need to be qualified.

Among the apparent similarities of behaviour of the Pharaoh Hound and the golden jackal, the strong family bond demonstrated by the jackal is also found in the behaviour of the Pharaoh Hound, though in a less highly developed form. This is possibly the result of domestication, but breeders state that a Pharaoh Hound bitch will 'call' to a pup which has wandered away; similarly, elder sibling bitches will share the bringing up of puppies, cleaning them and guarding them. A Pharaoh Hound bitch will sometimes choose one of her daughters to remain with her, in effect as a permanent companion;[18] this, again, may be an echo of the long period in which a golden jackal's offspring will stay with the family. These particular practices are not as fixed in Pharaoh Hound families as they are in those of the golden jackal, but even these more occasional parallels are telling.

Wolves also have rituals of greeting that are practised by members of the pack. Thus, the Alpha male in the pack will be greeted by submissive behaviour by all the lower-ranking members; another practice, common to wolf packs as it is to the golden jackal, is that all members of the pack will share in the upbringing of the young.

Another notable African canid is the so-called African Wild or Hunting Dog, *Lycaon pictus*, or, as it sometimes inaccurately called, 'the painted wolf'; it is a separate genus and is distinct from the *Canis*. It is entirely wild and has never been domesticated. Like the golden jackal it is strongly familial with certain distinct habits that are peculiar to it.

The dog that is known today to the Kennel Club in Britain and to other international registration bodies as the Pharaoh Hound[19] appears to have been

known by that name only since the 1960s. It will already be clear that some
controversy attends the hound's nomenclature. The breeders of the Maltese
Hound, Kelb tal-Fenek ('Rabbit Dog'), for example, from whose carefully
protected hounds the modern breed was derived, who believe that Malta
should have the credit for the hound's survival, evidently and understandably
resent the Pharaonic (that is to say, Egyptian) label.[20] It is not difficult to
have some sympathy with this view, and it should be noted in parenthesis
that were the belief in the dog's descent from Egyptian ancestors confirmed
the dog that bears this name would be older by far than the title 'Pharaoh',
for the king of Egypt only became known by that epithet during the New
Kingdom, in the second millennium BC. It is derived from a circumlocution
that was used when speaking of the king or the centre of government, a
hieroglyphic group meaning 'Great House' (in Egyptian per-aa), much as
'Whitehall' or 'The White House' are employed today as shorthand terms for
the centres of government of Britain and the United States. It has achieved
general acceptance as a result of its use, generally in a pejorative sense, in
the annals of the Old Testament, the product of a tradition that had little
enthusiasm for things Egyptian or, for that matter, for dogs.

The King of Egypt's most frequently employed title is transliterated as
nswt-bity, literally 'he of the sedge and the bee'. It is now rendered as Dual
King, for the sedge and the bee are symbolic of the two kingdoms into
which the Valley was notionally divided, Upper and Lower Egypt. It is not
difficult to accept that 'Pharaoh Hound' rolls off the tongue more easily than
the alternative, 'Nswt-bity Hound' and will probably remain in common use,
though it is so evidently anachronistic; 'Pharaoh' is also obviously a more
marketable term, though that observation is not of much consolation to the
Maltese breeders.

Although 'Pharaoh Hound' has achieved a wide acceptance since its
adoption by the Kennel Clubs of the United Kingdom, the United States,
Switzerland, France and others, historical accuracy and justice to the Kelb
tal-Fenek urges the restitution of that name to the breed. That this should
be seriously considered will become clear if one of the central contentions
of this study, that the breeds considered here, whilst irrefutably sharing
similarities of morphology, coloration and behaviour, are each distinct and
indigenous to their homelands, a consideration that also applies to the tjesm
itself. The populations were in all probability established in late Neolithic
times, in the migrations that followed the increasing desiccation of that

period. There is simply no evidence at present that any of the hounds descend directly from the tjesm, though it is certainly not impossible such evidences of descent will be found by further, more precisely focused, genetic studies.

The Pharaoh Hound, accepting that it is the Kelb tal-Fenek under an Egyptian alias, has a coat with the distinctive ochreous tan, suffused with gold, a coloration that the examples of mummified tjesm share (Figure 26). Only one dog is known to the present writer which was entirely black, doubtless a sport, an example of the phenomenon of melanism, a reversion to a black coloration that occurs occasionally in many domesticated species. This dog, a spectacularly handsome animal, instantly recalled the most celebrated of all canine gods, the great god Anubis, who is represented as black but with golden embellishments. However, the dog in question, though in appearance a typical Pharaoh Hound, was not pure-bred as his dam was not of the breed;[21] nonetheless, the Pharaoh Hound strain was clearly dominant. In Chapter 5 the experience of Howard Carter, the excavator of the tomb of Tutankhamun, will be considered when he reported having seen two jet-black 'forms of the Anubis jackal', indicating that melanism is certainly not unknown among these canids; the black tjesm on the Hemaka disc will also be recalled. The archaic Ethiopian wolf, Canis simensis, is a canid that sometimes throws puppies with an entirely black coat, as a result of cross-breeding with domesticated dogs; it is one of the larger canids, with a rougher coat than the tjesm. It is now in danger of extinction, the consequence apparently of its promiscuous interbreeding, not a behavioural trait associated with the island hounds or presumably with the tjesm; it would have been difficult to sustain the bred over so very long a period if it had been so.

The Pharaoh Hound has the same strange faculty of 'calling' as the golden jackal, though this now survives with no immediate or apparent purpose or utility, other perhaps than as an entertainment for its human companions. It will sustain a 'conversation' over an extended period using a widely differentiated 'vocabulary', expressing itself in its high, keening whimper that is constantly modulated. It has the very jackal-like propensity of mimicking the sounds which its human interlocutor produces, just as the young golden jackal 'replies' to the call of a parent or sibling. It appears to repeat 'phrases' or groups of sounds in the course of a 'conversation'.[22]

Figure 26   The Pharaoh Hound, International Champion Ezhar Nickel Coin (breeder, Mrs S.M. Simm; owner, Mr. A. Okk, Estonia).

Another behavioural characteristic that has been reported in a published study of the Pharaoh Hound describes the dog's habit of giving a small, consistent ritual 'nodding and groaning', when it meets a human for the first time.[23] Generally the dogs are diffident with strangers and this example of vocalisation may be a technique adopted to suggest reserve, though it is expressed with what appears to be the breed's habitual and characteristic politeness, perhaps a manifestation of that same reserve with strangers. When greeting humans outside its immediate family it rarely displays the typical ebullience of the domesticated dog, but rather conducts itself with something remarkably like quiet dignity. According to the observations of shepherds and other owners of Kelb tal-Fenek in Gozo in the past, the bitches will not mate with breeds other than their own. Some Pharaoh Hound bitches will also discourage the attentions of males that are not of the breed when in oestrus, a response perhaps analogous to the monogamous nature of the relationship of golden jackals in the wild.

Such behavioural traits of the Kelb tal-Fenek/Pharaoh Hound as these may go some way towards providing an answer to what has hitherto been one of the uncertainties of the hounds' descent. 'Calling', coloration, the position adopted whilst micturating, the tendency to maintain an exclusive attitude to the transmission of its genes and the behaviour of both Pharaoh Hounds/Kelb tal-Fenek bitches and golden jackal females are all forms of behaviour that are certainly not endemic to all canids but that do seem to be shared by them.

✦

Some of the characteristics displayed by the Pharaoh Hound, bred from the Maltese stock, are possessed by various of its 'cousins', the dogs of the islands where populations of prick-eared, golden-tan hounds were found, on Gozo, Sicily and Ibiza. Each of the dogs is slightly different, the result no doubt of their isolation, but they look to be related, to the extent of being drawn from a common stock that may antedate their division into distinct groups. The differences, principally in size and the coloration of their coats, are doubtless the result of each founder stock being separated from others and inbreeding; each population has developed its own characteristics but they are discernibly similar.

The hound from Gozo is the truest to the form and appearance of the original Egyptian hound, to the extent virtually of replicating the ancient dog of the tomb reliefs and the painted representations, which extend over more than 2000 years. There is some uncertainty about the actual point at which the first dogs from Gozo were exported to northern Europe. One of the few studies written specifically about the breed, in its nomenclature as 'Pharaoh Hound',[24] states that this occurred in the early 1960s. It is possible that some dogs were brought to Britain and Scandinavia at a date somewhat earlier in the last century, but it seems likely that the European founder stocks of the modern breed were not established until later, when dogs were brought to England by the wife of a senior British officer serving in Malta, one of the authors of the study referred to here. The Maltese dogs are still to be seen in their native habitat, in the farms and country areas, where they sustain their reputation as formidable predators of rabbits. It seems likely that they have been indigenous to Malta for a very long time and are regarded by the Maltese as their national symbol.

Of the other island dogs that replicate the appearance of the tjesm, the Sicilian Hound, Cirneco dell'Etna,[25] is slightly smaller and lighter in build, but otherwise is identical with the hounds of the tomb reliefs (Figure 27). This dog is the most interesting of the island hounds, not least because it evidently held a very special significance for the Greek-speaking inhabitants of Sicily in the fifth and fourth centuries BC, by which time the Egyptian hound had declined in status and popularity in its homeland. Interestingly, the Cirneco enjoyed a status comparable with the Egyptian Hound in that it was a manifest divinity, and had long been recognised as a god (or the

Figure 27 Cirneco dell'Etna Hadranensis Fedra (breeders and owners, Jane Moore and Domenic Tricomi).

manifestation of a god), playing a significant part in the mythology of archaic Sicily.

Many of the principal Sicilian cities had their own mints and produced very fine coinage. The designs of the coins and the quality of their striking is exceptional, even for a time when handsome coins were typical of Western Greek cities. The designs incorporate a number of mythological themes which are peculiar to the island. The Cirneco is depicted on many of the coins from this period minted in several of the principal towns, including Agrigento, Camarina, Messina, Eryx, Palermo, Segesta, Selinunte and Syracuse.[26] One of the towns from which several examples survive is Motya, an island city said to have been founded by the Phoenicians in the eighth century BC. This is suggestive, given the lingering belief that it was the Phoenicians who brought the dogs from Egypt to the islands, though this is an idea for which there is no independent support whatsoever and which, indeed, is most improbable. The populations of hounds on the islands must predate the existence of the Phoenicians by many centuries, for they did not enter Sicily until the late eighth/early seventh centuries BC.[27] Sicily had been inhabited for millennia before this time and the skeletons of dogs have been found in

Figure 28 A hound that certainly looks as if it were the ancestor to the living Cirneco dell'Etna appears frequently on coins minted by the Greek-founded Sicilian cities in the middle centuries of the first millennium BC. A coin from Panormus (Palermo) with, on the obverse, the hound surmounted by the murex shell, and, on the reverse, the hound 'scenting' (see text for connection).

excavations of early Neolithic Stetinello (of which more later), including a dog of 'a medium small species, possibly resembling a spitz'.[28] Once again, a compact terrier-like canine is identified from an early site where later slender prick-eared hounds would be dominant, strengthening the possibility that, like their Egyptian counterparts, the later specimens evolved from the earlier strain, encouraged by human selection and no doubt conditioned by the environment in which they found themselves.

Hilzheimer illustrated a coin from Panormus (now Palermo), also from the fifth century BC[29] (Figure 28), which shows a hound, with its tail tightly curled over its back, the carriage favoured for their hounds by the Egyptians of thousands of years earlier, which is still displayed by the Basenji. The dog is depicted on both faces of the coin: on the obverse rather majestically, on the reverse shown 'scenting', with ears of barley behind it. A coin from Eryx[30] shows the hound in a conventional pose, standing over a hare that it has brought down. Several of the coins, including examples from Palermo and Segesta, depict the hound standing alertly, ears pricked and tail raised, like that from Palermo.[31]

The designs of the coinage incorporate a number of themes which reflect the island's rich and very particular mythology, in which dogs play a very important part. At Segesta the hound is a manifestation of a river god; in at least one case it is said to be the personification of the River Crimisus.[32] This

29a   A young huntsman-god, identified as the personification of the River Crimisus, attended by his hounds, which are also mystically identified with the river.

29b   The hound is often shown in association with ears of barley.

29c   A hound 'scenting', a frequent episode that has been cited as explaining the breed's modern name, *cirneci* being the Old Sicilian word describing the sifting of the husk from wheat.

Figure 29   Coins from the Sicilian cities.

identification of the dog with the river god reveals the underlying significance of this otherwise odd equation of river, god and hound. In the *Aeneid* Virgil relates that Crimisus (the river that is also a god) seduced a Trojan woman, Egesta or Segesta, coming to her in the shape of a bear – or of a dog. She bore Crimisus a son, Acestes, who founded cities in Sicily and welcomed Aeneas and his followers to his kingdom. His mother became the eponym of the city that bore one form of her name.[33] Crimisus was said to be near where Timoleon, the Tyrant of Sicily, defeated an army of 70,000 Carthaginians.

Sometimes the hound is shown in the company of a young, naked huntsman who is said also to be a manifestation of the river god; thus river, hound and huntsman are one, the river in human form with his hounds at his side as if the god is about to set them on their prey (Figure 29a). On a coin from Segesta[34] the hound is depicted in the process of scenting, its head and muzzle to the ground. There are other examples of hounds in this stance, sometimes in association with ears of barley (Figure 29b), as in the case of the coin from Palermo illustrated by Hilzheimer.

This position adopted by the hound evidently had its own symbolic significance to the people of Sicily and an elaboration of the Cirneco's mythical relationships may be hidden here. The hound with its muzzle to the ground (Figure 29c) may well have inspired the idea of a symbolic connection with the act of sifting wheat from the husk; the threshing floor itself had a powerful mythical and symbolic significance to the Greeks. It is thus possible that the name by which the dog it is known today is derived from an archaic Sicilian word, cirneci, used to describe the act of sifting wheat from the husk.[35]

There is another possible reason for the Cirneco's appeal to the Greeks. The Sicilian cities, particularly Motya and others such as Segesta and Palermo which have been very fruitful in yielding examples of coins depicting the hound, were important centres for the manufacture of the richly coloured dye popularly known as 'Tyrian purple'. The dye is made from the shells of a sea snail, the murex, which when crushed and heated provide the substance of the dye. The Cirneco seems to have been identified with the dye and its production. The Roman author Pliny the Elder described the legend on which the link between the hound and the dye is based.

It is related that a shepherd lived near Tyre, the city on the Levantine coast where the Phoenicians originated and from which they colonised the western Mediterranean islands and the city of Carthage in North Africa. Carthage is traditionally recognised as the home of the purple (or scarlet) dyes that were so greatly admired in antiquity. The shepherd had a dog that accidentally bit into a murex, a mollusc found in great quantities in the warm seas off the coast of Lebanon, and in consequence became stained with the dye. The shepherd brought his dog before the king of Tyre, who forthwith adopted the colour as an attribute of royalty. The dog was thus commemorated in Tyre and in its daughter cities colonised by the Phoenicians and the Carthaginians. The appearance of the murex on the coins that also bear the image of the hound confirms the connection between hound and Tyrian purple dye, the river and the god and the cities of Sicily — a complex mélange of associations which suggest the existence of an equally complex and probably ancient corpus of myth that brought all of these elements together. The possibility of such a myth underlying the Cirneco's place in the society of early Sicily also suggests that the breed may indeed be even more ancient than the mid-First Millennium dateline that the coins confirm.

Another version of the legend concerned with the murex, related by Nonnius in his *Dionysiaca*, written in 48 books, has Herakles as its hero. Herakles was identified with the Phoenician god Melkart and according to this legend he was walking on the shore with his dog and a nymph of the locality, of whom he was enamoured. The dog found a murex as in Pliny's tale and the nymph, delighted with the rich colour with which Herakles' dog was now marked, refused to yield to him until he provided her with a mantle dyed with the same bewitching colour.

Whilst it may only be coincidence, it is a fact that many of the names of hounds recorded in Egypt in the Old and Middle Kingdoms, long before the appearance of the Phoenicians, have their origins in that part of North Africa that is now Libya. It has been suggested that 'Cirneco', is derived from the Greek *Kairenaikos*, identifying it with ancient Cyrenaica, in Libya. On balance this seems unlikely, though the ancient North African connection of the early population movements should perhaps not be forgotten. The dog's habit of scouring the ground referred to above, reminiscent of the process of husking, seems an altogether more probable etymology – given the evident, probably mythological, significance attached to the act of sifting or husking, as illustrated by the mid-first millennium coins of the Sicilian cities. Whatever may be the eventual explanation for these enigmas it is evident that the Cirneco seems to be an ancient hound, whose existence is overlaid with a very substantial symbolic meaning. That it was so important in late antiquity in Sicily, at the time when the tjesm was in decline in Egypt, is striking.

The question of these hounds' possible survival from antiquity is as complex as the same question attending the survival of the tjesm. It is interesting in this context that the Cirneco is described in its official breed standard in the following terms:

> This dog belongs to a primitive type of hunting or hound dog that is one of the few ancient breeds that has undergone very little manipulation by man. It has been selected by nature, by the environment and the use to which it has been put over the three thousand years it has been present in Sicily.[36]

The official standard of the breed in the United States reiterates the description of the Cirneco as 'a primitive type of dog of elegant and slender shape'.[37] It should be said that there is nothing remotely primitive about the Cirneco, nor indeed about any of these hounds. A better term might be 'archaic', expressing the dogs' ancient lineage, without burdening them with the faintly pejorative sense of 'primitive'.

Of all the breeds that have been claimed to be related to or derived from the ancient Egyptian Hound, the Cirneco was the first to be acknowledged as a distinct breed by the international canine registration community; it was recognised by the American Kennel Club in 1939. This was long before there was any sustained interest in the descent of the tjesm and substantially earlier than the attested importation of the Kelb tal-Fenek hounds to the United Kingdom. Only Hilzheimer's article, published a few years before the registration of the Cirneco in America, was current and, as noted above, he mentions the connection between the hound and the coinage of the Sicilian cities; he does not refer to the Cirneco by name, however.

The antiquity of the Cirneco was confirmed, at least to the satisfaction of its protagonists, by the discovery at the major Neolithic site of Stetinello, a short way up the coast, north from Syracuse, of the head of an animal in pottery with a long muzzle and the remains of two large protuberances on its forehead.[38] The figurine was broken off at the end of its long neck and the protuberances, which the breed's enthusiasts considered the remains of its prominent ears, were also broken.[39]

Stetinello is the type-site for the Sicilian Neolithic. The level from which the head was recovered has been dated to the beginning of the fourth millennium BC; this would certainly make it the contemporary of the Golenishchef dish with the four leashed hounds, which is dated to Naqada I in Egyptian chronology, circa 3800 BC. With the best will in the world, however, it is difficult to accept the identification of this fragmentary head as that of an archaic Cirneco. It looks much more like the head of a horned animal, a view which is supported by the wide and heavily moulded bases of the two broken protuberances on the forehead, which are much more reminiscent of the curving horns of a caprid, such as the ibex or a large goat, than a hound's ears, even such prominent ears carried by the hounds discussed here.

The authenticity of the claim for the Cirneco's longevity seems assured, however, by its importance to the cities on the island, which flourished in the middle of the first millennium BC, and it is therefore clear that the hound has an ancestry at least of 2500 years and very possibly considerably more; there is certainly no evidence that the dog has been manipulated in

Figure 30   The Ibizan Hound
Chahala Ivory Duchess Ezhar
(owners, Mr and Mrs
N. and S. Simm).

more recent times by its breeders to mimic the ancient strain, of which
they would only have become aware relatively recently, an observation that
applies to all the breeders of the modern strains examined here. The Cirneco
is not a well-known or popular breed; it is not recorded in all the works
of reference that claim to list the principal breeds of modern dogs. It is not
registered at the Kennel Club of Great Britain and has never been publicly
identified with the Egyptian Hound, except by implication in Hilzheimer's
article. It is not mentioned in the Chicago report (Parker et al.).

The Ibizan Hound (Figure 30) is generally taller, more rangy, with a pelage
often strongly marked with white, a coloration that occurs only occasionally
in its cousins. The Ibizan is the only breed that includes both rough- and
smooth-coated hounds. It is very like another dog that is often portrayed in
Ancient Egypt, though it appears less frequently than the tjesm, a tall hound
with its coat blotched with white. The *Kennel Club's Illustrated Breed Standards* states
of the Ibizan Hound 'The breed has been known not only on Ibiza but also
in the neighbouring island of Formentera for something like 5000 years.'[40]
It is not clear whether this statement is based on archaeological evidence,
rather than the mythology that has attended the Mediterranean hounds.

The local myths of origin of these hounds, referred to above and still
repeated in books and articles that describe them, is that they were brought
to the islands by Phoenician seamen; as mentioned earlier, there is no
evidence whatsoever to support this contention. The Romans, who controlled
Egypt after the death of Cleopatra VII, were interested in dogs and because
they bred them selectively they have been described as the pioneers of the
process, although the Egyptians must certainly have understood and pursued
the practice many centuries before the Romans adopted it. The presence of

the Cirneco in Sicily again discourages the idea of so late an introduction as would be required were the Romans to be involved.

It seems clear that the population of tjesm attenuated in Egypt at the end of antiquity whilst the dogs of the islands must be presumed to have flourished. The founder stocks of dogs that were established in the islands during the migrations of the early Neolithic period, at the same time as the ancestors of the Egyptians and their dogs were moving towards the Nile Valley, must have been derived from the same pool as one of the putative founder populations of the Egyptian Hounds, which traced its ancestry to the dogs that worked with the hunters of the Sahara, thousands of years before it appeared in the Nile Valley. Whilst it would be unwise to read too much into the presence of the 'dog of a medium-small species' in Sicily at an early date, its description certainly recalls the appearance of the dogs in the rock engravings of the Egyptian deserts.

The possibility of the survival of individual breeds of dogs over very long periods of time has been a matter of contention for many a long day in academic as well as in dog-breeding circles. Ancestries of hundreds of years have been advanced for many breeds, the product, often enough, of the loyalty and affection of the breeds' protagonists, rather than the consequence of scientific analysis. The possibility of a long ancestry has always seemed the more problematic given the relative rapidity with which major changes in the secondary characteristics of dogs can be produced over comparatively few generations of selective breeding. This fact alone makes the absence of any significant change over 20 and more centuries (let alone the 50 centuries that span the earliest representations of the tjesm and the present) seem improbable with or without human intervention. It is well, therefore, to note the comment of one of the principal authorities on canine descent and the perpetuation of canine strains.

> It is difficult to determine, however, whether the mastiff and the greyhound are really breeds with an unbroken line of 4000 years or whether the genetic diversity inherent in the species causes similar characteristics to re-combine so that the same type of dog is bred in different regions at different periods when selective breeding is carried out for the same need, this being to provide hunting, racing and guard dogs.[41]

This point has also been made in a recent study of the Saluqi.[42]

In the cases of the Pharaoh Hound and the hounds from the Mediterranean islands, however, there does seem to be strong evidence for the breeds' survival or, having in mind the caveat above, for its recurrence, when similar conditions of climate, environment and purpose will replicate the same or similar physical forms and characteristics. The breeds described here – tjesm, Kelb tal-Fenek, Cirneco dell'Etna, possibly the Ibizan Hound and the Basenji – all appear to have retained evidence of their kinship, effectively over all of recorded history. This suggests that a very remarkable process may have been at work. A telling consideration about this phase of the hounds' history is that they appear not to have miscegenated with local populations of dogs, either in Egypt or in the islands, but maintained the purity of their lines. Given that those that have lived for centuries in the islands were employed for hunting and as shepherd dogs, thus running free for much of their lives in a relatively restricted area, this must surely be significant.

It is clear from the reliefs, paintings and other representations of the hound that the Egyptians retained a very specific and distinct conception of the tjesm's morphology over something like 2000 years (conservatively expressed, from c. 3000 BC to c. 1000 BC) and, whilst account must be taken of the Egyptians' evident care of the breeding lines, this indicates that the dog had qualities of survival considerably greater than might generally be expected for a domesticated breed. This in turn suggests that the tjesm may have been closer in this respect to the wild canines – wolves and jackals, notably – whose basic structure does not change over many generations. Given this level of the breed's survival in antiquity it is surely not wholly impossible that it survived into the modern age in the form of the islands' hounds.

The dogs that constitute this example of biological archaeology would seem to represent a distinct and homogenous group. It is now surely time to engage the resources of modern science in order to establish whether there is a biological or genetic connection between them, based on the examination of DNA from the living hounds and from mummified tjesm. At the same time it should be possible to establish whether these hounds carry any evidence of even a partial descent from a canine ancestor other than the wolf alone.

Pharaoh Hounds today tend to be managed by breeders who in general will wish to see puppies weaned and separated from their dams as soon as reasonably possible; after all, though the breed is generally well served by its breeders, they are not primarily in business to build up and retain large packs of the dogs. However, it would possibly be rewarding if bitches could be allowed experimentally to determine when a puppy should be weaned and when it should leave the family den. In the circumstances attending the modern breed, the dogs tend to be less dominant than the bitches and there is no evidence of the monogamous behaviour displayed by the golden jackal pair. Again, it would be rewarding to know whether a Pharaoh Hound 'family' would manifest the same or similar traits if left to themselves, though in this age it would probably be difficult to bring about the conditions of seclusion that would be necessary.

Whilst this consideration would not apply so strongly to the island populations, domestication, selection and controlled breeding inevitably will lead to changes in particular to the Pharaoh Hound's character and doubtless its morphology; already the temperament of the hounds is said to be becoming more tractable, less strongly individual and independent as the earlier representatives of the breed were always said to be in their Maltese habitat. The breed is becoming physically more robust and its average size is said to be increasing; this would be attributable to a controlled diet and veterinary care.

A feature of the Pharaoh Hound/Kelb tal-Fenek's physique which it may have inherited from its putative (jackal) ancestors is its large, upstanding, triangular ears. The ears are remarkable, for they seem to be possessed of an independent life of their own. They are hardly ever still but seem always to be in movement, turning this way and that, often independently of each other, presumably tracking the sound of potential prey.

Selective breeding under domestication produces changes such as the flop or drooping ear, which can result in a loss of the exceptionally keen hearing of some breeds. Thus far the very distinctive ears of the Pharaoh Hound remain resolutely pricked, a characteristic which is also the result of selection, as it presumably was with the tjesm of antiquity; with the changed lifestyle of a cosseted favourite whose meals are served to it regularly by its human attendant, it is a matter of speculation whether its ears may go the same way as those of other breeds. This would be regrettable, both because the huge, alert ears of the breed are its most distinctive physical characteristic and seem to link it across the many centuries to its ancient Egyptian counterpart, and because the ears are obviously so much a part of the dog's equipment for enjoying its life and its hunting avocation. That it has kept its ears cocked so firmly over this long time-span may also provide evidence of its connection with the world of antiquity and with its putative forerunner.

All of these observations serve to demonstrate that it is a matter of regret that there is very little published or otherwise available reliable research material on the character and behaviour of these hounds for which such a long descent has been postulated. The Kelb tal-Fenek/Pharaoh Hound in particular is a dog of a highly individual nature; its possible connection with a dog so well identified as the Egyptian tjesm would make the prospect of controlled research attractive. With the scientific advances that have been made into all the aspects of genetics it should be possible now to determine whether the similarities between the behaviour of the golden jackal and the Pharaoh Hound are anything more than similarities, the product of chance and the generalities of canine behaviour, and whether there is any reality behind the belief that the tjesm still lives in the modern dogs which appear to share so many of its attributes.

The report of the researches conducted by the Fred Hutchinson Cancer Research Center, with the participation of the Canine Studies Institute, published in the journal *Science* (Parker et al.), must be cited particularly in the context of the descent of two of the dogs described here and their putative relationship with an ancient strain. In the concluding paragraphs of the report the authors summarise the breeds represented in one of the groups of dogs whose DNA was analysed. These include the Basenji, Saluqi, Afghan, Tibetan Terrier, Lhasa Apso, Chow Chow, Pekinese, Sharpei, Shi Tzu, Akita, Shiha Inu, Alaskan Malamute, Siberian Husky and the Samoyed. The report concludes 'Thus dogs from these breeds may be the best living representatives of the ancestral dog gene pool.' It then goes on to observe

> It is noticeable that several breeds commonly believed to be of ancient origin, such as the Pharaoh Hound and Ibizan Hound, are not included in this group. These are often thought to be the oldest of all dog breeds, descending directly from the ancient Egyptian dogs drawn on tomb walls more than 5000 years ago. Our results indicate, however, that these two breeds have been recreated in more recent times, from combinations of other breeds. Thus, although their appearance matches the ancient Egyptian sight hounds, the genomes do not.[43]

This emphatic rejection of the popular claim for the antiquity of these two dogs, singled out for this distinction, is a trifle surprising. This review of the Egyptian Hunting Hound's career and the possibility of a genetic connection of living breed with it has treated the question of its descent with caution. A 4000-year pedigree is a formidable claim, but this reservation will be offset by the Chicago report's acknowledgement of even older lines discernibly descending from the ancestral wolf.

The suggestion that the two breeds have been recreated or modified in modern times calls for some comment. The modern Pharaoh Hound is derived from the founder stocks of Kelb tal-Fenek exported from Gozo, one of the Maltese islands, in the 1920s and again in the 1960s; it appears that it is from the latter group that most of the living animals descend. Prior to the recognition of the breed it had been established in Gozo well beyond the nineteenth-century origins of most modern breeds, though admittedly it does not have the documentary evidence of the ancient coinage that provides the Cirneco with an impeccable lineage. But recent research[44] has suggested that the Maltese islands were uninhabited prior to 5000 BC and that their occupation dates from that time. This was also the time of the first 'village' settlements in the Nile Valley. It is tempting to speculate that the ancestors of the Kelb tal-Fenek were brought to the islands by migrants after the increased desiccation of North Africa forced them, like the ancestors of the Egyptians, to seek new living space. Having in mind the remarkable antiquity of the temples and shrines of the Maltese islands and the sophistication of their construction, the care and management of a strain of hunting hounds, trained for small game, would doubtless have been a comparatively easy matter.

It will have been clear from the early chapters of this study that Egyptology did not draw any marked attention to the tjesm, certainly not to the extent of alerting the very few breeders involved to the possibility of re-creating the ancient breeds. The representations of tjesm in Egyptian funerary contexts come, in the oldest examples, from the early Old Kingdom (2686–2125 BC) and later from stelae and decorated coffins in the Middle Kingdom, circa 2000 BC. As this study has demonstrated, a direct descent is not likely and at best the Pharaoh Hound today descends from the Maltese Kelb tal-Fenek; the descent of the latter hound may be an altogether different matter. The suggestion that the Pharaoh Hound has been subject to 'designing' by breeders cannot be applied to the Kelb tal-Fenek, which has been kept and bred by peasant farmers in the Maltese islands who, for most of the breed's existence, will never have heard either of the Pharaohs or of their hunting hounds.

If the descendants of the Kelb tal-Fenek, transmuted into the Pharaoh Hound, may, for whatever reason, be considered vulnerable to the interference of professional breeders, there is the reassuring evidence of the Cirneco's existence. The Cirneco is still extant in its native environment and, though slightly smaller, is as convincing a replica of the tjesm as any of its peers. It has not, however, attracted anything like the same degree of interest and attention associated with its Maltese 'cousin'. It does not appear that the Cirnechi provided their DNA to the authors of the Chicago report, either.

The Ibizan Hound is a somewhat different case. It is an exact replica not of the tjesm but of the taller, more rangy dog with a speckled pelage, like Khui's Iupu. As noted earlier, there appears to be no archaeological evidence to support the claim that the Ibizan has been known on Formentera for 5000 years. Equally, there is no reason to doubt that it is indigenous to the Balearics and further research would probably show that it has a lineage comparable with those of the Kelb tal-Fenek and perhaps with the Cirneco.

The high days of the tjesm's life in Egypt matched the centuries of Egypt's own greatness. In the Old Kingdom it was ubiquitous, an appendage apparently of every royal or noble family and present in every scene of the hunt. In the succeeding Middle Kingdom, Egyptian society, which was never very rigid in its social classifications and in which movement was always possible from one level of society to another, even the highest under the king, became still more open to the talented and well-fortuned. The accomplishments of the individual were recognised as significant in all strata of society, just as the hound was highly valued, a beloved companion that would be honoured in life and mourned in death. Breeds other than the tjesm became popular, as witnessed by Khui's dog Iupu and Djehutyhetep's Ankhu, to name but two examples.

The New Kingdom (c. 1550–1100 BC) was the time of Egypt's greatest prosperity and international influence when, in the middle of the second millennium, for the first time in her history she set out to build an empire. The world outside Egypt's frontiers was changing rapidly. New powers were rising in the Middle East, many of them aggressive and envious of Egypt's seemingly impervious assurance and prosperity. In what was probably a reaction to the pretensions of these newly established potentates in Mesopotamia, Anatolia and, on a much lesser scale, in the Levant, Egypt's kings adopted a policy of the acquisition of foreign territories as much for the purpose of imperial assertion and profit as for the more simple issue of the control of frontier lands to assure the integrity of Egypt. In this more martial phase of her history the tjesm, like the Saluqi, which also appears in the art of the time, once more attended the kings, in war as much as it had always done in the hunt. Rameses II and his buttock-seizing bitch 'Anath is a defender' demonstrate the regard in which the dog's fighting qualities were held.

The policies pursued by the kings of the New Kingdom opened up Egypt as never before to foreign influences and even to new breeds of dog, especially the heavy breeds of Mesopotamian and Anatolian fighting dogs like the mastiff of earlier times, which were favoured once more. In the Eighteenth Dynasty a most important development occurred when the techniques of hunting in Egypt changed radically, a consequence of the introduction of the horse. The horse was unknown in Egypt and its introduction had occurred in the seventeenth century BC during the so-called 'Hyksos' period when these 'rulers of foreign lands', who were probably Canaanites,[45] invaded Northern Egypt from Palestine and the desert regions to the north-east of the Nile Valley. They provided the kings of the Fifteenth and Sixteenth Dynasties (1650–1550 BC) and were generally execrated by the Egyptians when they were finally expelled by the founders of the Seventeenth and Eighteenth Dynasties, who were drawn from another family of princes originating in Thebes. The horse, however, remained and became an important element in war, in the panoply of the kings, of life in the countryside and in the hunting field. The Egyptian interest in animals probably accounts for the apparent rapidity with which the horse was taken into the community. Clearly, there must have been controlled breeding programmes for it to have survived after the Hyksos were driven out. It was widely distributed throughout Egypt during the later New Kingdom.

The hunting hound now became less important than once it had been when it was the companion of hunters who, in the absence of the horse, hunted on foot. Then it had the virtue of speed and the ability to separate the quarries and run them down till, exhausted, they could be dealt with by the hunters. When hounds are depicted in New Kingdom contexts they tend more frequently to be Saluqi rather than tjesm, perhaps a consequence of the Saluqi's speed over short distances. Tutankhamun, for example, is always represented as being attended by Saluqi, distinguishable by the breed's feathered lop ears and feathered tail, when hunting and in scenes of battle.

After the Twentieth Dynasty (c. 1168–1069 BC), local magnates, always quick to take advantage of a decline in the fortunes of the monarchy, awarded themselves royal titles and prerogatives. It was only when the Kushite kings of the Twenty-Fifth Dynasty from Nubia (747–656 BC) ousted the rival claimants to the kingship that the immemorial values of Egypt were partially restored, the declared objective of the conquerors. Again, in the Twenty-Sixth Dynasty the rulers of the city of Sais in the Delta managed to assert their rule over much of the Valley. Harking back to the great days of the Old Kingdom, they sought, rather touchingly, to recall the times of Egypt's greatness, the evidence of which lay in ruins all around them, by producing magnificent pastiches of statuary and architecture that were conscious attempts to restore the ancient glory of the Two Lands of two millennia earlier.

The relatively sudden eclipse of the *tjesm* after the end of the New Kingdom may be attributed to the reduction in the ancient values that had made Egypt so very great. Now the country began its long decline, to become very much like the generality of Near Eastern states: insecure, fractious and disunited. Influences came into the Valley from the north and east, represented by peoples for whom the hound was not a creature to be loved and admired but was rather to be held in contempt, aspects of its character attributed to despised humans and employed as terms of insult and abuse.

The hound no longer appears in the art of these later periods to anything like the extent that it had in earlier times. In contrast to the alert, jaunty companion of princes and hunters alike, the dog is now often identified only as a scavenger, cringing, dangerous and a thief. At the end of Egypt's historical period, which also marked the end of the ancient world, the Egyptian Hound appears again, this time as wholly domestic, a household pet, sometimes to be mummified and buried in a double sarcophagus with its familiar companion, the house cat. Gradually it disappears from occasions of high prestige; only the canine gods, Anubis and Wepwawet, are still honoured, Anubis as the companion of Osiris and the master of ceremonies of the rites attending the journeys of the dead to the Afterlife, and Wepwawet as the mystical companion and guide of the king. These are further considered in Chapter 5.

So far as the dogs were concerned, it was almost as if they realised that the glorious days of Egypt's history, in which they had had so honourable a place, were past and that the generations of dog-loving kings, nobles and more humble Egyptians were to be replaced by harsher, less agreeable masters. At this point, remarkably, it seems that the Egyptian Hound largely disappeared from Egypt. There is occasional archaeological and iconographic evidence (Figure 31) for the Hound's presence in Egypt in the Late Period, less after the termination of the Ptolemaic era, which ended with the death of Cleopatra VII in 30 BC and the following period of Roman domination.

Figure 31 In the later centuries of Egypt's history the tjesm lost some of its status as the nature and technique of the hunt changed. However, this Late Period head is exceptionally fine and shows that some Egyptians still cared for the hound that had been so much a part of history of the Two Lands. Its quality is such that it is difficult not to believe that it is a portrait of a favoured hound.

The Romans were interested in dogs and bred them selectively, giving them distinct names; Pliny records that sight hounds, of which the tjesm and its peers were examples, were classified as *pedibus celeres*. There is no evidence, however, that they were aware of, or interested in, any tjesm that may have remained in Egypt.

The disappearance of the hound from Egypt is a small mystery; it may be that there was some sort of epidemic that destroyed the bulk of the canine population, only those that (some would believe) somehow made their way to the Mediterranean islands surviving the larger catastrophe. The recent discovery of a mosaic of a surprisingly modern-looking dog from the Library of Alexandria, in late antiquity, though only one example (and having a remarkable resemblance to the dog in the famous painting 'His Master's Voice'), may indicate that a more comfortably built dog was favoured, though its commemoration in a handsome mosaic roundel suggests that it was loved.

At the end of antiquity, when much of Egypt became first Christianised and later largely Islamised, the tjesm either disappeared or was subsumed into the packs of pariah dogs that roamed the oases and the outskirts of the towns. There is no evidence of the hound maintaining its ancient place, either in the hunting field or in the hearts of the Egyptians. The only evidence available comes from outside Egypt.

The proscription of the dog is revealed in the writings, assembled mainly in the second half of the first millennium BC and attributed to the congeries of Hebrew-speaking tribes, in the books of the Old Testament. The beliefs and customs they demonstrate are rooted in the pre-exilic, mainly hill nomadic, tribes, which, after the Babylonian captivity, adopted a religious system that became rabbinical Judaism. The post-exilic structure of Hebrew communities was largely town-based; it may be that the attitude to dogs was influenced by this circumstance. By contrast it is notable that Bedu communities, which retain much of the way of life of the non-urban peoples of the Arabian peninsula and the Levant, still honour to this day the Saluqi and integrate it into their society, to the extent that it often sleeps in its human companion's tent.

In the days of the Muslim empires packs of hunting dogs were maintained by the Islamic amirs, but the dismissal of dogs by many Muslims is attributed, apparently, to the Prophet Mohammed's dislike of them. The Prophet was said to be very sensitive to odours and his rejection of dogs seems mainly to have been based on the requirement of Muslims to observe ritual cleanliness five times each day before prayer. In fact, the dislike of dogs seems particularly to be a trait of semitic-speaking peoples.

The Saluqi, which seems always to have been excepted from the Muslim proscription of dogs, became the favoured hunting companion of the amirs and has remained so to the present day, the amirs having been replaced by the shaikhs, at least in the Arabian peninsula and, in the recent past, in Jordan, Syria and Iraq. The people of Iraq have kept the Saluqi breed alive when otherwise it might have declined perilously in what was probably its native land. It is, however, at some risk in the conditions prevailing in Iraq at present.[46]

The Prophet's reservations about dogs are not generally supported in the Quran. Dogs were commended as hunters and their training for the chase encouraged. A problem arose here in that Muslims are required to eat only the meat of animals that have been slaughtered in the prescribed manner. The early Muslims accommodated themselves to this requirement by establishing that it was lawful to eat the meat of an animal that had been run down by hounds if the hunter recited the rubric 'In the name of God' over the hound as it was unleashed.

There is a celebrated episode in the Quran that describes the miraculous preservation of the 'Seven Sleepers'. These were youths who sought to protect their submission to the faith by hiding from their enemies in a cave. God sealed their ears and put them to sleep until the danger of their faith being corrupted had passed. Their dog was with them and it is clear that he counts as one of the companions thus protected by God.

A notable defence of the dog exists in an Arabic manuscript of the tenth century AD (the fourth century of the Islamic calendar) written by a Baghdadi man of letters who is known by the name Ibn al-Marzuban. In the English translation his text is called *The Book of the Superiority of Dogs over Many of Those who Wear Clothes*. A modern edition[47] is both scholarly and a delight. The text, a collection of stories, poetry and anecdotes from a wide variety of sources, praises dogs and commends their loyalty and their selfless and loving behaviour as distinctly superior to the qualities of many humans; it emphasises how important the dog has always been to the Bedu of the desert, where the dog is not only a hunting companion but equally a member of the family, sleeping in the tent with its master. The text is embellished by a number of engaging illustrations, drawn from Arabic and Persian manuscripts of the period of the Muslim empires, which preserved so much of the literature and scientific knowledge of the ancient world and ensured its transmission to the world of today.

The early Islamic period witnessed on the part of Muslim savants a considerable interest in alchemical practice and philosophy, much of which was believed to have been derived from ancient Egypt. At this time, corresponding to the early Middle Ages in Western European terms, Muslim geographers, historians, philosophers, travellers and poets enshrined much of the intellectual speculation and investigation that captivated the world that succeeded late antiquity. The dog features frequently in alchemical texts and symbolism. One of the most influential of Muslim alchemists was Ibn Umail, a tenth-century scholar who visited Egypt extensively. He wrote of the dog in highly commendatory terms, 'And it is the key and it is the dog to which they [the ancients] pointed in their books, and it is the hidden with which the work should start and finish, and in it not outside it...'

> The dog in it is a guard for our souls
> And the dog drives away the violence of the fires.
> The dog protects their spirits in their bodies
> And the dog is in them, immovable....

And the dog opens every lock that is difficult to open
And the dog is called the sheikh in their temples.
And the dog is called the lion in their texts....
And the dog is the dog.[48]

Whilst the Arabs' affection for the Saluqi ensured that it remained a valued
and valuable part of their society, surviving into the present day as a coursing
hound whose lineage is carefully controlled, its cousin, the Egyptian Hound
of antiquity, effectively vanished. But, as has been shown here, what were
declared to be remnant populations of the hounds, which many believed
were descended from Egyptian progenitors, were discovered flourishing
in the Mediterranean islands. This study, though it is entirely convinced of
the beauty, nobility and strength of character of the hounds concerned,
has reservations about this assertion, at least to the extent that the modern
hounds might have a direct line of descent to the tjesm. Whatever the reason
for their eclipse in Egypt at the end of antiquity, the long-enduring survival
of the tjesm as a graceful and valued adjunct of ancient Egyptian society
came to an end, leaving the dogs of the islands to maintain their distinctive
appearance and, just conceivably, some trace of shared, ancestral genes on
into the present day.

CHAPTER 5

The Canine Gods of Ancient Egypt

Perceptions of the Divine

The profound sense of identity with the natural world felt by the Egyptians is nowhere demonstrated more explicitly – if paradoxically – than in their employment of animals as manifestations of the divine or suprahuman principles governing the cosmos. The entities which it is customary to refer to as 'the gods' of Ancient Egypt are subtle and complex creations and are seldom, if ever, quite what they seem to be and, more rarely still, what they have been declared to be. Masking them in animal forms added convincingly to what, for the Egyptians, represented reality in a dimension other than that of the reality which surrounded them in their daily lives.

It is difficult for the modern world to comprehend the nature of these entities or powers, however they may be described. Although it will be seen that the term is inadequate when referring to the powers that the Egyptians believed ensured the balance of the cosmos, 'gods' and the word's cognates will have to be employed here, for the sake of clarity. Such terms have long been employed for lesser theogonies, the colleges of gods in which most more or less complex societies since the time when Egypt was the first of nations have contained their projections of the divine principle. To set the role of the divinities who manifested in canine form into some sort of context it will be necessary here to turn aside for a moment's space from the hounds, to consider something of the nature of Egyptian cults and of the people who practised them.

The Egyptian hieroglyph that is transliterated 'god' in English and equivalent words in other languages, is *neter*; it is a very ancient symbol (G.R8, 'probably a cloth wound on a pole')[1] that expresses a most elaborate and complex concept. Sometimes, when the name of the god is given, the hieroglyph (G.A40)[2] representing a seated divinity, who is shown to be divine by the form of his beard (also worn by kings), acts as its determinative, the seal that is set at the end of a hieroglyphic group to indicate its broad meaning or context. In the early period of Egypt's history this word, certainly in its plural form, seems best to convey the sense of 'powers', immutable, beyond space and time, not to be conceived in human form, despite their occasional anthropomorphic or therioanthropic representation.

In the early historic periods the gods were distant, remote from humankind, the concern only of the king and his immediate coadjutors, expressions of power in nature and the dynamics of the cosmos, rather than individual beings with specific characters or attributes. The king was one of them, their equal at least in early times, and sometimes was represented as their ruler. He was the conduit between the land and people of Egypt and the powers that could influence the prosperity, fecundity or security of the Two Lands.

The people were not represented in the worship of the gods; indeed it is questionable if, in these early times, the gods were 'worshipped' at all, in any sense that later cultures would understand the term. Egyptian superhuman entities never displayed that curiously neurotic anxiety of later Near Eastern divinities, under the influence perhaps of semitic-speaking peoples whose gods seem peculiarly subject to this condition, always to seek all manner of reassurance and cajolement, to the extent that the praising of the god became the most compelling act of his or her service, as if the divinity would only respond to the enticements of sacrifice or to expressions of shameless flattery. This is an attitude of mind that seems still to persist among many of the adherents of revealed religions to this day.

When the gods or divine powers were first represented it was often as abstractions, in forms that have led some commentators to call them fetishes: it was thought that in this form they represented particularly ancient concepts. On the other hand, some of the most ancient of the early Egyptian gods, Ptah the supreme artificer for example, or Hathor the cow-goddess of whom Isis was a manifestation, appear in human or part-human form. Some of the very earliest were represented in animal forms, at least from the First Dynasty.

They were often the most powerful of the gods. They included the falcon, the symbol of the god Horus reincarnated in the person of every king, a baboon known as 'The Great White', an ibis, several divine bulls and the canine gods Anubis, Wepwawet and Khentiamentiu, who will be the particular subjects of this chapter, along with a more equivocal divinity Set, represented graphically by an ambiguous creature with canine characteristics. Sometimes the powers might assume an anthropomorphic appearance as readily as they did zoomorphic form; such was the great artificer god Ptah, who generally was represented as a mummified but evidently living man: yet again, a paradox. He could also reveal himself in the form of a bull, in Memphis as the Apis, in Armant as Buchis and in Heliopolis as Mnevis. The Apis is recorded in the First Dynasty.

This aspect of Egyptian mystical practice has been the cause of a profound misunderstanding of their culture and beliefs. It is a matter of history, but none the less regrettable, that the adoption of animal forms at once to represent the divine powers and to conceal their true natures – a very Egyptian procedure indeed – was seized upon by people from beyond the Valley to traduce the entire relationship of Egypt with the transcendental, especially in the later centuries of her history. When this occurred the situation was further compounded by many of the great entities of Egypt's theogonies being recast in the familiar anthropomorphic Near Eastern modes, or in zoomorphic shapes that had their origins in the animals that may have been chosen, as some commentators have suggested, as the symbols of the predynastic divisions of Egypt. Recent research, however, suggests that there may be a still more powerful psychological imperative underlying the Egyptian practice of creating zoomorphs or, perhaps more accurately, therianthropes. The conflation of animal forms and humans and of animals alone to signify the presence of a particular divinity is a practice common to all societies and may be a universal product of the human psyche.[3] It is is bound up with the recognition that all humanity in all ages shares the same neuropsychological processes and the same neuropathological mechanisms. (See also the quotation from C.G. Jung below.)

It is a particular circumstance of the history of ancient Egypt that much of the information relating to the gods and to the practice of their cults has come down to us from the Late Period of Egypt's dynastic history in the second half of the first millennium BC. Such descriptions as do survive, most often in the form of the reports of visitors to Egypt, are mediated to the modern world through cultures such as those of Greece and Rome and, most significantly, by the redactors of the books of the Old Testament, in which Egypt generally receives a singularly bad press. This often problematical transmission has tended to influence adversely all subsequent understanding of this unique aspect of the Egyptian experience. In the later periods of Egyptian history, gods in animal forms came to dominate, both in the representations promoted in the temples and, most notably, in the minds of many of Egypt's neighbours. Fascinated by what they saw as the mystery of Egypt, the neighbours sought to understand the agency of the divine in nature that the Egyptians demonstrated. 'Egyptian religion' came to be represented as a procession of fantastic monsters, an extraordinary and unappealing menagerie of therianthropes, conflations of humans and animals, birds, reptiles, insects, fish, often the creatures if not of nightmare at least of either overheated imaginings or a child-like simplicity of mind. Through the writings of the Hebrews, travellers such as Herodotus and later Greek and Roman historians and geographers, this view of Egypt, patronising when it was not dismissive, became the criterion for the world outside the Valley, seeking to understand the Egyptian attempt to express the inexpressible.

The cults of the Mesopotamians, Levantines, Hittites and the inhabitants of the Mediterranean islands, all of them in general vastly more naive than the archetypal beliefs of the Egyptians, began to infiltrate the Valley in the second millennium and especially during the early centuries of the first millennium BC. In doing so they changed profoundly and for ever the perception of what underlay the Egyptian understanding of the cosmos. Those Egyptians who did still understand the ancient concepts that had powered the astonishing growth of the culture and achievements of the Old Kingdom were doubtless little inclined to enlighten foreigners when they questioned them. Such people, they must have argued, could not be expected to comprehend that which they sought to have revealed to them, their very questions demonstrating a lack of understanding to an extent that would preclude them from comprehending the 'answers' they might be vouchsafed.

This is not to suggest that the Egyptians had some form of 'ancient wisdom' that they hid from outsiders. They may have done, but there is no certain evidence to indicate that this was so; in its absence it is naive to argue that they possessed a corpus of esoteric 'wisdom' that the world has lost. However, it is not naive to assert that the Egyptians were wise and that their perceptions of nature and of the world around them were of great profundity, just as their practical achievements seem sometimes to go beyond the talents of mere mortals. Where those perceptions were acquired is hardly as important as the possession of them. Despite the counter-arguments of scholars in the past, the Egyptians did enjoy a profound philosophical understanding of the world and of the place of humans in it, which arose, as did the finest evidences of their culture, from within their very particular collective unconscious.

To judge by the reports of Herodotus and other travellers, who sought to obtain information about Egypt's past and its *mores*, the priests were as adept as modern tourist guides in providing unlimited access to wholly inaccurate information about the origins, past history and national character of Egypt throughout antiquity. As the centuries passed, the obscurity that surrounded Egyptian cults, rehearsed in the depths of the temples, became impenetrable, probably as much to the majority of their practitioners as to any outsider who might have observed them.

The attitude of mind revealed by these skewed and prejudiced attributions of travellers to Egypt was supplemented by the bitter fanaticism of early Christian clerics, and to a lesser degree of their Muslim counterparts who generally did not consider Egypt's ancient gods worthy of notice. The dismissive and contemptuous attitude, demonstrated by the disparagement of this deeply significant aspect of the Egyptian experience by Christian apologists in particular, was, most remarkably, carried over into our own times. The records and opinions set down late in Egypt's history have also influenced the comprehension of Egyptian belief and practices in the minds of many modern observers, including scholars devoted to the study of Egyptian *mores* and culture.

In the early decades of Egyptological scholarship most of those who were engaged in such work were themselves the products of one or other of the great monotheistic faiths, Christian or Jewish. Many of them sought, on the one hand, to find elements in Egyptian religious cults or beliefs that anticipated their own beliefs or, on the other, to demonstrate the manifest superiority of their beliefs by pointing to the grotesque character of the gods of Egypt, the evidence of which they were uncovering with such dedicated application. Important scholarly institutions were founded specifically to study the history of ancient Egypt to prove the historicity of the Bible.[4]

Often enough, scholars of the day seemed simply to be embarrassed that the culture by which, perhaps despite themselves, they were so profoundly moved and whose unique qualities they recognised and celebrated, should at the same time be entangled in a cavalcade of animal-headed monstrosities, whose very existence mocked their own ideas of the divine order. It must sometimes have seemed that the very people who were presenting to the world the extraordinary achievements of the Egyptians in antiquity were disposed, at the same time, to represent those achievements as little more than the work of a primitive and deeply misguided race.

This attitude is the more inexplicable when it is realised that, in the opinion of many commentators, behind the multiplicity of divine images and the entities that they are taken to represent lay a concept of something very close to that of the one universal divinity. This is brilliantly expressed in the rubric 'I am Horus the Falcon who perches upon the battlements of Him whose name is hidden.' But it would not be correct to imply that the Egyptians were, at heart, convinced monotheists, even before the highly doubtful instance of Amenhotep IV/Akhenaten. However, there is no doubt that all the forms in which they conceived the presence of a supreme guiding principle in the cosmos, including all the animal and animal–human conflations, were taken to be expressions of this ultimate singularity.

It is only comparatively recently that the study of analytical psychology, the branch of psychoanalytical discipline and practice developed by Carl Gustav Jung and his followers, has contributed much to the understanding of why divine entities in so many cultures tend to be manifested in or represented as animals. The phenomenon is universal: all the ancient Eastern religions had divinities or divine beings that were recognised in animal forms, both real and imaginary. Among the great Near Eastern cultures only the Sumerians depicted their divinities predominantly in human form: from them the gods of Greece and Rome descend, but even Mesopotamian gods had their attendant animals, each sacred to a particular divinity. Thus the lion was the sacred animal of Ningirsu, Nintal and Inanna. In an astronomical dimension Enki, the Lord of the Abyss (and his later, Babylonian and Assyrian form, Ea), ruler of the subterranean waters and the archetype, among others, of the Trickster, had the goat–fish as one of his symbolic animals, the origin of the Zodiacal sign of Capricorn, an imaginary or fantastic invention. Nearer to the theme of this book the Sumerian goddess Gula was attended by a dog; she was the goddess of healing, and the association between the dog and medicine and healing is also found in Egypt.

Jung wrote extensively of the animal–god fusion. In developing his theory of the archetypes he observed, when considering the nature of Zarathustra:

Zarathustra is an archetype and therefore has the divine quality, and that is always based on the animal. Therefore the gods are symbolised as animals: even the Holy Ghost is a bird, all the antique gods and the exotic gods are animals at the same time. The old wise man is a big ape really, which explains his peculiar fascination.[5]

The last sentence is especially relevant to an understanding of the essential Egyptian ethos for it explains both the appeal of the 'old wise man', always a figure of admiration in Egyptian society, and the importance that was attributed to the admonitions of Egyptian sages, real or imaginary, which were preserved and repeated for centuries. But, more than this, Jung's insight explains also the immediate recognition by the Egyptians of the role of the king, the inheritor of the position and rank of the Alpha male in primate communities. It is almost as if they recognised the fact of the descent of humans from the apes that are our ancestors; if they did not in fact acknowledge it, like the Chinese in later times, they would not have considered the idea of such descent remarkable or tendentious. One of the enduring representations of wisdom was the cynocephalus divinity Thoth, who brought the teachings of the sages of the ancient past to the service of Egypt; he was also depicted as an ibis. An extremely early example of a theriomorphic divinity is 'The Great White', a sacred baboon known from the First Dynasty.

Jung also considered the origins of the universal phenomenon of the conflation of human and animal forms. That he did so relatively early in the last century is remarkable and indicates how very advanced was his understanding of the value of the psychoanalytical principles that he had developed (or, more accurately, to which he had given expression) when they were applied to basic human experience, even those removed from specific therapeutic practice:

If the regression goes still further back, beyond the phase of childhood to the preconscious, prenatal phase, then archetypal images appear, no longer connected with the individual's memories but belonging to the stock of inherited possibilities of representation. It is from them that arise those images of 'divine' beings, part animal, part human. The guise in which these figures appear depends upon the attitude of the conscious mind: if it is negative towards the unconscious, the animal will be frightening; if positive, they appear as 'the helpful animals' of fairytale and legend.[6]

In writing of those images of 'divine' beings, part animal, part human, Jung asserted the principle of the common nature of the underlying psychology of all men at all times. He demonstrated that the archetypes are common to all peoples, in all cultures and epochs; he also defined this specifically in one of his most enduring, if still controversial, concepts, the collective unconscious, another phenomenon which is common to all humanity at all periods.

> This deep level I call the 'collective unconscious'; I have chosen the term 'collective' because this part of the unconscious is not individual but universal; in contrast to the personal psyche, it has contents and modes of behaviour that are more or less the same everywhere and in all individuals. It is, in other words, identical in all men and thus constitutes a common psychic substrate of a suprapersonal nature which is present in every one of us.[7]

Research in the fields that bear directly on the origins of the conflation of human and animal in manifestations of the divine or the transcendental, more recent than Jung's work but as significant in its particular context, has been that conducted by scholars at the University of Witwatersrand, notably David Lewis-Williams and his colleague Thomas Dowson, now of the University of Southampton. Their work has been augmented by other scholars, especially in the study of hunter–gatherer communities.[8] Lewis-Williams and Dowson have been primarily concerned with the life of the !Kung San people, a hunting community of the Kalahari desert who preserve many of the characteristics, beliefs and rituals typical of Neolithic hunter–gatherer communities, of which they are one of the last to survive.[9]

Like their predecessors in the south-west European caves, the hunters and herders of the Sahara and the pastoralists of the Egyptian and Arabian deserts, the !Kung San sustain dedicated artists among their communities. These artists are also shamans (as perhaps all real artists are), to whom the practice of art plays as important a part in their culture as it did for the artists of the European painted caves; it is certainly not unlikely that all or most of the creators of the painted caves were shamans too. The significance of the work of several anthropologists in addition to Lewis-Williams and his colleagues is that they appear to have discovered the psychological mechanisms which trigger the art of the hunters and in doing so have provided a convincing mechanical explanation for the universal conflation of the animal and the divine.[10]

By the study of a living group such as the !Kung San it is possible to demonstrate evidence for psychological phenomena that Jung postulated and, in the immediate context of this book, how in at least one respect the

Egyptians, like other peoples in a similar state of psychological engagement, 'saw' the conflations of humans and animals and then recorded what they saw. To comprehend this point fully, it is necessary to know that the !Kung San practise a form of shamanism that requires the shaman to enter stages of trance; in each state of trance he is able to communicate with the spirits of the ancestors and of the animals that the people hunt and on whose well-being they depend for their own survival. The shaman – priest, magus, magician, what you will – is Jung's 'old wise man' in another, authentic guise. He enters into deep trance and brings back to his own world the images and understandings that he gains whilst in a state of altered consciousness.

One of the most arresting of Lewis-Williams's and his colleagues' conclusions in this ground-breaking and important field of study has been the replication of the shamans' trance states by volunteer subject under controlled laboratory trance conditions. This suggests that trance itself proceeds through three stages, from a light to a deep state. In the lighter stages of the trance the subjects see and replicate what the researchers call 'entoptic' phenomena – that is, images that are seen, as it were, within the eye. These are comparable with the effects often produced by migraine: jagged, intermittent streaks of light, streams of dots and broadly geometric shapes passing before the eyes. It can be demonstrated that all these entoptic phenomena are to be identified in the art produced by the societies that practice shamanism, all over the world. In the second stage of trance the geometric shapes begin to take on forms that will be identifiable to the subject, familiar animals for example, or symbols of apprehension or distress.[11]

Returning from the deepest level of trance the !Kung San shamans produce drawings of the eland, the animal on the hunting of which the people very largely depend for their sustenance.[12] Sometimes the scenes that the shaman brings back are directly related to the hunt, suggesting that, as has long been suspected about the art of the European painted caves for example, such paintings are propitiatory, intended to honour and to placate the spirit of the animal which is to be hunted and which – paradoxically perhaps to modern understanding – is venerated even as it is hunted and killed. By eating the animal, which scholars of an earlier generation might have referred to as a totem, the people take in the animal's spirit and become one with it in death; thus it possesses a quality greater than in life. The essential idea is, after all, not so far removed from the ingestion of the body and blood of the Redeemer in Christian rituals.

In a deep trance state the shaman will see and record conflations of the animal and human. In the art of the !Kung San, frequently the body of the eland is depicted, surmounted by a human head, sometimes a human body with the head of the animal. It is surely from this type of experience that the therianthropes recorded throughout history from virtually every ancient culture in the world derive, and this must include those of ancient Egypt.

There is no direct evidence of the early Egyptians having practised shamanism, though of course the reputations as powerful magicians of the high priests, of which order there were many, may be rooted in the use of consciousness-altering substances and some form of trance-induced or artificially stimulated and heightened states of awareness. It is probable also that Egyptian surgeons in early times, whose practice included amputation and other quite complex surgical procedures, will have employed some form of narcotic or anaesthetic during the procedure and in the process of recovery. Patients survived what even today would be regarded as major surgery, such as trepanning, with its attendant trauma.[13] The Egyptian pharmacopoeia was extensive, and given their interest in every aspect of the natural world it is difficult to believe that, acute observers that they were, they would not have become aware of the analgesic properties of the plants, fungi and roots with which they were familiar; similarly, they would have known of their consciousness-altering propensities.

It is thus entirely possible that hallucinogenic substances and mind-altering drugs would have been known in Egypt and used from early times. It is interesting, however, that !Kung San shamans are said not to use hallucinogens or mind altering substances but to enter trance by the employment of hyperventilation techniques, deep concentration and, sometimes, dance. Such techniques might well have been adopted in Egypt in antiquity; it should not be forgotten that, even into comparatively recent times, there were wise men and women always to be found in the Egyptian countryside who were considered to be in possession of powers beyond the normal and who were thought to be in touch with forces beyond the purely human ken. There have been reports in the past of secret meetings in the Egyptian countryside where adepts were said to communicate with the spirits or with extra-human forces; dance was said to play an important part in such events. Every village had its wise man or woman and many of the festivals celebrated outside the principal cities have elements of magic and wonder-working even to this day.[14]

Many of the images that appear in Egyptian art replicate the elements of fantasy and the surreal which typify much of the art that known shamans have recovered from their deep trance states. Such images will have been mediated through the artistic conventions which the Egyptians devised in conditions far removed from shamanistic trance and which were formulated by highly skilled professional artists. This may make the origins of the designs employed less immediately evident than the more directly related phenomena of the shamans.

One of the most frequent episodes represented in the graphic art produced by the Egyptians in antiquity is the descent into the Underworld. Whilst in later times this is represented as inherent in the journey of the soul to judgement and eventual happy fulfilment in the pleasant landscapes of the Afterlife (which are notably like the Nile, transfigured), this may be a later synthesising of experiences gained during trance states. The descent into the Underworld is a universal product of the trance, and a study of the multitude of its representations will reveal many that are not related to a *post mortem* state but are associated with time, the appearance of the gods, the night and the stars. The Egyptian image of the justified soul as a human-headed bird, the *ba*, flying down the corridors of the route to the Underworld would be a particularly powerful expression of the recovery of a shamanistic experience.

The existence of trance-induced visions of therianthropes in the art of peoples with a powerful surviving hunting tradition (which seems to be the essential prerequisite) coheres very well with Jung's insight into the power and universality of the collective unconscious. It explains convincingly the appearance of theriomorphs and therianthropes in ancient Egypt as readily as it does those recorded by known shamanistic societies. Because of the close integration of the dog, and hence of the genus *Canis* at large, with human societies in Egypt, in some cases the conflation of canid and human would have emerged from the collective psyche of the people, probably induced by states of altered consciousness. In other circumstances, the apotheosis of cattle would reflect the preoccupation of the community with its most important food resource and, in early times, its principal quarry in the hunt, particularly the giant aurochs. The many hieroglyphic groups that commemorate the bull as the manifestation of divinity are always based on the wild bull.

The bull's paramountcy among the divine animals was doubtless because of its identification with the Divine King in the early centuries and the fact that the king was always hailed as 'Great Bull' and similar epithets.[15] In a particularly potent instance this identification reveals the intimate connection between animal and divinity. Thus, the many bull gods, such as those already named here, Apis, Bochis and Mnevis, were regarded as 'heralds', whose divine afflatus announced the presence of a god whose beneficence could be invoked through the medium of the divinely favoured animal.

For whatever reason, some of the divine animals became more important than others, in the sense of being accepted as manifestations of the divine principle across the whole of Egypt. Thereby they achieved national status, in addition to what had probably been an ancient local standing. When the animal concerned was ubiquitous and of evident value to the community, apparently sharing in the life of that community by its own volition, the relationship with its human companions became especially powerful. It is thus that the widespread acceptance by the Egyptians of canids as conduits to the divine may be appreciated. The designation of the canine gods as 'guides' for the dead on the way to the Afterlife, and of the king in the exercise of his office, is particularly significant in this context.

The animals that express the presence of divine cosmic powers in the Egyptian system are archetypes, the great universal, primordial principles that well up from a community's collective unconscious, an irresistible process that gives form, substance, reality and meaning to the otherwise suprahuman. The archetypes are the universal expression, common to all humanity at all times, of the great forms and images that are contained in the unconscious and that are given life and meaning simply by their recognition.[16] The hawk, the bull, to a lesser degree the lion but certainly the canids, were among the animal personae that were taken to represent archetypal forms of a greater, most ancient and hidden reality.

The summoning of virtually every living creature known to the Egyptians to manifest the presence of one of the greater or lesser divine entities shows how the Egyptian spirit shines most steadfastly when they depict the natural world and the animals around them. In this, again, they were the first: other cultures have painted and engraved their view of the world as they saw it, but it was always, as it were, from a distance, never from within. Even the painters of the great caves of south-western Europe and the artists of the Sahara seem to have stood apart from the world that they recorded. The depiction of humans in Upper Palaeolithic art is comparatively rare and similarly only appears significantly in the Sahara in relatively late times, whereas the Egyptians during the historic period always represented themselves in a joyful interaction with their animal companions: it is one of the more definite differences of the art of the predynastic period compared with that of dynastic times that humans are much less important than the animals (and the suprahuman entities) in the rock art of the Egyptian desert. They worked from within, as if they wished to demonstrate that the animals were sacred, like themselves.

The Egyptians did not restrict the representation of the gods to the larger or more handsome or formidable animals. To the modern mind, the identification may sometimes seem perverse, even comically inappropriate. It is tempting for us today to see the play of something like irony in their apparent attribution of divinity to the mongoose, the scarab beetle, the goose (in which the high god Amon, the national god of Egypt in the time of her imperial greatness, was accustomed to manifest himself), the cat and the hare.

But what, to modern eyes, may seem to be a child-like lack of sophistication or sensitivity is merely another expression of the Egyptians' sense of the oneness of nature, of the interconnection and the interdependence of all living forms. When they wished to do so they could achieve an astonishing synthesis between the animal and the conceptual divinity. The identification of the divine king with the falcon, soaring high into the remote reaches of the sky, is a brilliant encapsulation of an audacious idea and its symbolic expression.

This absorption of early dynastic Egypt with the natural world and the total identification with it are demonstrated by a profoundly significant and abiding preoccupation with the concept of duality. This was expressed in every aspect of life in the Valley. Everything, animate and inanimate, human and animal, light and dark, night and day, storm and fair weather, all natural phenomena and all philosophical tenets, consisted of the One and the Other, in perpetual counterpoint, neither being capable of existence without the other. This applied too in what might be called, though with distinct reservations, the moral sphere: good was balanced by evil, evil by good, order by chaos. This concept of an essentially dualistic world was carried over, most intensely, into the perception of the world that the Egyptians themselves inhabited, the Dual Kingdom.

The idea of the Two Lands, as Egypt was always described by convention after their supposed Unification, of the Two Crowns, the Dual King, Upper and Lower Egypt and so on, through all the departments of Egyptian life, constantly reiterates this almost Manichaean understanding of the binary nature of the cosmos. An essential component of the Egyptian world-view was the constant seeking for the reconciliation and balancing of opposites and, by their achievement, the attainment of stasis. The king himself was literally the embodiment of this process of reconciliation in that, in addition to the injunction that he should 'rule in Ma'at', thus in justice and truth, he was the living incarnation of the two great divine powers: not only Horus, with whom he was ever identified as the reborn king, but also Set, the principal of chaos, without whom Horus could not be fully realised. As with every other dimension of the Egyptian existence the role of the king as the conduit to the divine is crucial. In this representation of the cosmos being kept in balance by two opposing but complementary powers, the Egyptians anticipated by several thousand years more familiar dualistic creeds such as Manichaeism and the Iranian duality of Ahura Mazda and Ahiram. These systems, however, tended to represent the duality as a conflict between good and evil, whereas the Egyptians, demonstrating perhaps a greater maturity, saw it as the opposition of order and chaos.

Canines brought their particular qualities of trust, guardianship and the mildly mysterious to the Egyptian conception of the divine involvement in nature. Anubis, the hound or jackal – in any event the archetypal canine – Khentiamentiu, Wepwawet and, less definitively, the ambiguous creature that represented the god Set in his most equivocal manifestation were all divine entities that were manifested in canine form. It is now timely to consider their roles in the Egyptian scheme of sacred matters.

The Great God Anubis

The divine entities begin to cluster round the king and the office of the kingship at the very beginning of the historic period, at the commencement of the First Dynasty, in the thirty-second century BC. From this point onwards they come and go, some surviving from still more remote times, others drawn into their service from the various localities up and down the Valley, as the rulers of such localities came to greater power, bringing their gods with them. One of the most ancient, probably coming from times long before the creation of the kingship, was the most celebrated of the canine gods, Anubis, Lord of the Necropolis.

The term 'canine' is here used in connection with Anubis quite specifically, because there is little agreement among scholars as to what species he belongs to. Various authorities have seen him as a jackal, others as a hound; even his coloration is diverse, though he is often shown as black, a colour rare in mammals as we have seen, though not unknown in nature. The representations of the god particularly in three dimensions seem to show him in a form closer to the jackal, but even here the representation is not absolutely literal and, as we have seen, the determinative which seals the hieroglyphic group that declares his name is a hound.

A very ancient symbol, represented by jet-black canines, replicas of the Anubis archetype, is known as 'The Souls of Nekhen', legendary kings of Upper Egypt who were said to have reigned in remote predynastic times, before the Unification by the kings of the First Dynasty. Nekhen was the ancient Egyptian name for the stronghold of the Falcon princes, known to the Greeks as Hierakonpolis and the site of a very ancient temple consecrated to Horus, who was sometimes conflated with Anubis. Four black canines also drew the solar boat on its journeys through the sky, bearing the god Re. These animals are generally described as jackals.

Anubis himself was said to have been king of Egypt in legendary times.[17] His cult centre was located at the city which the Greeks called Lykopolis, 'Wolf City', now Asyut in Middle Egypt; it was probably the Greeks who were responsible for the introduction of the idea of Anubis as a wolf, presumably being unaware that the wolf was never native to or established in Egypt. The reservation regarding this view expressed earlier in relation to *Canis lupaster* should be borne in mind, however.

There is no doubt that the Egyptians identified Anubis with the dog, and indeed the dog with Anubis. This is confirmed by the rubric that appears in the funerary inscriptions of which there are many examples dedicated to a favourite hound buried in its own tomb, like Khufu's Abutiyuw, or in its own handsome sarcophagus. The deceased dog is commended specifically to the care of 'The Great God Anubis', and it is prayed that the dog 'will be honoured before him'. That Anubis is regarded as the patron divinity of dogs is plain, indicating that the Egyptians, though they doubtless understood the difference between the hound and the jackal, recognised them all as belonging to the same family.

Canine-bearing standards were carried before the kings of the First Dynasty when processing; Wepwawet (see below) appears on the palette of King

Narmer, and earlier still a canine standard leads King Scorpion as he opens
the canal, on his great macehead from Hierakonpolis. Anubis himself appears
on a sealing of King Djer,[18] the third king of the founding dynasty. Prayers
were addressed to him on the walls of the Old Kingdom mastabas and he
is frequently mentioned in the Pyramid Texts, which were first set down
in permanent form at the end of the Old Kingdom but parts of which
probably descend from much earlier times. In historic times Anubis was
honoured throughout the Two Lands, for his priests were responsible for the
management of the obsequies of the king and the Great Ones as well as for
the preparation of the dead for burial, including the rites of mummification.
When the practice of mummification became universal in Egypt for all ranks
in society, the Anubis priests became, predictably, very powerful.

Anubis became especially identified with Abydos in northern Upper
Egypt in later times, by reason of his association with Osiris, the Lord of
the Underworld. According to one of the prevailing theogonies concerning
the origins of the gods, most of which are late recensions heavily edited,
probably corrupt and thus suspect, the goddess Nephthys, the sister–wife
of Set became the mother of Anubis, although according to other myths he
was the son of a divine cow, the goddess of milk. He was also said, perhaps
pertinently in the present context, to be 'the son of a jackal and a dog'.[19]
Set never acknowledged his paternity of Anubis; the myth suggests that his
brother, Osiris, seduced Nephthys (or, a little improbably, mistook her for
Isis, her sister and the sister of Osiris as well as his consort) and fathered
on her the Lord of Graveyards, whose duty it became to lead the dead to
judgement before Osiris.

Though a far more ancient divinity in Egypt than Osiris, from the Middle
Kingdom onwards Anubis was taken into his retinue and attended him in the
Underworld. He was honoured as the dog which, after the murder of Osiris,
became the protector of Isis, the mother of Osiris' posthumous son, Horus.
He had been introduced to Isis by dogs that found him after his birth and
brought him to the goddess.

This review of the origins of Anubis and his engagement with the Osirian
family is contained in the writings of Plutarch, the Greek author and friend
to the Emperor Hadrian, who wrote in the second century AD. Plutarch
is one of the principal sources for the cults of Anubis, though it must be
remembered that his life was passed very late in the history of Egypt and
there is no knowing how recognisable would have been his descriptions of

the rites associated with Anubis to an Egyptian living in the earlier periods. The god Typhon, of whom Nephthys was afraid in this extract, is the Greek form of Set, who was her husband and brother.

> They also relate that Isis, learning that Osiris in his love had consorted with her sister through ignorance, in the belief that she was Isis and seeing the proof of this in the garland of melitote which he had left with Nephthys, sought to find the child; for the mother Nephthys had exposed it because of her fear of Typhon. And when the child had been found, after great toil and trouble, with the help of dogs which led Isis to it, it was brought up and became her guardian and attendant, receiving the name of Anubis and it was said to protect the gods just as dogs protect men.[20]

'Anubis' is the Graecized form of the god's name, in Egyptian 'Inpw[21] (G.D15); he may have come originally from Abydos and probably owed much of his later celebrity to the importance that Abydos acquired in the early development of the kingship. All the kings of the First Dynasty were buried there, in immense funerary palaces; some of the kings of the Second Dynasty also chose Abydos as their burial place. The great lowering mud-brick walls of the area outside Abydos known as Shunet ez-Zebib and, erroneously, as 'the Castle of Khasekhemwy', was the burial place of that king, the last of the Second Dynasty, which has miraculously survived for nearly 5000 years. Anubis would have been the natural choice as guardian of the royal dead.

After the end of the Old Kingdom, Osiris became the dominant presence in the cults practised in Abydos, which was one of the centres of the early kingship, and the fact of its choice as the burial ground of the earliest kings ensured that Osiris became identified with the royal dead. He rapidly became one of the principal divinities of Egypt, Lord of the Land of the Dead and King of the Underworld.

Osiris came to be recognised as the father of Horus and hence the divine father of the king in whom Horus was reincarnated. According to a relatively late myth Osiris was murdered by his brother, Set. Horus avenged his father's death and succeeded him on the throne of Egypt. This myth was presumably concocted to identify Horus as the heir of the supposedly once living king who was reputed to have brought the arts of civilisation to Egypt in legendary times, though in fact Horus of Nekhen–Hierakonpolis was the supreme god of the kingship long before Osiris came to prominence. Osiris was assimilated into a much older god of the Abydos region, Khentiamentiu, who was also identified as a canid.[22]

Another hieroglyphic form of Anubis' name is (G.E16),[23] where the animal, described by Gardiner as a dog, is recumbent on his shrine: in this form it is used in the group which expresses one of Anubis' titles, 'He who is over the secrets', the secrets in question being concealed in the shrine. This image will be further considered in the context of Anubis in the tomb of Tutankhamun.

Anubis presided over the rites which attended the funeral ceremonies conducted on the deceased's behalf, especially the process of mummification. Many representations exist of Anubis actually performing the mummification rites; it is usually accepted that the tall figure with a canine's head is a priest of Anubis wearing a dog or jackal mask, examples of which have survived from later in Egypt's history.[24]

Anubis is one of the most appealing, if also one of the most mysterious, of all Egypt's gods. He was known as one who prowled by night around the graveyards that in every community, even in early predynastic times, were set up in close proximity to the settlements. By the sort of poetic transposition of which the Egyptians were always supremely capable, in this lonely nocturnal prowling of a canine which was not above scavenging for its sustenance, Anubis came to be recognised as the protector of the dead, and their guide to judgement. That he was also a scavenger gave further witness to his divine powers, for he was able to transform putrefaction into living substance and so was considered especially competent to restore the dead to life.

In his role as psychopomp, the guide and guardian of the dead on their post mortem journey, Anubis' most important function in all probability originated in predynastic times, before the practice of mummification became as sophisticated as it was to be in the Old Kingdom. It may well be that the control of graveyards had originally been attributed to Anubis, representing all feral canines, as a propitiatory gesture to protect the dead buried on the outskirts of the early settlements. It was the aspect of the responsibilities that Anubis discharged which appealed most to the people of late antiquity, when he enjoyed great popularity and was absorbed into the religious beliefs of the Graeco-Roman world.

Anubis was the guardian of the boundary between the worlds of the living and the dead, which only the canine divinities could traverse. He was a further example of the Egyptians' perpetual concern with the expression of the duality of all forms, principles and entities. Because he was able to move freely between the two worlds he was both a solar divinity and a god of the Underworld. He was familiar with, and equally at home in, light and darkness, a quality on which Plutarch commented. Not infrequently he was conflated with gods even greater than himself, to form a composite divinity: Anubis–Re for example, or with Set, whose canine appearance would make the identification particularly plausible.

The belief that canines could move between the worlds of the living and the dead is another example of the Egyptians' ability to transpose ordinary events and appearances into highly poetic concepts and also of the almost uncannily sophisticated understanding of the scientific realities underlying the natural world that frequently they display. The Egyptians' sensitivity to the natural world will have alerted them to an aspect of canines' optics whereby dogs, especially feral dogs, are known to be particularly active at dawn and dusk and therefore their sight must be adjusted to semi-obscurity. This observation will have led them to invest Anubis and his like with the ability to see in the half-light, which no doubt would characterise the boundary between the two worlds.

Dogs' eyes are indeed conditioned to operate in half-light, by reason of the distribution of the two light-sensitive cells, cones and rods, on the retina; cones respond in good light whilst rods are better adjusted to dimness. The dog's retina has a proportionately higher ratio of rods to cones. One consequence of this cone-favoured distribution is that dogs do not respond to colour as clearly as do humans, though their vision is not wholly monochrome.[25]

Another factor affecting the dog's optics is the light-reflecting layer at the back of the eyes, the *tapetum lucidum*. This structure acts like a mirror, reflecting light back through the retina and serving to increase the effect of light rays on the rods and cones;[26] dogs share this faculty with cats. The eyes of a dog, reflected in moonlight or by firelight, would have been a powerful influence in suggesting its slightly uncanny quality and would have enhanced its reputation for being licensed to move between the worlds of life and death. All of these factors would have augmented the canines' mythological character, suggesting that they could enjoy access to regions not penetrable by humans.

As with so much of what are described as the cults and rituals conducted in Egyptian temples, our knowledge of Anubis' responsibility for the rites of the dead and of the process of mummification comes from Herodotus and other writers of late antiquity, long after the end of Egypt's pristine culture. His reputation has also been formed by what it has been possible to deduce from the myriad representations of the performance of the rites in the illustrations in papyri and in the reliefs and paintings of the tombs and sarcophagi of the New Kingdom and later.

The rites attending the process of mummification lasted for 70 days, during which prayers and incantations were said whilst the processes of evisceration and embalming were carried out. Many of the liturgies that descended ultimately from the Pyramid Texts of the Old Kingdom and the Coffin Texts of the Middle Kingdom were designed to ensure the safe passage of the justified soul to the Afterlife, the first for the transit of the king from this world to the next, the second for all those who, in later periods, could claim 'justification'. The various texts surviving from the later centuries of Egypt's history are known popularly as 'The Book of the Dead', though each recension has its own specific title; together they contain much material relating to Anubis and his responsibilities. Little, however, is known of the rites conducted in the temples that were consecrated to him, or of those which attended the burials of huge numbers of mummified dogs at Lykopolis (Asyut), at Abydos and at Saqqara, where the cemetery of dogs, one of the largest in Egypt, is known as the Anubeion.

There is a considerable repertory of invocations to Anubis in his capacity as the guide to the judgement before Osiris. There are also many representations of him participating in the process of judgement, when he is responsible for maintaining the accuracy of the scales on which the soul of the deceased is weighed. The supervision of the actual mummification process, an operation that is frequently depicted in Egyptian sources, was performed by his priests who were trained specially in its techniques. The process has been described in loving detail by Herodotus, who, like all Greeks, was fascinated by what he saw as the Egyptians' macabre preoccupation with the preservation and revivification of corpses. By his time and even later, when the writers of Greece and Rome who came after Herodotus similarly lingered over the cults of the dead, many of the rituals performed in the temples and the funerary ceremonies had become debased, just as the original pristine spirit of Egyptian belief and ritual practices had been diminished by contact with peoples from outside the Valley.

It is a curious fact that the actual techniques of mummification seem to have declined markedly after Old Kingdom times. Then, the body was wrapped in fine, gauze-like linen and washed in a substance similar to gesso.

When the 'package' dried, it shrank and moulded itself to the body of the deceased with extraordinary precision. Cosmetic touches to the face, limbs and genitals completed the making of a remarkable simulacrum of the living body, with little of the qualities of nightmare which attend the mummies of the New Kingdom and later. Unfortunately, it is these that are best known, and because vastly more survive than the earlier forms it is these that have contributed to the images of delicious horror which cling to the examples of Egyptian mummification processes, filling museums as well as movie-houses across the world today.[27]

In writing about aspects of the cult, Plutarch revealed much of Anubis' significance in the Graeco-Roman world, where he experienced a considerable revival, becoming one of the fashionable Egyptian deities that the Alexandrians and then the Romans cultivated enthusiastically. By the time that Plutarch claimed to have witnessed some of the rituals associated with the god in the second century AD, Anubis had been recognised as a universal archetype, but it is not clear how much of what remained descended from earlier times and how much represented the incorporation of later influences from outside Egypt.

Plutarch does have some notably interesting observations to make, especially in his identification of Anubis as the guardian of the boundaries between the two worlds and in associating him with the concept of time. This last, admittedly, sounds more Greek than Egyptian, though the Greeks always acknowledged their indebtedness to the earlier civilisation for many of their most deeply held beliefs;[28] indeed, they were convinced that the Greek pantheon was drawn from Egyptian prototypes. The canine gods seem always to have been associated with time and the seasons, with the hours and the movement of the heavenly bodies. It is possible that, as he hints, Plutarch was privy to a degree of secret or concealed knowledge about the rites of Anubis known only to initiates, though once again the very late date of his evidence must be borne in mind.

The text of the Plutarch extract does suggest that he knew more than he was prepared to divulge, though this was a technique not infrequently adopted by Classical writers when describing the mysteries of foreign religious beliefs and practices. It will be noted that Plutarch here obviously recognises Anubis as a dog.

> When Nephthys gave birth to Anubis Isis treated the child as if it were her own; for Nephthys is that which is beneath the earth and invisible, Isis that

which is above the earth and visible; and the circle which touches these, called the horizon, being common to both, has received the name Anubis, and is represented in form like a dog: for the dog can see with his eyes both by night and day alike. And amongst the Egyptians Anubis is thought to possess this faculty, which is similar to that which Hecatê is thought to possess among the Greeks for Anubis is a deity of the lower world as well as a god of Olympus. Some are of the opinion that Anubis is Cronos. For this reason, in as much as he generates all things out of himself and conceives all things within himself he has gained the appellation of 'dog'. There is therefore a certain mystery observed by those who revere Anubis; in ancient times the dog obtained the highest honours in Egypt; but when Cambyses had slain the Apis and cast him forth nothing came near the body nor ate of it save the dog; and thereby the dog lost his primacy and his place of honour above that of all the other animals.[29]

There is a considerable and complex symbolism here. Anubis is represented as reconciling the several opposite characteristics in the natures of Isis and Nephthys. Anubis is the circle of the horizon embracing that which is above and below ground; in this he is comparable to Horus, who was also identified with the horizon. That he can see equally well by day and by night shows him to be a creature in which the opposites are reconciled, hence a fitting exemplar of both the kingship and of the Two Lords, Horus and Set. He is a god of the Underworld and at the same time one of the high gods. He is a form of the Demiurgos, generating all things within himself and out of himself. This last carries echoes of the Gnostic beliefs that were current in Egypt at the time when Plutarch was writing.

The reference to the loss of standing that the dog experienced when it ate the body of the sacred Apis bull allegedly killed by the Persian king Cambyses appears nowhere else in Egyptian texts. It may be that it is a rationalisation of the loss of status experienced by the dog in the Late Period, when the tjesm and the several other 'breeds' that had been known in Egypt for so long seem to diminish in representation and hence, presumably, in importance and acceptance.

The story of Cambyses and the killing of the Apis is disputed by scholars.[30] It has been questioned whether Cambyses was the monster which Egyptian propaganda portrayed after the Persians had finally been driven out of the Valley following the defeat of the last Persian Great King, Darius III, by Alexander the Great. Rather, scholars today point to Cambyses' concern to respect and protect Egyptian temples and the rituals and other observances carried out in them.

If the once high standing of dogs in the affections of the Egyptian people had declined, it would be entirely within the Egyptian way of explaining events obliquely to propose that the hound's loss of place was due to its opportunistic ingestion of the murdered sacred bull. If the Apis was not murdered by Cambyses, the story falls to the ground; it should also be remembered that Plutarch was a Greek. Whilst the comment is speculative it may simply be that with the infusion of alien influences that penetrated Egypt in the first millennium BC, the hound declined in the regard of the Egyptians.

The linking of the goddesses and Anubis with the sky is also rich in symbolism. Isis was represented in the night sky by one of the most important heavenly bodies in the Egyptian consciousness, Sopdet (G.N 14),[31] which the Greeks called Sothis and is known to the modern world by its Latin name, Sirius. This was the dog-star which for the Egyptians announced the coming of the New Year and the beginning of inundation of the Nile.

Sirius is the brightest star in the constellation Canis Major. Indeed, it is the brightest star in the night sky, with a magnitude of 1.6. It is distant from earth by a mere 8.7 light years; it is not the nearest star, a position occupied by Alpha Centuri, but it is one of the closest. The association between the constellation and the dog is very ancient, said by some to date at least from the third millennium BC; however, it was the Greeks and later the Romans who publicised the connection most assiduously. It seems to derive from the idea of another canine divinity, Wepwawet (see below), as 'the leader' of the procession of the gods.

The reappearance of Sirius marked the return of the inundation which throughout Egypt's history was the most important event of the year; this return of Sirius promised the beneficial flooding of the banks and canals on which Egypt's prosperity and indeed the survival of the people depended. The heliacal rising of Sirius, when it appeared on the horizon immediately before the sun came up at dawn, signalled the commencement of the New Year. Again, the function of leadership is invoked, with Sirius leading time and the seasons. Popular superstition in later times identified the appearance of Sirius with the 'Dog Days', the time of relentless summer heat which was thought to drive dogs mad. One of the meanings of the name Sirius is 'scorching'. Anubis was the epitome of the summer solstice.[32] Curiously, the Chinese also identified Sirius with a jackal.

In addition to his links with the constellation of Canis Major, Anubis was also identified with Canis Minor, the Lesser Dog, whose appearance in the night sky was also seen as providing a signal for the arrival of the 'Dog Days'. Its principal star, Procyon, like Sirius a first magnitude star though less bright, lies 11.4 light years from Earth.

The Greeks and Romans were fascinated by Egypt. Even before the Macedonian Ptolemies had established themselves in Memphis and later in Alexandria, Egyptian religion and, most particularly, what was believed to be 'Egyptian magic' had seized hold of the imaginations of the emerging Mediterranean cultures. Apuleius' wonderful and fantastic novel *The Golden Ass* is heavy with magic.[33] Most of its adventures related in the story culminated disastrously and always embarrassingly for its effete hero, Lucius, the peak of whose misfortunes is to be transformed, like Bottom, into an ass, though in his case totally, not merely his head. Bottom was a therianthrope; Lucius is metamorphosed, translated into another creature entirely. After a series of miserable experiences in which Lucius, in the person of the poor beast, is tormented by all manner of malignant forces, the goddess Isis, who was by this time a favourite among the Europeans ready to experiment with new cults, appears to him in a dream and promises his redemption and restoration to his human form.

Lucius' restitution is to be brought about during a high religious ceremony when he is enjoined to eat roses from the high priest's garland. In his asinine form he watches the procession in honour of the goddess with dancers, priests and the entire pious assembly. He describes the procession and one part of it which relates directly to Anubis, who it will be remembered was particularly associated with Isis.

> Next in the procession followed those deities that deigned to walk on
> human feet. Here was the frightening messenger of the gods of Heaven and
> of the gods of the dead: Anubis with a face black on one side, gold on the
> other, walking erect and holding his herald's wand in one hand and in the
> other a green palm-branch.[34]

Since Anubis was as much revered by kings as by the ordinary people, he was one of the most frequently depicted of all the divine entities in paintings, sculpture, carvings, reliefs, in bronze, silver and gold, all the media which the genius of Egyptian artists had at their disposal. He was one of the earliest to be represented, his image carried in royal processions, a distinction he shared with his canine colleague, Wepwawet, who will be described below.

A jackal image which might be interpreted as being in honour of Anubis was said to have been dedicated in the reign of King Aha, the first king of the First Dynasty.[35]

Anubis appears again in another context that has been cited as evidence for the survival of this rite of the forecasting of the king's appointment with ceremonial death. This comes from the Third Dynasty; it involves the role that has been attributed to an influential, if somewhat mysterious, figure of the time, the priest Khabausoker.

The Third Dynasty was one of the most significant periods in the formative stages of the high Egyptian civilisation, at the very beginning of the Old Kingdom. It provides the bridge between the Early Dynastic Period, a time of rapid social and political change, which moved on to the dawning of the distinctive Egyptian culture at the end of the Second Dynasty with the beginning of the Old Kingdom. This was the point at which life in the Valley was no longer the concern only of the king and his immediate coadjutors but was broadening out to touch the whole of society. The Third Dynasty was of the greatest importance in determining many of the most enduring characteristics of Egyptian society and the Egyptian state. It was also notable for the appearance of a group of powerful state servants who surrounded the king, (Djoser) Netjerykhet. These included Imhotep, the vizier and architect of the Step Pyramid complex, and Hesy-Re the dentist, who was also the vizier and who is remembered by some exceptionally finely carved wooden panels from his tomb, illuminated by very beautiful hieroglyphs and handsome portraits of Hesy-Re himself.

Another of the leading figures of this period of most rapid development in Egypt was this same Khabausoker, who held a number of offices of very high rank under King Netjerykhet. He was a senior priest of Anubis, perhaps ranking as a high priest of the cult. He was also very advanced in the hierarchy of the temple of Ptah at Memphis, perhaps also ranking as High Priest. In his capacity as High Priest of Anubis (Figure 32) he was entitled to wear a curious piece of regalia: a necklace consisting of two parts, probably separate from each other.[36] The underpart fastened round the throat with a flat piece of metal: to this were attached three flat, zigzag strips that reached from the throat to the chest. The middle is finished by a wide loop, the two side pieces by small knobs. Attached to these strips and reaching from shoulder to shoulder is another long piece of metal, described by the excavator of Khabausoker's tomb as intended to represent a jackal or other canine. The animal has its two front

Figure 32 Khabausoker, a powerful figure in the hierarchy of the Third Dynasty, was connected with the cults of Anubis, perhaps being the equivalent of the High Priest of the Cult. His status and rank are indicated by the elaborate and unusual metal collar that he is wearing in his portrait in his tomb at Saqqara. The collar seems to represent the god himself, recumbent with his paws outstretched, a position repeated hundreds of years later in the tomb of King Tutankhamun.

paws raised in an attitude of worship, and also has six legs placed at intervals along the body. The whole device must have been absolutely rigid, judging by the width of the metal strips. Over it is placed a necklace of interlaced chains that are threaded through small circular discs and ankh signs. The 'jackal' of the necklace, referred to in the original report of the excavation of his tomb at Saqqara, which he shared with his wife, Hatorneferhetepes, is a representation of Anubis. This prompted one scholar to conclude that Khabausoker was a 'death-priest' in the service of Anubis, who was said to have announced the number of years that the king might reign.[37]

There is something slightly sinister about the portraits of Khabausoker displayed in his Saqqara mastaba. He has the look of a determined, perhaps arrogant man.[38] That he was ever the custodian of this very fanciful rite, supposedly charged with numbering the years permitted to the king before he was to be sacrificed, is certainly not remotely proven; indeed, as there is no evidence for its existence, other than these two instances on which such a theory could be constructed, it can surely be disregarded entirely.

Khabausoker was also engaged in the cults associated with the equivocal god Set. It has been suggested that his name means 'The glory of Soker shines'; Soker was the tutelary god of the district of Saqqara. Later he was assimilated with Ptah and Osiris ('Ptah–Soker–Osiris'), this portmanteau divinity giving rise to the composite god Serapis, who established for ever the image of the supreme god as a forceful, bearded man of mature years.

Khabausoker's responsibilities, as recorded in his tomb, included ones of a frankly rather banal quality, which in any event would certainly be at odds with these more sinister speculations;[39] he had charge of the court dancers and the management of the breweresses. As a high official in the temple of Ptah he was responsible for the direction of the carpenters and craftsmen who served the king. As a near contemporary of Imhotep, he may well have been involved in the building and equipping of the Step Pyramid complex. In this event his life will have been considerably more significant for the world that followed these events of nearly 5000 years ago than if he had been some sort of practitioner of the black arts, a Nile Valley Mephistopheles summoning a royal Egyptian Faustus to his doom.

In the succeeding Fourth Dynasty, which drew extensively on the advances, technological and philosophical, that had been made by its predecessor, the prevailing concern of the Egyptians always to achieve balance, the eternal counterpoint of opposites or complimentary entities, is demonstrated by one of the most sublime works of art from the Old Kingdom. This is one of the schist or greywacke triad statues of King Menkaure, recovered from his mortuary temple at Giza. The king stands, eternally young, energetic and forceful, between his queen on his right hand and on his left Anupet the tutelary goddess of the Seventeenth Upper Egyptian Cynopolite nome.[40] She is the feminine form of Anubis and carries his symbol on her head.

As the goddess of the nome, Anupet was particularly identified with the cults of Anubis; its principal city, El Qais in Egyptian, was called by the Greeks Cynopolis, 'Dog City'. Its remains lie at Shaikh el-Fadl, some 20 miles downstream from Minya, in Middle Egypt. According to Ptolemy the city was located on an island in the Nile. The figure of Anubis which Anupet wears on her head shows the god lying on his belly, front paws outstretched before him, 'He who is over the secrets', one of his most familiar manifestations.

Representations of Anubis of particularly high quality are known from the period of transition from the Fourth to the Fifth Dynasty (c. 2494 BC), when it would seem that he was especially important in the cults attending the king. They combine canine and human elements, in the treatment of the eyes, for example, though the overall character is unquestionably that of a hound. Several of the animals wear a voluminous scarf, which will be seen to be similar in form to that worn by Anubis in his most famous appearance, in the tomb of King Tutankhamun, 1000 years later.

One of the earliest formal portraits of Anubis, and one of the most majestic of all, comes from the reign of King Niuserre of the Fifth Dynasty, at a high point in Egypt's prosperity and splendour.[41] The king is enthroned, attended by one of the goddesses, and Anubis stands before him, presenting him with seven ankhs, the symbol of life which gods always carried and with which they would bless their favoured devotees. This is an unusual scene and it prompted the suggestion that the god was setting the term of the king's life;[42] this was at a time when Egyptology still believed that the king was liable to be sacrificed after he had completed the term allotted for his reign.

Though the scene is strange, there is certainly no reason for attributing this rather baroque explanation to it. Niuserre's regnal years, like all those of the Old Kingdom, are imprecise; one authority gives his reign as lasting for 24 years (2445–2421 BC), another reckons a longer duration (2420–2389 BC). In either event the dates would not appear to have any correspondence with the various cycles which were once proposed by those who believed that the Divine King, in cultures other than Egypt, was sacrificed after their completion. That such sacrifices did take place in many early societies is certain, but there is no evidence that Egypt was one of them.

The representations of Anubis, both three-dimensionally and in graphic form, follow a fairly prescribed course. His coat is predominantly black, sometimes with gold embellishments and, as we have seen, Apuleius records that in processions in his time the priest of Anubis wore a mask, the two sides of which were black and gold respectively, which he displayed as he turned his head from side to side as he walked in procession. Thus he emphasised his mastery over the light and dark by the dual coloration of the god; one scholar indeed has proposed that Anubis is 'the black and gold god'.[43]

In the statues of Anubis seated, robed as a king with the attributes of divinity, he is most clearly – if paradoxically – a dog; the determinative that seals the hieroglyphic group, an alternative to that reproduced earlier, which spells his name, 'Inpw, is of a seated god with a dog's head[44] (G.C6). He wears a collar like that worn by the tjesm when hunting and sometimes in the household.

The most famous of all Anubis' representations is the magnificent black and gold dog which, for more than 3000 years, guarded the entrance to the inner chamber of Tutankhamun's tomb. He lies, alert and watchful, on his gilded shrine. When the tomb was opened Anubis was found in the room beyond the burial chamber; Harry Burton's photograph, the first ever to be taken of what was to become one of the most frequently photographed and reproduced of all Egyptian icons, is immensely impressive, even today. Anubis lies on the top of his pylon-shaped shrine in an open doorway in the tomb, facing to the west. His head is held high, his eyes bright and vigilant. The shrine is mounted on runners as a sledge.[45]

Howard Carter's description of the discovery of the Anubis shrine and of the nature of what he found is still the most immediate and compelling of all the millions of words that have described the finding and excavation of this, at once one of the most obscure and yet the most celebrated of Egypt's kings.[46] Anubis had been set deliberately in his place in the tomb so that he could 'keep watch over the Burial Chamber and its occupant while he guarded his domain the "Treasury of the Innermost"'.[47]

Anubis' shoulders were covered with a linen shawl and round his neck was a long scarf, like the leashes which tjesm are frequently represented as wearing. The whole figure was covered with an ample linen shirt, with an ink docket dating it to a time long before Tutankhamun's death, in the seventh

year of the reign of his putative father, Amenhotep IV/Akhenaten.⁴⁸ The god
is carved in wood, varnished in black resin with gilded details, including
the inside of his sharply pricked ears. His eyes are piercing, made of calcite
and obsidian, set into gold surrounds and pricked out with gold. His claws
are of solid silver.⁴⁹

Between his paws was an ivory palette inscribed for Meritaten, the eldest
daughter of Akhenaten and Queen Nefertiti; she was Tutankhamun's half-
sister and may have been married to the shadowy King Smenkhkara, who
may have been Tutankhamun's immediate and short-lived predecessor. 'The
royal daughter, Mert-Aten [sic] beloved and born of the Great-Royal-Wife
Nefer-neferu-nefer-titi.'⁵⁰ The palette had evidently been used at some time;
it contained colours that had been employed in painting or in some form of
decoration. The colours were white, yellow, red, green, blue and black.⁵¹ The
shrine on which Anubis crouched contained a variety of materials relating
to the king's mummification, figurines and symbolic forms, and, in a special
compartment, 'eight large pectoral ornaments'.

Carter is perceptive in his discussion of the species to which Anubis,
as here represented, belongs. He suggests, first, that 'it is possible that it
originated from some form of domesticated jackal-dog of the primitive
Egyptians'. He goes on,

> It presents characteristics of several of the sub-orders of the canine family.
> It is represented black; as having a smooth coat; the attenuated form of
> the greyhound; long, pointed muzzle; long, erect ears; eye-pupils round;
> the fore-feet have five toes, and the hind feet only four; and it has a very
> long, straight, drooping, bushy, and club-like tail.... The numerous repre-
> sentations of this Anubis animal upon the Egyptian monuments resemble
> largely the bearing of the jackal and this specimen gives reason to entertain
> the idea that it may have been a domesticated form of the jackal crossed
> with another sub-genus of the canine family. The collar and the scarf-like
> leash that are invariably represented round its neck also suggest an animal
> brought under human control. And when one takes into account the quali-
> ties of the domesticated canine family – devotion to its master, knowledge
> and defence of his property, attachment to him until death – it may be the
> reason why these ancients selected this jackal-dog as the vigilant watcher
> over their dead.⁵²

He describes two encounters that he himself experienced with

> two animals resembling this Anubis form of jackal-dog. The first example
> was seen by me during the early spring of 1926, when in the desert of

Thebes I encountered a pair of jackals slinking towards the Nile Valley, as is their custom, in the dusk of the evening. One of them was evidently the common jackal (C. Lupaster) in spring pelage; but its mate – I was not near enough to tell whether the male or the female – was much larger, of lanky build, and black! Its characteristics were those of the Anubis-animal, save for one point – the tail was short, like the ordinary jackal. In fact, with the exception of its tail, it appeared to be the very counterpart of the figure found in this room. It may possibly have been a case of melanism, or sport deviating in both colour and form from the normal type, but I must admit that its extraordinary likeness to the Anubis beast brought to my mind the possibility of a throw-back or rare descendant of some earlier species in Egypt.... The second example that I saw was in October 1928, during early morn in the Valley of the Kings. It had precisely the same characteristics as the former example described, but in this case was a young animal from about seven to ten months old. Its legs were lanky; its body greyhound-like; it had a long pointed muzzle, large and erect, pointed, ears; but its drooping tail was comparatively short and of ordinary jackal shape. Long hairs of a lighter colour (greyish) under the body could be detected....

I have made enquiries among the inhabitants of Gurna (Western Thebes) regarding these animals. They tell me that individual examples of this black variety, though they are very rare, are known to them, and that they are always far more attenuated – 'of the Selakhi [sic] (a kind of greyhound) form' – than the ordinary species.[53]

Given Carter's observation of these two animals and the present writer's meeting with a jet-black Pharaoh Hound in rural England,[54] it seems likely that the canines, whatever their descent, do from time to time throw sports with black coloration; melanism is in fact a well-known phenomenon among domesticated species of all sorts. Carter speculates that the Anubis animal is principally a jackal strain, interbred with another 'sub-species of the canine family.' On this point it will be recalled that 'the evidence suggests that Anubis was modelled on the wolf-jackal of Egypt, C. aureus Lupaster.'[55] This Latin term is the zoological classification of the larger Egyptian subspecies of the golden jackal. It is possible that it was this animal that prompted the description 'wolf' being applied to it. However, as will be seen below, this does not wholly account for some of the attributions of 'wolf-pelts', for example, being used in temple ceremonies.

Anubis' lordship of the necropolis was also signified by his title 'Lord of the Holy Land', the Holy Land in this instance being Abydos and its outskirts where the early kings were buried and where generations of Egyptians sought to be commemorated; if they could not themselves be buried there, their spirits could undertake the journey to Abydos after death. Many of the more prosperous arranged for commemorative stelae to be set up there, as close as possible to the curious cyclopean structure which was known as the Tomb of Osiris and possibly dates from the First Dynasty; it is similar in form and construction to the equally enigmatic Valley Temple below the pyramid of King Khafre of the Fourth Dynasty.

Anubis was also 'Lord of the Divine Pavilion', indicating his control of the booth in which the rites of mummification were performed, over which he presided. An ancient sobriquet of Anubis was Imy-wt, 'He who is in his wrappings', which related to his supervision of the process of mummification. Imy-wt was symbolised by a headless animal skin, carried on a pole, which contained the solutions used for washing and embalming the corpse. This became Anubis' fetish. Some scholars have translated another of his soubriquets as 'Lightbringer', a title that would later acquire more equivocal overtones, though in Anubis' case it seems to have meant that, like Prometheus in Greek myth, the god brought light to the human race. It would be pleasant to think that this was a graceful acknowledgement of the part the dog had played in the civilisation of its human companions, in the course of their long association.

Anubis was invoked widely in the tombs in the Valley of the Kings at Thebes; he was especially popular in the New Kingdom. His image appears on the seals that were placed on the entrances to the burial chambers, lying over nine bound captives symbolising the traditional enemies of Egypt, from whose malice Anubis would protect the inhabitant of the tomb. Tutankhamun's tomb was sealed in this way.[56]

From this time onwards Anubis was one of the most frequently depicted divinities in Egypt, later in much of the ancient world. In many occasions he appeared with Osiris, in the countless paintings that decorated the tombs of the great and of the not so great who sought his protection. Thereafter Anubis never lost his appeal to the Egyptians, surviving until the end of Egypt as a distinct cult figure in the post-Roman period.

Khentiamentiu

One of Osiris' titles was 'Foremost of Westerners'. This had originally belonged to a very ancient canine divinity of Abydos, Khentiamentiu, but it appears that he lost his position in the local cultic hierarchy when the cult of Osiris, for whatever reason, became predominant. Before Osiris' rise to prominence Khentiamentiu was the god of the Abydos necropolis and hence 'Lord of the Dead', thus ruler of the Underworld. The earliest temple at Abydos was almost certainly dedicated to him. It survived throughout the Old Kingdom, and a new temple, dedicated to Osiris, was only built during the First Intermediate Period, a phase in Egypt's history marked by unrest and a decline in the power of the central authority of the kingship. It may be said that Osiris usurped Khentiamentiu and assumed his principal functions.

That Khentiamentiu was once of very considerable status is demonstrated by a cylinder seal, recently excavated from one of the royal tombs at Abydos, which lists the sequence of the early kings of the First Dynasty, from Narmer to Den, in their correct order. Queen Herneith is also named, seeming to confirm that she was accepted as a ruler of Egypt, though in all probability she was regent for her son, probably the same King Den.

Surmounting all the royal names is the image of Khentiamentiu, in the form of a canine, lying on its belly, with ears pricked and paws outstretched, in the stance that later the representations of Anubis were to make familiar[57] (Figure 33). It is clear that the divine rulers of Abydos acknowledged Khentiamentiu as their colleague, his presence confirming their royal status. But his place in the upper hierarchy of divine beings was taken over by Osiris after the end of the First Intermediate Period, circa 2000 BC. From that point on Osiris was the tutelary god of Abydos and identified with the king in death. Eventually he was seen as the assurance of life beyond death and

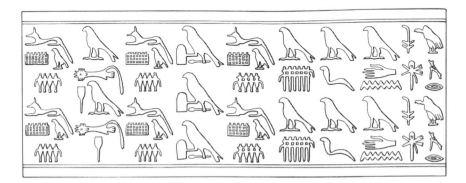

Figure 33 The names of the kings (and one queen) of the First Dynasty are displayed in this sealing from Abydos. Each of the royal names is preceded by the recumbent figure of the canine god Khentiamentiu, indicating his importance before he was supplanted by Osiris in the Middle Kingdom.

every justified person could become an Osiris. Occasionally a king would make a grant to Khentiamentiu's cult in Abydos; these included Neferirkare of the Fifth Dynasty, who relieved the god's priests of the burden of paying taxes, perhaps because of falling off in their revenues, and Pepi I gave orders for a few restorations to be carried out. But otherwise Khentiamentiu was largely forgotten, remembered only in archaic inscriptions.

Wepwawet

A third canine divinity, who was especially associated with the king, was Wepwawet (G.E18).[58] In this form his name is sealed with a determinative distinct from that used for Anubis; however, as with Anubis, the determinative for a dog-headed god can also be used. Wepwawet is a particularly intriguing entity, of great antiquity and originally more important than Anubis. The ideogram or determinative for his name is of a standing canine mounted on a standard. On this he was borne in procession before the king, certainly from the First Dynasty on the Narmer palette and very possibly from earlier still.

The earliest form of the Wepwawet standard, like the determinative that seals his name, shows the god with a balloon-like object in front of him, before which is a rearing cobra, the symbol of Uadjet, one of the Two Ladies, the ancient goddesses who protected the king from his enemies. The balloon-like object is known from the Pyramid Texts as the *shedshed*, which enjoys a close and intimate relationship with the king; it is generally accepted that it represents the king's placenta, which was especially sacred. The lance on which the standard is mounted is pierced by a pear-shaped mace; this demonstrates that Wepwawet is also a warrior-god, and in this capacity he also guards and guides the king in opposing his enemies.

Gardiner describes Wepwawet as a 'wolf (?)' in his comments on the hieroglyphic determinative of his name;[59] the query in parenthesis suggests that he is uncertain what species the determinative represents. The Greeks appear to have conferred the wolf-identity on Wepwawet, unaware presumably that there was no evidence of the wolf as indigenous to Egypt, though the possibility remains that an identification with *Canis aureus lupaster*, as mentioned earlier, may also apply here. It seems that, once again Wepwawet, like Anubis, must be regarded as an example of the composite or archetypal canine.

Figure 34 One of Egypt's greatest rulers, King Seti I had a splendid funerary temple built at Abydos, one of the wonders of New Kingdom architecture. Here the king is shown in the company of the god Wepwawet, whose embrace confirms the acceptance of the legitimacy of Seti's dynasty by the company of the gods. The image of Wepwawet is especially interesting as he is represented with a grey head, which might suggest that he is here identified with the grey wolf (see text for further observations).

Like his canine peers, Anubis and Khentiamentiu, Wepwawet was a very ancient entity; he was the patron of the XIII Upper Egyptian nome, with his capital at Asyut in Middle Egypt. Because of the cults involving canids there it was called Lykopolis, 'Wolf City', by the Greeks. Their belief that he was a wolf may have been derived from the fact that Wepwawet was sometimes shown with a grey or white head, suggesting that on some occasions he was considered wolf-like as well as being, from time to time, subsumed into a general canine identity (Figure 34). As he was apparently represented as a wolf and this identification persisted over time, it may be possible that he came to Egypt from outside, from a region where the wolf was indigenous. The Greeks would also have been familiar with wolves in their homeland and so may have decided that Wepwawet was one of them. It may equally be that the Greek commentators, geographers such as Strabo and historians like Herodotus, confused the jackal, particularly *Canis simensis*, with the wolf. However, it will be seen below that in rituals associated with Wepwawet there are references to wolves and to the participants in temple ceremonies honouring him in the Middle Kingdom adopting wolf-skin pelts, suggesting that there may have been an earlier association with the wolf, long before the appearance of the Greeks.

Lykopolis was particularly important in the IX/X Dynasties when the princes of Heracleopolis (ancient Henen-Nesut) were recognised as kings of Egypt. The city now has mostly disappeared, the only evidence of its architecture being found in the drawings made by the French savants in Napoleon's train during his invasion of Egypt at the end of the eighteenth century. These are contained in the monumental record of Napoleon's inspired survey of the wonders of Egypt, the first scientific exposure of the Two Lands' antiquity to Europe, *Description de l'Egypte*.[60]

Wepwawet's name means 'Opener of the Ways'. In the context of the mortuary cults with which he was associated this was a tribute to his acting as guide to the dead, like Anubis whom he resembles so closely. All the canine gods were associated with graveyards and the dead, the result of dogs and jackals alike prowling at night around the cemeteries on the outskirts of the settlements and towns.

Though Wepwawet was principally a funerary divinity, he was also a warrior. He 'Opened the Ways' for the king in his campaigns against Egypt's enemies. In Wepwawet's relationship with the king his responsibilities as guide also served him when living, as well as in the Afterlife. He is often mentioned in the Pyramid Texts, the most ancient ritual or liturgical texts in the world. During his transition from this life to his place in the glorified Afterlife, the king is said to undergo a process known as 'becoming Wepwawet', as he moves towards the acknowledgement of his divinity by the other gods, who are assembled to await his arrival.

Wepwawet appears in other festivals designed to emphasise the nature and majesty of the kingship. The Heb-Sed Festival was one of the most important ceremonies associated with the royal office. Its purpose was to confirm the king's mastery over the Dual Kingdom and, in an ageing monarch, to reinvigorate him and to show his fitness to continue to rule. The Festival was of great antiquity; it was depicted in the First Dynasty when King Den, the fourth king of the dynasty, is shown executing one of the rituals whereby he demonstrated his sovereignty over Egypt, by striding round a marked-out course, which enclosed a space representing the kingdoms in microcosm. In his hand he holds the flail, one of the traditional parts of the royal regalia, and he also carries a document, reputed to be the will, handed down from the gods, which contained his title to the kingship. The Festival was celebrated under the patronage of Wepwawet.

A particularly finely portrayed version of the Heb-Sed Festival is contained in the Step Pyramid complex at Saqqara, built for the Third Dynasty king (Djoser) Netjerykhet. In reliefs carved at the back of recesses in the passages in the pyramid's underground chambers, which are inlaid with strikingly beautiful blue-green tiles, the king is shown as a commanding and athletic figure. Like his predecessor Den, several hundred years before, he clutches the Flail as he strides away. Again, the whole ceremony is carried out in the presence of Wepwawet, whose standard bearing the royal placenta goes before the king.

As a witness of his concern with the affairs of the living king a powerful image of this aspect of Wepwawet's nature is engraved on an ivory label that shows the early First Dynasty king, Den, striking down an Asiatic chieftain, symbolic of the event which is called 'The First Smiting of the East'. Wepwawet's standard protects the king, both as he presides over the (presumably) symbolic execution of the eastern chief and as he shows the way forward, which the king will follow.

Wepwawet appears among the standards borne before the king in procession even before the First Dynasty; he appears on the monumental palette associated with King Narmer where he is carried in the procession that precedes the king as he reviews his foes defeated in the campaigns to bring about the unification of the Valley, in late predynastic times.[61] As much as he was the king's guide in life as in death he was also proclaimed 'Leader of the Gods', for he was the first in the procession of divinities who waited upon the king on great occasions.

Henri Frankfort, the brilliant Dutch Egyptologist of the first half of the twentieth century, wrote extensively of Wepwawet's relationship with the king in his influential study *Kingship and the Gods*.[62] He describes the significance of the processions shown in the sun-temple of King Niuserre at Abu Gurob in which Wepwawet is an important participant and where Anubis has already been seen presenting seven mysterious ankhs to the king. The ceremonies take place at the king's Sed Festival, held theoretically in the thirtieth year of the reign but in practice often more frequently, which was intended to renew the sovereign's vigour and restore his youthful vitality. Wepwawet was also associated with another very ancient canine divinity, whose name was Sed. It is possible that the great royal festival of Heb-Sed commemorates him.

A deputation waits on the king. It is led by 'The Herdsman of Nekhen', who is attended by two officers wearing wolf-skin caps and tails. 'The Souls of Nekhen', mythical kings of the south in legendary times, are represented iconographically as wolf-headed, revealing by this curious reference the attribution of a wolfish character to the god as early as the Fifth Dynasty. With 'The Souls of Buto', the equally mythical rulers of the putative northern kingdom, they were conflated as 'The Souls of Heliopolis', reputedly the great cult-centre of predynastic times; Wepwawet was proclaimed their commander.[63]

These references to wolves, and the fact that two important participants in so major a festival as the Heb-Sed wear wolf-skins and caps, suggest that it may be unwise to assume that the Egyptians, as well as the Greeks, were wrong to employ the term 'wolf' in this context. It will be recalled that the XVII nome of Upper Egypt, with its capital at This, whence came the eventual rulers of the unified Two Kingdoms at the beginning of the First Dynasty, was known in later times as 'The Wolf'. Again, it is reasonable to ask whether these apparently specific references to wolves, particularly these that relate directly to the kingship, indicate that the cult of Wepwawet and possibly of the other canine divinities had their origins outside Egypt, in a region where true wolves were known.

A long inscription survives from the Twelfth Dynasty in which a high official, Ikhernofret, the royal treasurer in the service of King Senwosret III, records the signal honour which was paid to him by the king, who commissioned him to travel to Abydos and there to represent him in the ceremonies dedicated to Osiris.[64] He was instructed to direct the entire festival in honour of the god and even to take the king's place when he would impersonate the god Horus. In this capacity he was appointed to a special high priestly rank to permit him to take on so great a responsibility.

As part of the programme, Ikhernofret organised 'The Coming Forth of Wepwawet', when the god arrives to fight on behalf of his father Osiris, who in fact had only recently come to major significance at Abydos. Osiris was already identified with the king and Wepwawet was called upon to act as his herald, announcing his presence. In this capacity Wepwawet becomes assimilated with Horus, whom Ikhernofret also represents as the king's reincarnated personification. As Ikhernofret himself set up in an inscription in stone, 'I conducted the Procession of Wepwawet when he goes forth to champion his father.'[65] Ikhernofret was a great noble at a time of Egypt's renewed prosperity and the re-establishment of the royal power. The recital of his titles is very sonorous:

> Prince, Count, Royal Seal-Bearer, Sole Companion, Overseer of the two gold-houses, Overseer of the two silver houses, Chief Seal-Bearer, Ikhernofret the revered.[66]

The especially close relationship that the king enjoyed with Wepwawet is shown by the divinity's occasional identification with Horus, just as the king was said 'to become Wepwawet' during his transit to the world of the gods after death. The meaning of his name 'Opener of the Ways' was sometimes taken to mean 'Opener of the Body', in which capacity Wepwawet was the king's first-born twin, who opened the way for the king out of the womb. Wepwawet was thus logically identified with the royal placenta, displayed before him on his standard. Twins were regarded by the ancient Egyptians as somehow slightly uncanny, an attitude that can still be found in the Middle East today.

As the king's afterbirth the placenta was especially sacred. It was regarded as the king's double, almost as his celestial twin, with whom he would be reunited at death; it was a measure of Wepwawet's importance that he was so closely identified with this most personal and intimate of the king's attributes. The king was said to travel to join the gods on Wepwawet's standard, the shedshed.[67] He was an important functionary in the king's obsequies, for his adze was used in the ceremony of 'Opening the Mouth', by which act the king's physical powers were restored.

Like Anubis, Wepwawet was frequently assimilated with the great gods. There are records of Wepwawet-Re, and one, admittedly very obscure, king of the late Thirteenth Dynasty who reigned briefly and probably ingloriously, at the time of one of the periods of decline in the royal authority, whose name was Sekhemneferkaure Wepwawetemsaf. He sat uneasily on his throne during the time when the Hyksos, the Semitic-speaking invaders from Palestine, occupied and ruled much of northern and central Egypt. His sole surviving monument is a sadly inexpertly carved stele on which he is honouring Wepwawet-Re.[68]

The XIII Upper Egyptian nome, modern Asyut, Lykopolis to the Greeks, was especially important during the First Intermediate Period. It formed a buffer between the Heracleopolitan rulers of the nome and the growing power of the princes of Thebes, who would eventually emerge as the rulers of a once-more united Egypt when they provided the kings of Dynasty XI. As Lykopolis was the cult centre of Anubis the nomarchs assumed the title of High Priest of Anubis and also of Wepwawet, indicating a fusion of the two canine divinities, at least in this context, since both were commemorated in the city and both were its tutelary gods. Extensive burials of mummified dogs have been found at the site of Lykopolis. Asyut is approximately halfway between Minya and Qena, some 400 kilometres south of Cairo. Its modern name is thought to be derived from its ancient Egyptian name, Z3wt or Z3wty, meaning 'the Guard', obviously commemorating both the role of its principal divinities and its strategic political function.

Wepwawet continued to be associated with the king into New Kingdom times. A stele erected by the great king of the Eighteenth Dynasty, Thutmosis III, is a poem of triumph glorifying the king placed in the mouth of the High God of the day, Amun-Re, Lord of the Thrones of the Two Lands.

> I let them see your majesty as southern jackal,
> the racer, the runner, roving the Two Lands.[69]

The southern jackal is Wepwawet.

Wepwawet also played a particularly prominent part in the ceremonies recorded in the temple of King Seti I, of the Nineteenth Dynasty, at Abydos, one of the towering monuments of the architecture of the New Kingdom (Figure 34). The ceremonies commemorate the king being received into the company of the gods and his coronation. Wepwawet presents the king with the royal insignia and participates in the ceremonies of purification and performs the recognition of Seti as the undoubted sovereign, the heir of all the kings who have gone before him.[70] In the relief from the Abydos temple Wepwawet is clearly represented with a grey head. It is tempting to see this as revealing knowledge of the grey wolf but in fact it is probably an accurate depiction of Canis aureus lupaster, the so-called 'Egyptian wolf' which in fact is a jackal.

That Wepwawet in this role, in which he is called 'of Upper Egypt, Controller of the Lands', is of special importance is shown by his address to the king as he presents him with the crook and the flail and gives him the breath of eternal life:

I come to thee bearing life and dominion: mayest thou be young like
Horus as king. I hand over to thee the sceptre and flail and the beneficent
office of Onophris (Osiris); may thy name endure by reason of what thou
has done. As long as the sky shall exist, thou shalt exist. Receive for thyself
the sceptre and flail which are in the hands of thy father Osiris.[71]

The founding family of the Nineteenth Dynasty was, in a sense, heterodox
in that its members were known to honour gods not usually so highly
regarded by most Egyptian kings, notably the god Set, who is considered
below. They originated in northern Egypt and may have been influenced
by some of the cults of foreign gods, who were assimilated with Egyptian
divinities. They did, however, celebrate Wepwawet, recognising him as being
particularly important to the legitimacy of the kingship. In the superb
and justly famous relief in the temple of Abydos, King Rameses II and his
eldest son, Prince Amunhirkhopshef, are shown lassoing a massive bull as a
sacrifice for Wepwawet. The young prince, evidently at this time his father's
heir, was not to live to succeed to the throne for he died young. The kingship and the throne instead ultimately devolved upon another of Rameses'
progeny, Merenptah, the thirteenth in the long sequence of sons begotten
by Rameses.

The relief is a work of consummate craft, the sense of power and vigorous
forward motion of the great bull and of the concentration of the king and
the boy being brilliantly achieved. The relief is paralleled by the sequence in
the temple at Abydos initiated by King Seti I that shows him with Rameses
his son contemplating the names of the kings of Egypt who have preceded
them, since the beginning of the kingship. Wepwawet's presence and his
approval of their succession would have been important for them as King
Seti, the father of Rameses II, was the son of a general in the army who was
named as heir by the evidently childless King Horemhab. He succeeded as
King Rameses I but reigned only briefly; neither Horemhab nor Rameses I
was royal by birth and so it was important for the heirs of Rameses I to be
adopted by their predecessors and accepted by Wepwawet. In the succeeding
Twentieth Dynasty, Wepwawet enjoyed another recognition of his ancient
status when Rameses III restored his temple at Asyut.

The two canine gods sometimes shared epithets that represented two
balanced aspects of a similar concept. Thus, Anubis was 'Opener of the Roads
of the South, the Power of the Two Lands'. Wepwawet was 'Opener of the
Roads of the North, the Power of Heaven'. Together they symbolise the two

halves of the year, the sky by day and night and the waxing and waning of the powers of nature in summer and winter. Anubis was the summer solstice, Wepwawet the solstice in winter.

Anubis and Wepwawet continued to enjoy acceptance as two of the great divine entities throughout Egyptian history. This is particularly true of Anubis; indeed, he is one of the very few divine beings who maintained his place in the affections of the people throughout the entire historic period. He came to be regarded as a god in the sense that later Near and Middle Eastern cultures recognised the term. Anubis was wholly benign and was regarded affectionately by the Egyptians from their earliest days to Roman times; he was one of the Egyptian gods who migrated to Rome, where he was much venerated, and on to other parts of Europe, including the sacred island of Delos in the Aegean.[72] Wepwawet had to wait until modern times for his name and august function to be recalled.

Set, God of Confusion

Anubis and Wepwawet were both more fortunate than the great god Set, who, from being first the tutelary god of Upper Egypt, whence came all the initiatives that gave Egypt its particular glory, ended his career vilified. By late in the first millennium BC, Set had, under the influence of foreign cults, become the nearest approximation that the Egyptians had to a truly malign spirit, whereas he had originally been an expression of the dualism that underlay all Egyptian theologies, the principle of chaos, contrasted with the order represented by Horus, the desert contrasted with the sown. The original inspiration of the kingship came from the south lands of Egypt, which acknowledged Set as the High God, and which was the locus of the processes which set Egypt on its historic path to the realisation of the Dual Kingdom. The Two Lands were eternally ruled by the incarnate Horus and the duality implied in an especially definitive manner the absolute necessity for the reconciliation to ensure the welfare of Egypt. Horus, the personification of the royal order, of the integrity of the cosmos, is balanced by Set, representing the elemental forces of chaos, but in neither case is a moral judgement implied.

The idea of the conflict of Horus and Set being determined by a judicial process, the form in which the myth of the contending of the two gods has come down to the present,[73] seems curiously un-Egyptian. The functions of the two immense, competing, yet complementary entities in achieving and sustaining reconciliation is of primary significance in apprehending the Egyptian understanding of the essential balance of the cosmos. It is an unusually subtle concept, just as Set is a subtle and complex archetype. Whilst he is not truly a canine divinity in the manner of Anubis, Khentiamentiu and Wepwawet, he figures in this narrative in one of his manifestations, as the divine and royal hound; like Anubis, he is capable of changing his shape at will and is a further instance of the power of the Trickster archetype,[74] of which he is a powerful representative and certainly the earliest known.

The centre of Set's cult was in the town of Nubt, 'Gold City', also known as Ombos; he was often designated 'the Ombite, Lord of Ombos'.[75] Set personified the random elements in nature, the unforeseen, the unpredictable, that which was to be feared in natural phenomena such as storm or drought. But in this role Set was morally neutral, as were all the divinities of Egypt in their earliest manifestations, as indeed was Horus himself. The gods of Egypt are not judgemental, nor do they require obedience from their adherents, at least not until relatively late times.

Just as Ma'at, the archetype of justice, balance and right-doing, is at once the most abstract of the divinities of Egypt and, in the form of a young girl with a feather in her hair, one of the most engaging, so Set is the most enigmatic, his nature the most occult, in the proper sense of the word. He is subtle, tempestuous and elemental; though sometimes despised and excluded, Set is still one of the most powerfully enduring of the Egyptian gods.

The origins of Set are lost in the remote past of Upper Egypt, perhaps to be looked for among the first migrants who moved up the Valley from the south, following the cattle and attended by their dogs. This seems most likely to have been the case, having in mind the inferences that may be drawn from the later traditions that speak of him in the predynastic, Early Dynastic and Old Kingdom periods. It has been suggested that Set was abroad during Naqada I times, though this is not considered certain.[76] The 'Animal of Set', an enigmatic representation of the god whose characteristics will be considered further, is clearly a standing canine when he appears on two of the standards carried before the late predynastic king Scorpion.

Figure 35   On the great mace head recording the opening of a canal by the late predynastic king Scorpion, standards proclaiming the support of the gods are carried before him, of which two show canine divinities, with the characteristics of Set.

The scene appears on the large ceremonial mace-head which shows Scorpion, crowned as king of Upper Egypt, presiding over a ceremony to mark the cutting of new canals.[77] The standards of Set may indicate the presence in Scorpion's entourage of the Upper Egyptian prince whose device it was (Figure 35). It is now considered that Scorpion may have been one of the predynastic rulers who had control of much of the Valley, even before the time of the acclaimed Unification.

Set has been described as 'the god of confusion'.[78] Certainly his ability to cause confusion, even chaos, is one of his acknowledged attributes and it is this faculty that identifies him as the archetype of the Trickster, whose capacity to change shape at will and whose indifference to moral persuasion makes him especially dangerous. The word *Åasha*, glossed by Budge as 'a kind of dog or jackal',[79] is also applied to Set (B.624), when it means 'the cryer' or 'the roarer'; in the case of the first group the determinative, the animal of Set, is pierced by a dagger to render it harmless, whilst in the second example the determinative is that of Anubis.[80] It may be observed that it is one of the characteristics of the Pharaoh Hound, a relic perhaps of Set as much as it may be as a putative descendant of the *tjesm*, that when hunting it sets up a loud, deep-chested belling cry, which could be described, perhaps a little freely, as 'roaring'. The Pharaoh Hound is notable for its capacity to howl, a practice that, as we have seen, it shares with the golden jackal, which howls readily and distinctively, part of its familial and social behaviour.

According to some of the various and often contradictory myths attending Set, he was one of the first of the generations of gods to be born, after the creator god Atum brought creation into being by masturbating and so forming the very first generation of the gods. Set was the son of Geb (Earth) one of the founders of the divine line, and of Nut, the sky. He was one of the pairs of divine twins (again the Egyptian obsession with dualism), born with his sister, Nephthys. But his violent and uncontrolled nature showed itself even before his mother was delivered of him; so impatient was he to come into being that he burst out of his mother's body. His sister Nephthys also became his wife. With Set's 'birth' the period of primeval time was ended, the time before Duality had arisen in the Two Lands.[81]

Horus, Set's immemorial counterpart, was born of the next generation of gods; as related in this relatively late theogony, he is thus Set's nephew, the son of Set's brother Osiris. It is the destiny of Set and Horus to be bound together, perpetually in opposition, perpetually in partnership. The myth of Horus and Set, the most developed version of which is very late in the date at which it was recorded, is the work of the Greek writer Plutarch. It is well known and not especially relevant here; it is readily accessible to anyone who wishes to study it. But Set's place in the order of affairs which bear on the place of the dog in Egypt is another matter for Set and Anubis, at least according to one of the genealogies of the gods, are closely linked.[82]

In the myth explaining the nature and origins of the gods, Set murdered Osiris his brother not, seemingly, because he was angry at Nephthys' seduction, which resulted in the birth of Anubis, but because Osiris conferred the succession to the throne of Egypt on Horus, when Set believed that as he represented the earlier generation of gods the succession should have been his. A violent and long-drawn dispute erupted between the two contenders, and the myth becomes further convoluted when Isis, the sister–wife of Osiris,

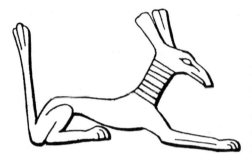

Figure 36 Though the mythical animal of Set is clearly a creature of fantasy, its canine characteristics are clearly evident in this hieroglyphic representation of the god.

mourns his death and she is sustained by Anubis. Osiris' murder is avenged by Horus, the perpetually reincarnated king.

The relationship between Set and his nephew Horus is very fraught, overlain both with high drama and with much that approaches knockabout farce. They are perpetually in contention, fighting for the Crowns of the Two Lands. The 'Conflict of Horus and Set' is an elaborate drama which was evidently staged in the temples and which portrays the titanic struggle between the two gods. It is probably the oldest surviving dramatic text intended for public performance.

There is no doubt that one of the earliest figurines to be associated with an Egyptian divinity is that of the enigmatic 'Animal of Set', representations of which are known from predynastic times. The very first known iconographic example in Egypt of the human–animal conflation, the therianthrope, is of the god Ash, a god of the desert who was identified with Set. Ash appears on the seal of a Second Dynasty king, Peribsen[83] (Figure 37), who has a particular significance in the cult of Set and his hound, which is described later. Ash is a tall, striding human figure, but his head is that of the Set animal, with its distinct, markedly curved muzzle clearly emphasised.

In the hieroglyphics associated with the god and in other representations, the Set animal is most readily identifiable as a tall, slender canine, with a long, slightly arched muzzle, upstanding ears that are strangely blunted, as though cropped, with a long tail, its tip divided like a feathered arrow, which is held upright (Figure 36). It is shown lying on its belly[84] (G.E21), its front paws outstretched in the manner in which Anubis is often depicted, or seated on its haunches[85] (G.E20), its head lifted proudly, its tail rising rigidly. It will be seen that the animal has several differences with the hieroglyph for the dog, G.E14.

Any attempt to identify the animal of Set from hieroglyphs is, however, likely to be disappointed; as in most matters Egyptian there are no simple solutions. At the end of the day, it is probably better to accept that the Egyptians were as capable as any other people (and indeed probably more so) of introducing elements of symbolism and invention in their epigraphy as much as in any other department of their complex culture and iconography. Set's animal has been variously described: as an ass, oryx, antelope, greyhound, fennec, jerboa, camel, okapi, long-snouted mouse, aardvark, giraffe, hog or boar, jackal.[86] Set's capacity to change his shape at will and to bewilder and confuse by his manifestations is clearly shared by the animal that is conventionally described as his. But the Set animal is unmistakeably a canid, though with characteristics which no living member of the species resembles exactly.

It seems reasonable to discard some of the more fanciful or obscure of the forms that have been attributed to the Set animal. The oryx was well known in Egypt, a respected nome-sign and associated, in the Middle Kingdom if not earlier, with powerful political interests in Middle Egypt. It was certainly identified as one of the animals sacred to Set and was occasionally sacrificed to him. The fennec fox and the jerboa are surely both too small to be identified with Set's animal. The camel was not important in Egypt until relatively late times after its domestication, which probably happened not before the early second millennium BC. The long-snouted mouse, like the fennec and the jerboa, can be discarded on grounds of size; the giraffe was known in Egypt but its identification with the animal of Set is unlikely.

P.E. Newberry, a respected Egyptologist of an earlier generation, suggested the connection of the animal with the pig.[87] Certainly, in parts of Egypt the pig was proscribed and on occasion regarded as one of the animals reserved to Set and sometimes sacrificed to him. Such animals included, in addition to the oryx and the pig, the ass, the gazelle, the crocodile, the hippopotamus and certain fish. At other times the auroch, the wild bull which was venerated in Egypt and which, in early times, was one of the manifestations of the Divine King, was similarly sacrificed, as was the snake, usually a creature of ill-omen in Egypt. The dog-like appearance of the hieroglyphs that are used to denote the animal of Set and the manner in which the animal is depicted generally in art cannot be described as typical of the comportment of pigs, a consideration which rules out many of the other attributions also.

The Animal of Set, in its hieroglyphic form, appears in contexts that suggest a divergence from the normal order of things in a well-ordered universe. It is, for example, the determinative in the group 'rage, storm, disaster'.[88] This indicates that the animal with which Set is so frequently identified, whilst it is predominantly canine, is also a product of something approaching poetic fantasy. In this it resembles the strange, monstrous creatures that seem occasionally to have haunted the imaginations of the Egyptians, notably in the late predynastic period at the end of the fourth millennium BC when 'serpopards', with their saurian necks and feline heads, and winged griffons appear on the schist palettes that are so significant at that time. Similar creatures are depicted in tomb reliefs and paintings during the Middle Kingdom. The Animal of Set is the most enduring of these monstrous forms, visible during virtually the whole of Egyptian history.

Set was sometimes depicted as a 'red dog'. In parts of Egypt dogs with ochreous-tan coats were on occasions sacrificed, in one case at least to the constellation Sirius, which was identified sometimes with Anubis and sometimes with the goddess Isis;[89] it will be recalled that it was a dog or dogs which led Isis to find the newly born Anubis, who later became her protector. A sacrifice of a red dog was performed on the festal day of the baboon or ibis-headed god Thoth.[90] Red was most important in Egyptian colour symbolism, which was subtle and pervasive in all aspects of their philosophy, decoration, coloration of hieroglyphs and architecture. Red was associated with Set's desert domain, the 'Red Land', as distinct from the 'Black Land' of the Valley.

There can be little doubt that the animal of Set was at least in part inspired by the tjesm hunting hound. One of the most compelling features of the Set animal is the curved or arched muzzle (sometimes, erroneously and gracelessly, referred to as a 'snout') that was also characteristic of the hunting hound's physiognamy, as it is of the living Pharaoh Hound's.

As the centuries went by Set's character changed, from a violent and unpredictable god but one who ranked with the greatest divinities and whose attributes were essential to the maintenance of balance in the management of the cosmos, to a much darker persona, in which the dangerous, uncontrollable nature of the god became identified with evil. This was never the view of him in most of Egypt. Set's demotion to the position of malignant spirit (a role which was reinforced in Christian times) obviously derived from the infiltration of alien concepts of the gods in the late second millennium

BC and afterwards. Most proponents of Near Eastern religions, unlike the Egyptians, relied heavily on the concept of guilt arising from the neglect or wilful disobedience of the god's instructions, and the condemnation of deviation from the precepts determined by the principal divinity or group of divinities, as promulgated by their human representatives. The sense of guilt, an emotion that had no part in the pristine Egyptian ethos, became dominant, and with it the threat of perpetual punishment for any departure from the form of conduct that had been determined and promulgated by the servants of the presiding divinity. With the inculcation of guilt and the threat of punishment came the need for a Devil-figure to preside over the fate of those condemned to eternal suffering for transgressing the precepts of the divinity and his or her earthly representatives.

In the Late Period, Apopis, a latter-day addition to the ranks of Egyptian composite monsters, fulfilled some of the tasks of a vengeful spirit, destroying wrongdoers who failed the examination conducted by Anubis in the presence of Osiris. When he attacks the barque of Re as it sails through the Underworld at night Apopis is repulsed by none other than Set, in this case the defender of order and the right.

Whilst Set may not be included among the ranks of the unequivocally canine gods of Egypt like Anubis, Khentiamentiu and Wepwawet, there is one episode, a rather mysterious one to be sure, in which his manifestation as a hound raised him to the ultimate height of identification with the king, the acknowledged peer of Horus and, for a brief interlude, his supplanter. This was during the Second Dynasty, which lasted from 2890 to 2686 BC. Despite rather more than two centuries of the royal power, the Second Dynasty is obscure, even the succession of its kings having only been established in relatively recent years.[91] It has been speculated that during this period there was a reaction against the imposition by the kings of the First Dynasty of their control over the whole of the Valley and that something approaching a rebellion was raised by forces in the south opposed to the victorious Falcon clan.[92]

It has already been remarked that, almost without exception, the tombs of the First Dynasty kings and of their most senior supporters, the great nobles who were the holders of the highest offices in the Two Lands, were destroyed by fire, not long after the dynasty's end; this was a particularly frightful calamity in the Egyptian canon since the destruction of the body would prevent its *ka* from ever being able to return to it, a necessary condition for the renewal

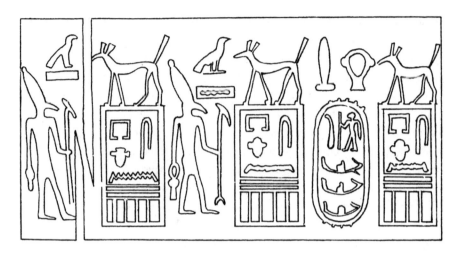

Figure 37   The seal of King Peribsen, proclaiming his adherence to the cult of the god Set, replacing his earlier allegiance to Horus.

of life. No such opprobrium as the destruction of the First Dynasty tombs would suggest seems to have attached itself to the Second Dynasty.

Any familial relationship of the kings of the Second Dynasty to their immediate predecessors is not known, but it is safe to assume that there would have been at least the semblance of continuity, to provide a warrant for the new line of kings to assume the divinity that went with the Horus kingship. The first king of the Second Dynasty was Hotepsekhemwy and he was followed by eight attested successors, of whom most have left little substantial evidence of their reigns, a fact that has been interpreted as indicating a period of unrest in the country. As against this, nine kings in two hundred years indicates reigns of unusual length and therefore presumably a considerable degree of security of tenure surrounding the holders of the kingship. It is the last two of Hotepsekhemwy's successors who concern us here.

The seventh king of the dynasty assumed the thrones of Egypt under the Horus name Sekhemib. Later in his reign, however, he appears to have changed his principal royal name to Peribsen.[93] When he was Sekhemib his name when proclaimed in the *serekh* was surmounted, as with all Horus kings, by the royal falcon. When he adopted the style Peribsen, his name was surmounted by the hound of Set, standing proudly, who proclaimed the royal divinity: the king was now 'The Set Peribsen' (*Figure 37*) where previously

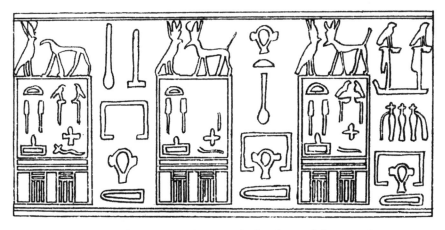

Figure 38 The seal of King Khasekhemwy, the last king of the Second Dynasty, showing his royal name surmounted by the two contending gods, Horus and Set, Falcon and Hound, united in his person. He was honoured throughout the history of Egypt as one of its greatest rulers and one who reunified the Valley.

he had been 'The Horus Sekhemib', and the adoption of the hound in the *serekh* was a unique event in the titulary of ancient Egypt. As The Set he was frequently awarded the epithet 'Conqueror of Foreign Lands', the lands in question being particularly to the east of Egypt, which were traditionally considered to be under the dominion of Set; one of the god's titles was 'Lord of Foreign Countries'.[94] Peribsen was buried in a great tomb at Abydos, the burial ground of the First Dynasty kings, in which the last kings of the Second Dynasty had also chosen to be interred.

Sekhemib/Peribsen was followed in the kingship by one who is marginally more celebrated than his immediate successors, though information relating to him is still sparse. At first he adopted the throne name Khasekhem; later in his reign he became Khasekhemwy. The addition of the extra syllable gave his name the meaning 'In Him the Two Lords are Satisfied'.

Khasekhemwy was one of the most important of the early kings of Egypt. In his time the development of all manner of skills and crafts reached their highest level yet. The country entered upon a period of unequalled prosperity and progress, which was carried forward into the dynasties of the Old Kingdom, when Egyptian civilisation reached its zenith. The power and status of the king became acknowledged as transcending all human bounds; in the early part of Khasekhemwy's reign the first monumental statues of the king enthroned as king and god appear, to become the matrix for all such works, even into the distant future.

Most significantly, Khasekhemwy adopted both gods as the guardians of his *serekh*, another heraldic event unprecedented in all the annals of Egypt. Horus and Set, Falcon and Hound,[95] stand together above the king's most sacred name, thus signifying the reconciliation of the two, which it was always the king's duty to bring about (*Figure 38*). In the circumstances of the time, when Egypt may have experienced something approaching a rebellion, such a reconciliation must have been of an especially profound importance. It was also another of the extraordinary coups of the royal propagandists, whose often inspired designs marked the early centuries of the evolution of the kingship.

The Horus and Set Khasekhemwy has claim to be one of the most important of the Unifiers of the Dual Kingdom and is thought to have reigned for more than forty years. When he died he was probably succeeded by the great King Netjerykhet, with whom the most astonishing monument in Egypt, the Step Pyramid at Saqqara, is always to be associated. Netjerykhet was the son of Nemaathap, who was Khasekhemwy's daughter and possibly his wife. As it appears that Netjerykhet presided over the ceremonies held after the death of Khasekhemwy, it is possible that he was his natural son, though in the annals a new dynasty seems to have been recognised as being inaugurated with Sanakht.[96]

It is pertinent that in Netjerykhet's temples the animal of Set is unmistakeably a dog, despite his still somewhat extravagant tail. Whatever may have been the original inspiration for the animal of Set, there can be little doubt that the Egyptians of later periods considered it to be a canine. Very occasionally in the future Set would be represented, in statues for example, with a dog's head on a human body, making the identification quite explicit. In one exceptional case he is shown as bull-headed when he has been admitted back into the upper ranks of the gods once more.

In the New Kingdom (1550–1069 BC) during the XIX and XX Dynasties the Ramessid kings honoured Set virtually as the equal once more of the greatest gods of Egypt. The founder of the XIX Dynasty, who succeeded King Horemhab was, like him, a soldier and took the throne name Rameses. His son and successor was Seti I, whose name directly honours the god. Their devotion to another, assuredly canine, divinity, Wepwawet, has already been described. The family originated in the west of the Delta, a long way from Set's original kingdom of Upper Egypt, but his influence must have been strong there because he became effectively the royal family's tutelary divinity. In the period that preceded the establishment of the New Kingdom, Semitic-speaking invaders, known as the Hyksos ('rulers of foreign lands') and execrated by the Egyptians when they were eventually driven out, came into Egypt from the north and brought with them some of their own gods. One of these was Reshef, a storm god like Set, and he became identified with the elder divinity. As Ramesses' family came from the northern part of Egypt it is possible that some remnant of the Hyksos' attachment to Reshef–Set survived and explains their loyalty to Set, Reshef having largely been forgotten.

Set is the outsider, the 'Great Roaring God'. He stands for the power and menace of the desert, where he howls and wreaks destruction. Howling, of a god-like nature, was evidently not despised by the Egyptians, for it is recorded of King Rameses III of the Twentieth Dynasty, one of the last of the great native-born kings of Egypt, that, 'Like Seth, the chosen of Re, his roaring is heard like that of a griffon, another mythical creature.'[97] The griffon, a mythological creature that appears in the art of the late predynastic period and is probably of Western Asiatic origin, is sometimes associated with Set. This inscription was displayed in the king's funerary temple at Medinat Habu. It indicates clearly that on some occasions, even quite late in Egypt's history, Set, having been proclaimed 'the Chosen of Re', assumed a much higher standing than he was awarded later still, when he became the victim of the priests' need to fabricate a vengeful, punishing high god.

The Survival of the Gods

One of the mysteries associated with the canine as divinity in Egypt is that, for the next thousand years after the end of the Ramessid period and the slow disintegration of the Egyptian state, Anubis continued to grow in strength and popularity, despite Egypt's steady decline from its days of greatness. He appears in countless tombs, in myriads of papyri, in Books of the Dead and in every other medium available to Egyptian artists. His presence is always benign, even comforting; together with Isis he was one of the Egyptian gods most readily adopted by the newly emergent societies of Greece and Rome. Just as the dog could not be kept out of human habitations, so it seemed that the archetypal dog-god would continue to have a lair on the Palatine or in Athens and the other cities and sacred sites of the Graeco-Roman world, which, as we have seen, included a shrine even on the sacred island of Delos. In the culture of the Mediterranean lands that succeeded the Macedonian Ptolemies' rule of Egypt, ending with the death of Cleopatra VII in 30 BC, Anubis enjoyed a surge of popularity. Whilst he continued to fulfil his solemn vocation as psychopomp, his popularity was unmistakeably suffused with affection.

That Anubis sustained his popularity as Egypt diminished in relative importance in the Mediterranean world was in part the consequence of the phenomenal rise in the influence of esoteric cults which swept the ancient world at this time. The traditional rituals of the temples had become debased into increasingly unappealing and meaningless displays of magic and illusion. Religion, in the sense that the word was to have meaning in the centuries to come, became more and more populist in appeal. Anubis' role as the protector of the dead and as the artificer who would ensure perpetual life became one of the most popular of all the gods. His cult was further enhanced by the acceptance that the various brands of gnosticism achieved and into which Anubis, for little more reason than his association with esotericism, had been drawn.

His migration to Europe was not universally applauded, however. Not all Romans, for example, were enthusiasts for things Egyptian as were the Greeks. However, now it was Isis who was the 'Opener of the Ways', for her cult became almost universal, presaging the acceptance of the cult of the new Mother of God, when Christianity asserted itself over the ruins of the ancient temples. Anubis, however, was dismissed as 'barking' by some and in places his cults were officially banned. But his popularity survived nonetheless, despite the mockery that was not infrequently heaped upon his worship and the cults which attended it. Among such severe Roman critics was Virgil and, perhaps unsurprisingly, Josephus. But that his appeal was strong still is demonstrated by the scandalous story of the Roman knight who took advantage of a lady, Paulina, in the temple of Isis, by disguising himself as Anubis. In Alexandrian tombs of the Roman period Anubis appears, somewhat incongruously, accoutred in armour as a Roman soldier. His cult was evidently popular among the military.

Even in the Middle Ages Anubis was still a presence, still visible. A dog-headed divinity, usually described as a portrait of the god, appears in a manuscript of the encyclopaedist Rubanus Maurus (776–856) of Monte Cassino.[98] Here he is identified as Mercury Anubis, a frequent conflation which served to make him acceptable to a Roman audience, as Hermanubis, his conflation with Hermes (the Greek prototype of Mercury), did in the Greek world.

From these and like circumstances Anubis was carried on into the world of the Renaissance, preserved in magical texts and other writings. These were seized on by the savants of the fifteenth, sixteenth and seventeenth centuries when they discovered the riches of the ancient world and in their pursuit of the arcane wisdom that they were thought to conceal. In these latter-day manifestations there is much less doubt about the nature of the Anubis archetype than there had been in his native Egypt. He is a dog or, more precisely, dog-headed since in these later times he is almost invariably depicted as a therianthrope, with a dog's head on the body of a man. Jackals are not indigenous to northern Mediterranean lands and the dog was a more familiar and readily acceptable incarnation.

The reason for Anubis' long-lasting appeal and support, which transcends boundaries of time and nation, is clear: he is one of the most fully realised, multi-faceted archetypes whose recognition, at the very beginning of the Egyptian state five thousand years ago, echoed so exactly the part that the dog had played in the development of the larger human society in times still more remote. Anubis is indeed one of the greatest of the archetypes: he is the Night Lord, Grave-Watcher, Soul-Guide, a being who bridges the worlds of the seen and unseen. In this he is one of the most fully realised of all the animal divinities, brought out of the collective unconscious of the early inhabitants of the Nile Valley, who gives meaning and explanation to the entire community of animal-human conflations. The theriomorphic archetypes of Egypt are the first to be recognised and recorded by any complex society; in this lies their power, for the archetype only requires recognition to assume an independent existence.

The Egyptians were not the only people to give life to supranatural entities who combined the physical characteristics of animals and humans, but they were the first to do so on a universal scale and, by the power of their invention, the first to give them enduring and universal forms. These have resonated down the centuries. One of the most powerful of these inventions of the unconscious, which has held the imaginations of European artists for many centuries, is not Egyptian: the Minotaur, the man–bull therianthrope who is the archetype of the sorrowful, blameless monster, who induces revulsion and pity in equal measure. He is also, most potently, the most specific expression of the Shadow, the realisation of all the negative and fear-inducing qualities which inhabit the unconscious of all humans. Although they represent almost entirely polarised qualities, the Minotaur is one of the very few archetypes in animal–human form that bears comparison with the enduring power and significance of Anubis.[99]

Other societies have created images of magically endowed dogs, wonder-workers, astral beings or messengers moving, like their Egyptian counterparts, between the worlds. Only the Egyptian canine divinities, however, have had the power to become universal symbols of the bond between humans and the animal world and to give expression to its unique significance.

CHAPTER 6

Tail-end

A number of interrelated preoccupations run through this book. They have grown out of the intention to present a popular study of the Egyptian hunting hound and the very special place in the community that the hounds occupied, as much as they did in the hearts of the Egyptians. The closeness of that affection, reflecting the bond that had been established probably millennia before but transfiguring it, is wholly consistent with what is now known about the extent and antiquity of the human–canine relationship, but conferring on it a new dimension.

The last two hundred years have seen the creation of an immense scholarly resource on every aspect of ancient Egypt and of the lives and achievements of its people. The bibliography of ancient Egypt is vastly greater than that of any other ancient culture; only the study of the Greek contribution to the intellectual heritage of Europe perhaps begins to approach it and the considerable extent of the Greek debt to Egypt is now being increasingly recognised. Yet on this episode, the story of how the Egyptians brought their dogs into a close mutually dependent relationship, which is unique in the history of human social evolution, only a few sparse but welcome studies have appeared in recent years which make some mention of this aspect of the Egyptian experience.

It is clear from the several studies in the history of canine domestication published in recent years that the relationship between canids (tamed wolves or evolved dogs) and hunters must considerably predate the Epi-Palaeolithic horizon suggested by archaeology, where the earliest surviving evidence of the domestication of the dog in the Near East derives from burials at the end of the last Ice Age, with the evidence from Europe somewhat earlier, dating from the latter Magdalenian period. Whatever may be the answer to this intriguing question, there is no doubt that the principal subject of this book, the acceptance by the people of Ancient Egypt, very early in their historical development, of the hunting hound into a close and enduring affection, was a unique and very special event in the social evolution of the humans, at least as much as it was of the hounds, which grew out of a long-established sequence of observation and contact.

The idea that the human–dog bond and its consequent development must have contributed, to a degree not remotely matched by any other human–nonhuman species' relationship, to the psychological and cultural development of both species is particularly attractive. In the dog it contributed to its physiological development too, resulting in the multitude of subspecies, breeds and mongrelisations over the past ten thousand years and more. For the human partners to the bond it may have been influential in the stimulation of oral communication in the hunting field, as important as the hunt itself in the promotion of cooperation-planned organisation. The lessons that would have been learned in these circumstances, all of them serving to inculcate a sense of social and community responsibility, must have been of considerable value in devising what were otherwise untried techniques in the management of settled societies, when they emerged around 12,000 years ago when the archaeological evidence begins to show an acceleration of the human–canine bond. The human element in the relationship also gained in the expansion of the horizons of affection and compassion that concern for another nonhuman species will have engendered. It may even have stimulated the humans involved to recognise, as later on the Egyptians surely did, the extent of their place in nature and their responsibility to their fellow creatures.

Two aspects of this remarkable relationship in its Egyptian dimension are especially intriguing: the first is the plausibility or otherwise of a genetic connection of the living breeds of hounds derived from canine populations in the Mediterranean islands and hence with the historic tjesm of ancient Egypt. Whilst a survival over this formidable period seems problematic, the evidence of the longevity of some living breeds, including the tjesm's likely near relative the Saluqi, at least make it difficult to believe that the modern dogs are not directly related to the ancient one, though whether it is by direct, unbroken descent is much less certain. The possibility of an ancient lineage for the Pharaoh Hound and the Ibizan Hound has been dismissed by Parker et al., who argue that the evidence of the living hounds' genomes precludes an ancient ancestry. The report supports an extended lineage for a number of other breeds whose genes contributed to the research. Most of those dogs are Far Eastern in origin, further strengthening the contention that canine domestication first occurred in the Far East. As against that assertion, the evidence provided by the Cirneco in Sicily has been advanced here to suggest the propriety of some reservation of the emphatic rejection of the possibility of a line linking the ancient and modern hounds.

For a moment, let us assume that a relationship between the ancient and modern dogs is feasible. This assumption would require that relationship to have been the consequence of human intervention, having been sustained over a timespan almost as long as that maintained by the ancient Egyptians themselves in protecting the authentic tjesm strain, which they seem so remarkably to have done. The question that must then be asked, how such a connection between two distinct subspecies of domesticated dog might have come about over such a formidable timescale, is another matter entirely. The mechanisms by which a 'breed' (to use an anachronistic term) such as the tjesm could seem to have disappeared and then apparently to have resurfaced two millennia later are very far from clear. One possible explanation is particularly persuasive: that similar circumstances of climate, context and environment may bring about the replication of the characteristics of an earlier domesticated canine, in the behaviour and morphology of another, later, example of the species. This process is known as *convergence*, whereby animals and plants have the tendency to assume similar characteristics under like conditions of environment. Thus sight-hounds, bred for the chase particularly of small game, in a predominantly hot or arid climate, over a desert terrain, would display common morphological characteristics and possibly similar conditions of coloration and behaviour.

On the face of it, this would seem to be an explanation more likely than that the breed was somehow preserved intact in conditions of relative isolation, though, as we have suggested, this is certainly not impossible. It must be remembered that the Egyptian tjesm, to judge by the iconographic evidence and by that of mummified specimens, retained its essential physical characteristics from the early third millennium BC until at least the end of the second, some two thousand years in all. It should also be remembered that Egypt is a land that seems peculiarly to retain its genetic strains. It is only necessary to walk down a street in Cairo or in a village in the countryside to see living faces that could have come straight off an Old Kingdom relief.

The question of the descent of the tjesm itself and the observed similarities of behaviour between the Pharaoh Hound/Kelb tal-Fenek and that of the golden jackal are arresting but equally controversial. These factors bear directly on the whole question of the domestication of the dog and whether its ancestry is exclusively descended from the wolf. This is an area of academic debate where opinions are exchanged vigorously and where the intervention of an outsider is likely to be unwelcome. But the similarities of behaviour between the modern hounds and the golden jackal *are* there. Whether there are genetic connections between the tjesm and the jackal may now be capable of resolution by examination of the genomes of mummified tjesm.

The importance of the degree of correspondence is that the most striking similarities are behavioural. This touches the issue of the inheritance of wolfish behavioural characteristics that the majority of zoologists believe to be decisive in excluding the possibility of any modern dog having a golden jackal forebear. It may be that the apparent similarities are merely common (or relatively common) canine characteristics. But a reading of the reports of the recent scientific symposia on the origins of the domestic dog reveals a number of scholars who now accept the possibility of a diversity of its origins and, in some cases, specifically the possibility of a contribution to the dogs' genes being derived from the golden jackal.

This issue is one on which scientific opinions have long differed. Reading again one of the most influential studies of animal domestication, *A History of Domesticated Animals*,[1] written nearly fifty years ago by F.E. Zeuner, one of the founders of the science of archaeozoology, it is clear from the section of his work dealing with the domestication of the dog that he does not entirely reject the possibility of a jackal component in the dog's ancestry. Like most of his colleagues and those who have followed him, he believes that the wolf is the primary ancestor. In analysing what he sees as the several options from which canine domestication might derive, he writes:

> So far there are four alternatives. The domesticated dog is descended (1) exclusively from the wolf, (2) exclusively from the jackal, (3) from both, with the dominance of a small race of wolf, or (4) from a wild dingo. Of

these (4) is the best formed theory, (1) the second best, whilst (2) is no longer considered probable.[2]

It is curious that Zeuner did not comment on (3), which might be thought to be the most feasible, at least so far as the ancestry of the tjesm is concerned. The advent of mitrochondrial DNA analysis is a valuable means of unravelling the matrilinear descent of a species and has put an entirely new dimension of knowledge within the scientist's reach. No doubt the investigation of the DNA of mummified tjesm, living Pharaoh Hounds and other of the stocks of hunting dogs in or from the Mediterranean islands would indicate whether, somewhere along the line, there had been an infusion of golden jackal genes into the stock of early domesticated dogs. Given the fact that all canine species are interfertile, it would perhaps be surprising if this were not the case. Such intermingling most likely would have occurred in the times when the populations of the Near East in the Epi-Palaeolithic period and the early Neolithic were coalescing, and in those migrations that led to the establishment of the Egyptian kingdoms in the Nile Valley. The dominance of the golden jackal in North Africa will be recalled and the incursion into its domain of another canine species would hardly have gone unnoticed – and unexploited – by so long-established a resident species.

It must be remembered that the study of the mitrochondrial DNA of the dogs included in the research published by Vilà et. al in 1997, which excluded any of the dogs mentioned here with the exception of the Basenji, only defines descent in the maternal line. It does not reveal evidence of paternity and it is probable that if the golden jackal did intervene in the lines of descent considered here, it would be from a male jackal mating with a domesticated (or semi-domesticated) bitch.

The correspondences between the behaviour of the golden jackal and the observed behaviour of the Pharaoh Hound/Kelb tal-Fenek (there is no comparable evidence at present for the behaviour of either the Cirneco or the Ibizan Hound) raises the possibility not only that the Pharaoh Hound/Kelb tal-Fenek possesses genes inherited from the golden jackal cross with the ancestral wolf, but that such possession strongly predicates the tjesm, having provided the mediating intervention in the genetic transmission from jackal to modern breeds.

The exceptionally long period, more than 2000 years, over which the Egyptians managed and controlled the breeding of the tjesm, reproducing the strain's principal morphological characteristics and ensuring that it bred true, argues strongly, as does the evidence of the Chicago report in relation to those dogs whose descent stands closer to the wolf than others, for the survival of the dogs' genetic structure over many centuries. There is nothing inherently improbable in the survival of genes donated by the jackal to a wolf-descended strain of already domesticated dog in early Egypt. It may be that the sturdy, deep-chested 'pariah' dogs portrayed on the rock surfaces and overhangs in the deserts by predynastic hunters were crossed with the jackal strain to produce the taller, slender greyhound type of dog that became the tjesm. Given the Egyptians' proven abilities in the management of domesticated species, the cross between pariah and golden jackal could well have been deliberately induced or encouraged. Even if the possibility of direct descent from the tjesm to the modern breeds is dismissed, the possibility of recurrence remains. It is perhaps a more convincing argument than proposing the deliberate 're-creation' of the breeds, for which there seems to be no significant supporting evidence and much to suggest the contrary to be the case.

If there is any merit in the questions that have been raised here, it may be that future research will include other studies to focus on the specific descent of the Mediterranean and Near Eastern hunting hounds considered here. It might be borne in mind that, in addition to the availability of the genes of living dogs, there are communities of mummified tjesm that can now be called on to supply the genes of dogs living 4000 years and more ago.

This study also concerns itself with the importance of the canines in what is generally termed Egyptian 'religion'. This can only be understood by appreciating the Egyptians' overwhelming preoccupation with the integrity of the natural world, their fascination with and delight in the animals that they saw around them and their ability to see all aspects of existence as reflections of the same cosmic unity. This perception naturally led them to express the qualities of what they perceived to be the suprahuman as manifested in certain animal forms. Their motivation in choosing particular animals to represent divine entities is often obscure, perhaps deliberately so. One of the most compelling images that they created was of the humble scarab beetle, a creature neither beautiful nor portentous, earnestly rolling its ball of dung across the ground, which becomes a representation of the sun-god, no less, sailing majestically across the sky. More, the beetle was Khepri and stood for the concept of 'coming into being', the most absolute expression of the Egyptian recognition of the underlying dynamic of existence. Other creatures

might have been chosen to give life to this august conception: the noble
lion, once one of the personifications of the king, might have seemed to be
a more appropriate candidate, but it was the little beetle, perpetually rolling
its make-believe sun-ball across a limitless horizon containing the promise
of new life, which expressed more concisely, and certainly more poetically,
the mystery of the renewal of existence.

All the animals chosen to represent aspects of the eternal principles governing the cosmos and hence the life and prosperity of Egypt, the epitome of
the cosmos brought to earth, exhibit this disregard for any meaningful or
direct association between themselves and the principle that they express. The
ibis is not renowned for its wisdom, the ram seldom practises the making
of pottery, the fly is not notable for its courage in battle though it was the
symbolic award, fabricated in gold, which was given by the king to his most
notable military commanders and to warriors who distinguished themselves
in campaign. The soaring falcon has already been recognised as a brilliant
encapsulation of the idea of the divine king. This apart, only the baboon
perhaps shows its awareness and sagacity in greeting the sun each morning
as it rises above the horizon. That the animals are in fact rousing themselves
from their night-time torpor by beating their paws together does not diminish
in the least either the perception or the poetry of the image.

Canines particularly articulate this duality of literal appearance and hidden
meaning. Of all the animals in the Egyptian world, they alone shared totally
the lives of their human companions. They were not a food resource, unlike
the cattle, birds, the occasional fish and some of the creatures of the desert.
They participated in the daily life of the people and no doubt brought
pleasure and happiness to their companions as often as they served them in
the hunt or in protecting herds and property.

As we have seen, the canine divinities link the two worlds, the world of the
living and that which awaits the just after death; their ground is the frontier
between the seen and the unseen. As such they are creatures of mystery, on
the one hand loyal, loving and benign, and on the other possessed of unique
rights of access peculiar to themselves (and hence power), in regions from
which the living are excluded. They are Lords, not only of the Necropolis,
but also of time, the divisions between day and night, guardians of the
solstices and the cycle of the seasons. They are at once the most familiar of
all the animals and yet are possessed of the most complex symbolism, with
access to a compelling mystery.

For reasons that can only be guessed, the Egyptians (or perhaps their ancestors), in times and places remote and far distant from their eventual homeland, invested the canines – the dog, the jackal, possibly the wolf (if they knew of its existence) – with special qualities, seeing in them the realisation of some aspect of existence which needed the physical expression of a living creature. For several thousand years dogs enjoyed a dignity accorded to them, and an affection which they readily returned, with the most talented and creative race in the history of man. It is, all in all, a very mysterious and perplexing but distinctly satisfying encounter.

The mystery of that encounter can be sensed by the realisation that in the course of creating one of the most complex ancient societies, a vigorous and sophisticated administration and a political system that was the model for all royal and imperial administrations for the next five thousand years, the Egyptians found the time and the enthusiasm to bring another creature into their lives, care for it and to share all the joys and sorrows of life with it. Of course, not every Egyptian was attended by a loyal, loving dog, but very many of them obviously were. This first occasion of the election of a quite other species to share his world is a strange and wonderful event in the evolution of Homo sapiens as a social animal.

We are able to see more of the Egyptian world as the Egyptians them- selves saw it than of any other ancient people. Time collapses when we regard Egypt in the centuries of its greatest power. No other people until modern times even contemplated the recording of their world on the scale and with the commitment that the people of Egypt displayed, especially in the third and second millennia BC. Herodotus' amazement at the Egyptians' attitude towards their animals, particularly the dog (and, in later times, the cat), expresses so well what must have been a general bewilderment on the part of visitors to Egypt that a people obviously the heirs of a great past should so prodigally expend their affections on a creature not of their own kind. Certainly, the Greeks kept dogs and it was at least an artistic convention to represent young boys and athletes on funeral stelae as accompanied by a faithful hound, gazing at its master with adoration; but often the dog seems little more than an accessory or a guardian, not an integral part of the life of its human companions. For thousands of years before the Greeks existed, the Egyptians regarded dogs as one of the bounties with which a generous providence had provided them, to be enjoyed and cosseted.

That this curious, engaging preoccupation with dogs is so particular to Egypt in early antiquity is evident by a comparison with the situation of the dog in the society of the Egyptians' near contemporaries, the people of Sumer in southern Iraq. The Sumerians exhibit a warm humanity comparable in many respects with that of the Egyptians themselves; they are even more explicit in analysing their own psyches and the challenge of being human than did the Egyptians, who took a notably more relaxed and cheerful view of the world than did their Mesopotamian peers. Though they tolerated dogs and allowed the occasional minor divinity to have one as a companion, the Sumerians did not attempt to bind the dog to them and themselves to the dog, as the Egyptians did.

When Queen Herneith's dog went with her into her tomb and hence on to the pleasant, eternal life which awaited the justified dead (queen and dog in this case together, for the Egyptians would certainly have believed that all dogs were worthy of justification, just as modern cynophiles very reasonably insist that all dogs go to heaven), Egypt was just beginning on its long and valiant history, which was to be like the history of no other people or nation-state. When King Den's dog Nub was buried beside his master's tomb, the kingship was in the process of developing into a unique institution that was eventually to become worldwide in its extent, independent in the main of the Egyptian precedent, but replicating it in most particulars, an instance perhaps of the phenomenon of convergence in politics. Kingship was to endure, effectively until early in the last century, identical in significant detail with the audacious system created by the Egyptians five thousand years ago, though the concept of the king's divinity had generally been tempered with a more sceptical view of the nature of the king prevailing. When King Khufu's guard and companion, Abutiyuw, was given his sumptuous burial in his own tomb, fitting for the friend of so great a king, the first of the pyramids was being raised on the plateau at Giza, shining brilliantly white in the light both of the sun by day and of the moon and stars by night. Did Abitiyuw, one wonders, cock his leg comfortably against one of the polished casing stones of the lower courses of the pyramid, as his master watched the masons at work?

Kings, nobles and commoners all shared in the delight of dogs and their ways. Legions of artists – carvers of reliefs, 'outline artists', who sketched the content of a scene on the still damp plaster of the tomb walls for the painters to infill and complete, sculptors, carvers in wood and the fashioners of gold and bronze figures and jewellery – all recorded the ways of the dog. No other ancient people has left such a repertory of canine representations, their beauty and absorption in life, in the moment and in the task in hand, if not in paw.

But none of this explains why the Egyptians, at so early a moment in their history, brought the dog into their society, virtually institutionalising their mutual relationship not merely as an amiable pet but as a creature which represented to them qualities which they found admirable and worthy of praise. We can only guess: it may simply be yet another manifestation of the Egyptian delight in the natural world and all the creatures in it. In their commerce with dogs, in the early settlements when the canines prowled round the outskirts of what became quite large inhabited areas, they would have observed them keenly. They would also have done so in the hunt, and there they would have been impressed with the dog's ability to track, to im-mobilise game and to run to exhaustion the larger prey. They would quickly have come to appreciate the dog's intelligence and its ability to learn and to retain what it had learned.

Yet there may have been other, simpler reasons for the Egyptians' delight in their dogs. It must have been in the domestic context, in the family and in the household, when such an institution may be said to have existed, that the special bond between Egyptians and the dog developed. It may have come about in this way.

The early Egyptians (or, more probably, their ancestors before they took possession of the Valley) cannot have failed to notice that, unlike all the other animals with which they had contact and association, the dog alone displayed a range of emotions very similar, identical almost, to those which they themselves experienced. The dog demonstrates happiness, anxiety, humour (a highly subjective judgement, admittedly), certainly compassion and a concern, not only for its own kind but also for its human companions and their young. They will have recognised the dog's intelligence and its willing-ness, for whatever reason, to please its human companions. Just as humans will approach a potential benefactor with a friendly or respectful disposition, so the dog, though it may be accused of opportunistic sycophantism, will have sought to encourage the transmission of warmth, food and, certainly not the least important quality, affection, from its human companions. But they will also have known of dogs which risked their lives for their human companions and for the families of which they were part.

Whilst Egypt in the early centuries of its existence moved towards the making of such a complex, many-levelled society, the process of bringing the dog into the larger community must have happened as if by the dictates of nature. In a literal sense the Egyptians were the most domesticated of ancient peoples and at the same moment the most sophisticated. As they began to shape the perfection of the tjesm's physical form or brought about the elevation of the jackal to the Lordship of the Necropolis on the one hand, and on the other identified the canines as the guides of the gods and kings, they will have readily responded to the generosity of the dog's nature and its natural predilection for humans. These qualities, aligned with the emotions that they seemed to share, would have made their special place in the hearts of the Nile people secure.

It is this quality in particular that reveals the extraordinary dimension of the Egyptians' ability to give time and effort, over a protracted period, to the management and welfare of their dogs. It is extraordinary, because it is at base so simple and natural a commitment, and indee, so very unextraordinary, that for a people with the world-view possessed by the people of Egypt in antiquity it is entirely comprehensible. In the midst of designing the most advanced and complex culture in the world of their day they could turn aside from tasks of profound importance – the definition of the kingship, the building of a pyramid, choosing the symbols to be enshrined in their writing system – to select the qualities which produced speed, enhanced intelligence, even the twist of the tail of the dogs which they admired and loved.

There are few aspects of the Egyptian achievement that show more power-fully the extent of their humanity than this concern for another creature, which they sought to bond into the community that they were building. Although the people of ancient Egypt probably would have denied it, their care for the dogs that shared their world is a recognition of the essential loneliness of man in the cosmos and his need to secure all the friends that he can. The dog, the friend of man (indeed, perhaps his only friend, as poets have said), comprehended and most amply fulfilled that need.

The harm that the human race has wrought on the planet on which we live and on the other species with which we share it is now approaching the dimension of catastrophe. Species are continuing to disappear at an appalling rate and the destruction of so much life shows no abatement. However, it must be admitted that in the domestication of species humans have found some consolation, for themselves if not for most of the animals involved. Sheep, goats, cattle, domestic fowl have little cause to applaud their harnessing to the service of humankind; the countless millions of animals bred only for slaughter daily are the ultimate victims of those first farmers and husbandmen in the primitive settlements of the Near East at the end of the last Ice Age.

One species alone would, with few reservations, consider human efforts in this regard a good and positive achievement. Domestic dogs have prospered spectacularly and have swept across the globe, colonising it as completely as has man himself. Today their numbers must be reckoned in at least hundreds of millions; not all live a life as cosseted as did the dogs of ancient Egypt but, taken all in all, they probably have fared far better than the vast majority of domesticates. Only the cat, an animal of resource and supreme assurance, has equalled the dog in securing a warm and comfortable life, with the compliance of the Universal Provider of food and affection. It is not without point that the cat, perhaps with the example of the dog before it, attached itself with equal firmness to the Egyptians, though it was considerably later in doing so, from having perhaps been impressed by observation of the dog's success.

For the Egyptians, the experience of the partnership between human and dog was clearly a happy one, to be accepted as part of the pleasures of life, the benefits of what later ages would call providence and the Egyptians might sometimes call the gods. Of course, like all good things it could not last and, as we have seen, the day came when the dog no longer enjoyed the privileged place in the Egyptian world that once had been his. Now the wheel of fortune that governs the destiny of dogs as it does of people has turned full circle once again; dogs have once more secured a place of welcome in the habitations of humans, in the homes of supposedly advanced and sophisticated communities, in Europe, America and the lands where their traditions prevail, but also among the native Australians and the peoples of Polynesia. If there are collective memories in the world of dogs, they will surely recall the days when their most devoted protagonists, the people who colonised the Nile Valley, were also stalwart tribesmen, hunting vigorously and ensuring that their dogs shared in the success of the hunt, around a camp fire or in a sheltering rocky overhang in the limitless desert.

And what of the Kelb tal-Fenek/Pharaoh Hound (to restore for a moment the priority of the Maltese hound), the inspiration for this journey into the remote reaches of the Egyptian state and the byways of its peoples' enthusiasms? The question whether there is a genetic connection between the island dogs and the tjɛsm will ultimately be settled by closer genetic researches than have thus far been conducted. The connection between the island dogs and the ancestral wolf (not to mention the tentative golden jackal) cannot be dismissed by the present results which themselves may be anomalous, as they were drawn only from hounds removed generations ago from their homelands and hence exposed to the claim of genetic interference.

Yet even if no connection were to be ultimately established, it should matter little. The Pharaoh Hound, to consider it separately from its Maltese forebear, is a handsome, elegant and intelligent creature with an exciting and unusual repertory of behavioural traits. Perhaps it may be best to think of it as the reincarnation of the tjɛsm, in much the same way that the king was the reincarnation of the great god Horus, and to rejoice that so beautiful a hound has returned to proclaim the strange history of the ancient hound that it so strikingly replicates.

APPENDIX I

Hieroglyphs Relating to Dogs and Hunting

R eferences to Egyptian hieroglyphs are drawn either from Gardiner's *Egyptian Grammar* (3rd edn, 1963) prefaced G, followed by an intial letter indicating the appropriate section of the sign-list and the number of the hieroglyph quoted; or from Budge, *An Egyptian Hieroglyphic Dictionary* (2 vols, 1920) prefaced B followed by the page number of the entry and *a* or *b* indicating a left- or right-hand column.

The word by which the Egyptians named the hunting hound, *tjesm*, G.E14, seems simply to mean 'hound'. Gardiner's *Egyptian Grammar* gives the meaning of the determinative for 'dog' (transliterated as *tesm* [*sic*]) as 'greyhound', which he then glosses as '*slughi*', despite the fact that the hieroglyph clearly indicates the dog with pricked ears and a curly tail, both characteristics with which the *tjesm* rather than the Saluqi is to be identified. The word for 'dog' in ancient Egyptian is *iw*, sometimes transliterated as *oau-oau*, a word which is evidently onomatopoeic in origin: *bow-wow* might be a reasonable rendering.

In the art of the historic periods Egyptian artists did sometimes attempt to differentiate the hound and the dog from the jackal when seeking to record the living animal. The hieroglyph G.E17 is used as an ideogram or determinative and signifies 'jackal' quite specifically. It shows a tall standing canid with a heavy bushy tail, characteristic of the jackal rather than the dog, but it has been suggested here that the portrayals of canine tails are often unreliable pointers to the precise species of the owner of the tail in question. The word for jackal is transliterated *z3b* or *s3b*, naming both the animal and, rather oddly, perhaps by some sort of ironic association, also meaning 'dignitary', 'worthy'.

The hieroglyphs that were used to describe canids are revealing. In addition to the signs shown here a variety of other hieroglyphs or groups of hieroglyphs are employed. Some of the groupings are variant spellings of words which require the dog determinative. Thus *oau-oau* can also be rendered B.4a, whilst *Åasha* B.25b is glossed 'a kind of dog or jackal', maintaining the confusion between the two canines, though the determinative is specifically that for 'dog' B.10a. Another group, with the same phonetic value but relating to the god Set, appears in Chapter 6. A variant of *iw* or *oau-oau*, which appears in various groups, as in G.E9, has the meaning 'cry, outcry, wail'; the animal is 'a newly-born bubalis or hartebeest', according to Gardiner. Yet another is B.31a *uahr*, also glossed as 'dog', which may be onomatopoeic like *oau-oau*, perhaps suggesting the dog growling; another related form is where the determinative is a jackal. The gloss 'a kind of dog' appears for the group *sha* B.720a; the feminine form, indicated by the presence of the alphabetic sign for 't', B720a, expresses 'bitch'.

A particularly interesting group, glossed as 'The Hounds of Horus', is *Thesmu Heru* (sic) B.862b. Perhaps these were the hounds which came into Egypt with the legendary 'Followers of Horus' in predynastic times, one of the migrations from which the root stock of the Egyptian population in historic times sprang, as in all probability did most of the stock of hunting hounds.

APPENDIX II

Dogs Named in the Text

Nub	Dynasty I
Sed	Dynasty I
Abutiywu ('Pointed ears'?)	Dynasty IV
Peshesh	Dynasty V
'One who is favoured like an arrow'	Old Kingdom
Bekhir ('Gazelle')	Dynasty XI
Abaqer ('Hound')	Dynasty XI
Pehtes ('Black One')	Dynasty XI
Tegra ('Kettle')	Dynasty XI
Tekenru	Dynasty XI
Breath of Life to Senbi	Dynasty XI
Ankhu	Dynasty XII
Iupu	Dynasty XII
Anath is a Defender	Dynasty XVIII

Glossary

Abutiyuw The favoured hound of King Khufu (qv) who ordered the construction of a sumptuous tomb for him.

Abydos (Eg. Abdju) A city in Upper Egypt, one of the principal centres of power in the period immediately before the Unification. It was the site of the tombs of the First Dynasty kings and was always regarded as sacred and a place of pilgrimage. Its principal divinity was originally Khentiamentiu (qv) whose place was later usurped by Osiris.

Anubis (Eg. Inpw) The principal canine divinity: variously a jackal and a hound. Lord of Graveyards and the archetypal psychopomp, who led the dead to judgement before the god Osiris.

Archaeozoology A scientific discipline combining zoology and archaeological techniques in the study of animal remains, especially important in identifying skeletal evidence and tracing the descent of living animal strains.

Asyut (Eg. Z3wty) A town in Middle Egypt, known to the Greeks as Lykopolis, sacred to the god Anubis, whose principal temple was located there, as were extensive dog burials. It was the capital of the nome.

Badarian The earliest predynastic culture in Upper Egypt, c. 5000–4000 BC, named after El-Badari, where it was first recognised.

Bos primigenius The archaic strain of large, wild cattle, herds of which were found throughout much of the ancient world, including North and East Africa and Europe. They were extensively hunted and became extinct in the seventeenth century AD. The king of Egypt was indentified with the wild bull, as a symbol of power and several of the gods manifested in the form of bulls.

Canidae (Lat.) The family of all canines, including wolves, dogs, jackals.

Canis A member of the family *Canidae*.

Canis aureus The golden or common jackal (*see also Canis aureus lupaster*).

Canis familiaris   The domesticated dog. In Egypt represented principally by the tjesm, the hunting hound.

Canis aureus lupaster   The qualification *lupaster* added to the Latin designation of the golden jackal reflects its supposed wolf-like characteristics and size.

Canis lupus   The wolf, the generally accepted ancestor of all breeds of the domesticated dog.

Cirneco dell'Etna   A lightly built hunting hound, native to Sicily, which in colouration and other characteristics bears some resemblance to the Pharaoh Hound/Kelb tel Fenek (qv).

Crowns   The Crowns of Upper and Lower Egypt symbolised the sovereignty of the king over the Two Lands; by convention Egypt was always considered to be two kingdoms. The crowns were divinities.

Den   King, First Dynasty, c. 2950 BC. Two of his dogs were buried with him at Abydos

Dynasty   A succession of kings considered to have a familial connection. Egypt recorded 30 royal dynasties, from the First Dynasty, c. 3100 BC, to the Ptolemies, who were replaced by the Romans in 30 BC.

Dual Kingdom   Upper and Lower Egypt, the two kingdoms into which Egypt was always notionally divided. The king was sovereign of each.

Early Dynastic   The First and Second Egyptian Dynasties, c. 3100–2700 BC, previously termed 'The Archaic Period'.

Elam   South-western Iran and the apparent source of many design motifs and possibly regalia in the late predynastic period (qv)

Epi-Palaeolithic   The period of Near Eastern history following the end of the last Ice Age in Europe, which experienced the first permanent settlements in Mesopotamia and Iran and the domestication of cereals and animals.

Golden jackal   *Canis aureus, Canis aureus lupaster* (qv). A canine native to Egypt, North Africa, Ethiopia and other regions, with distinctive behavioural traits and communications techniques. Considered here a putative (but unproven) ancestor of the tjesm.

Hemaka   Noble, Chief Minister to King Den (qv) of the First Dynasty. His mastaba (qv) tomb at Saqqara produced the magnificent inlaid steatite disc depicting two tjesm hunting two gazelles.

Hierakonpolis   (Eg. Nekhen) A district and city in southern Upper Egypt, highly influential in the emergence of the Egyptian kingship. Sacred to the god Horus (qv) and the location of an important early temple and shrine.

Hieroglyphs   'Sacred Signs', the epigraphy of ancient Egypt. See also Appendix I, which describes the hieroglyphs relating to dogs and hunting.

Herneith   Queen, early First Dynasty. Buried at Saqqara in a large mastaba (qv) with her hound.

Horus   A god particularly associated with the Egyptian kingship. Each king of Egypt was considered to be Horus reincarnated. In later times he was mythologised as the son of Isis and Osiris; he was said to have succeeded the latter as king, after he was protected by Anubis (qv). Horus represented order in the cosmos and was perpetually linked with Set (qv) who represented chaos and disorder.

Hykos 'Rulers of Foreign Countries' who invaded Egypt *c.* 1650 BC and formed the Fifteenth and Sixteenth Egyptian Dynasties. They introduced the horse to Egypt and radically changed the methods of hunting in consequence.

Ibizan Hound A hunting hound native to Ibiza.

Kelb Tal-Fenek A hunting hound, native to the Maltese islands, from which the modern Pharaoh Hound has been bred.

Khentiamentiu An ancient canine divinity of Abydos, where his temple was located. He was supplanted by Osiris.

Khufu (Gk. Cheops) King, Fourth Dynasty, identified with the great Pyramid at Giza. He ordered the building of a tomb for his dog Abutiuw (qv).

Kush A kingdom in Nubia (qv) from which an African dynasty originated and ruled Egypt for more than a hundred years, Dynasty XXV (747–656 BC).

Late Period The Twenty-Second to the Thirtieth Dynasties *c.* 747–332 BC.

Magdalenian An Upper Palaeolithic culture in Europe, *c.* 15000 BC.

Mastaba An Arabic term, meaning 'bench', used to describe the rectangular, brick-built tombs originally designed for the elite of the First Dynasty and subsequently adopted by Old Kingdom royalty and nobles.

Middle Kingdom The Eleventh to Fourteenth Egyptian Dynasties, *c.* 2055–1650 BC.

Naqada (*Eg.* Nubt) A city in Upper Egypt, sacred to the god Set and the find-site for two important predynastic cultures, Naqada I (Amratian) and Naqada II (Gerzean).

Natufian An Epi-Palaeolithic culture in Palestine, *c.* 10000 BC, where the possible remains of early domesticated canines have been found.

Nekhen The city of Hierakonpolis (qv).

Neolithic 'The New Stone Age', succeeding the Epi-Palaeolithic in the Near East and Egypt, a period of rapid social development. Coterminous with the invention of pottery in the region.

New Kingdom The Seventeenth to the Twenty-First Egyptian Dynasties, *c.* 1550–1070 BC.

Nome (Gk.) Administrative districts in Egypt, ruled by nomarchs, many of whom became exceedingly powerful after the end of the Old Kingdom (qv).

Nubia The extreme south of Egypt and parts of Lower Sudan, rich in gold and other minerals. A highly developed 'royal' administration apparently flourished there in late predynastic/Early Dynastic times.

Old Kingdom The Third to the Sixth Egyptian Dynasties *c.* 2686–2181 BC. The high point of Egyptian civilisation and the care of the tjesm.

Palaeolithic The Old Stone Age, subdivided Lower, Middle and Upper.

Palette A soft-stone (chlorite, steatite) plate of varying size and formulations, originally used for the grinding of kohl, applied to the eyelids and upper cheeks to reduce the sun's glare, and later, in the late predynastic period, as dedicatory objects, decorated with scenes recording mythological and historical events.

Pharaoh The King of Egypt. A term derived from 'per-o', Great House, signifying the centre of government. Its use is anachronistic before the Eighteenth Dynasty.

Pharaoh Hound (Eg. tjesm ?) An Egyptian hunting hound of the greyhound type, with a characteristic ochreous-tan pelage, golden eyes and sharply pointed, upstanding ears.

Predynastic The period of Egyptian history from the first villages, c. 5000 BC to the Unification and the foundation of the First Dynasty of kings, c. 3180 BC.

Pyramid Texts A collection of spells, incantations, antiphons and rituals, some of which are thought to originate in predynastic times, which appear on the interior walls of pyramids at the end of the Old Kingdom. The texts were forerunners of the Coffin Texts of the Middle Kingdom and the Books of the Dead of the later periods of Egyptian history.

Rameses II King, Nineteenth Dynasty, c. 1279–1213 BC.

Saqqara A site in northern Upper Egypt, south of the modern city of Cairo, the location of important funerary complexes of the early periods of Egyptian history, particularly serving the capital of the Two Lands, Memphis, close to which it was located.

Serekh A heraldic device, thought to have originated in south-western Asia, which was adopted by the Early Dynastic kings to proclaim their most sacred royal name, as the reincarnated god Horus.

Set A powerful divinity, originally perhaps the principal god of the south (Upper Egypt), who represented the principle of chaos in contradistinction to Horus, who represented order and was identified with each King of Egypt. 'The Two Gods' stood for the balance of influences in the cosmos; in later periods Set was considered a malign deity.

Step Pyramid A monumental tomb built for King Netjerykhet (Djoser) c. 2667–2648 BC at Saqqara in the Third Dynasty. Other step pyramids were built throughout Egypt during the dynasty, to be succeeded by the true pyramids of the Fourth Dynasty at Giza.

Sumer Southern Mesopotamia (modern Iraq), the homeland of the Sumerians, the contemporaries of the Egyptians of the late predynastic, Early Dynastic and Old Kingdom periods. Various influences from Sumer (and from Elam, south-western Iran) have been detected in Egypt in the earlier part of Sumer's history.

Tjesm The Egyptian hunting hound (see also Pharaoh Hound).

Thebes The capital of Egypt in the New Kingdom.

Tulip Ears A term sometimes used by breeders to describe the pointed, upstanding ears of the Pharaoh Hound, Cirneco, greyhounds and similar breeds.

Unification The imposition of a unified political system throughout the Egyptian Nile Valley by the kings of the First Dynasty, traditionally ascribed to King Narmer.

Wahankh Intef II King, Early Eleventh Dynasty c. 2112–2063 BC, noted for his affection for his dogs.

Wepwawet A canine god, whose name means 'Opener of the Ways', particularly associated with Abydos and with the person of the king.

Notes

All works listed in the Bibliography are referenced here by author name and date of publication.

Preface

1. Vilà et al. 1997.
2. Parker et al. 2004.
3. Ibid.: 1163–4; Savolainen et al. 2002.
4. Rice 2003.

Chapter 1

1. S.J. Olsen, *Origins of the Domestic Dog: The Fossil Record* (Tucson 1985).
2. H. de Lumley, 'Une Cabane de chasserie acheulénne dans la Grotte du Lazaret à Nice', *Archaeologia* 28 (1969): 26–33.
3. J. Clutton-Brock and P. Jewel, 'Origin and Domestication of the Dog', in H.E. Evans, ed., *Miller's Anatomy of the Dog* (Philadelphia 1993): 21–33.
4. Zeuner 1963: 100; Clutton-Brock 1984: 205–6; Osborn with Osbornovà 1998: 59, Figs 7.19, 7.20.
5. Clutton-Brock 1984: 200.
6. Ibid.: 204.
7. Zeuner 1963: 83–4; Clutton-Brock 1984: 204.
8. Serpell and Jago in Serpell 1995: 79–102.
9. Zeuner 1963: 82; Osborn with Osbornovà 1998: 55–7.
10. Vilà et al. 1997.
11. G.J. Nobis, 'Der älteste Haushund von 14000 Jahren', *Umschau* 79 (1979): 610.
12. R. Musil, 'Evidence for the Domestication of Wolves in Central European Magdalenian Sites', in Crockford 2000: 21–8.

13. J. Hahn, *La Statuette masculine de la grotte de Hohlenstein-Stadel* (Würtemburg 1971): 75, 233–4.
14. A. Sinclair, 'Art of the Ancients', *Nature* 426 (18–25 December 2003): 774–5; N.J. Conard, 'Palaeolithic Ivory Statues from South-western Germany and the Origins of Figurative Art', *Nature* 426 (18–25 December 2003): 830–32.
15. D.O. Henry, *From Foraging to Agriculture: The Levant at the End of the Ice Age* (Philadelphia 1989): Fig. 7.19.
16. Davis and Valla 1978.
17. P.F. Turnbull and C.A. Reid, 'The Fauna from the Terminal Pleistocene of Palegawra Cave, a Zarzian Occupation Site in Northeastern Iraq, *Fieldian Anthropology*, vol. 63, no. 3 (1974): 81–146.
18. F. Safar, M.A. Mustafa, S.Lloyd, Eridu (Baghdad 1982): Fig. 66, grave 185.
19. Max Hilzheimer, 'Dogs', *Antiquity*, vol. VI, no. 24 (December 1932): 411–19, Pls I–XII.
20. Zeuner 1963: 82; Osborn with Osbornovà 1998: 55–6.
21. E. Neumann, *The Origins and History of Consciousness*, Bollingen Series (Princeton 1970), Appendix I, 'The Group and the Great Individual': 421–35.
22. Herodotos 1998: 66–7.
23. *Canidae*: the family of mammals that includes domesticated, wild and feral dogs, wolves, foxes and jackals.
24. For hyena, see Osborn with Osbornovà 1998: 97–104; for Old Kingdom relief see W.M.F. Petrie, *Deshshaheh* (London 1898): Pl. IX (Tomb of Anta [Inti]).
25. P. Vermeersch et al., 'Une minière de silex et un squelette du Palèolithique superieur ancien à Nazlet Khater, Haute-Egypte', *L'Anthropologie* 88 (1984): 231–44.
26. P. Vermeersch et al., 'A Middle Palaeolithic Burial of a Modern Human at Taramsa Hill', *Egypt. Antiquity* 72 (1998): 475–84.
27. D.R. Connor, 'The Kiseba Plateau in the Bir Murr Playa', in F. Wendorf and R.Schild, *Cattle Keepers of the Eastern Sahara*, ed. A. Close (Dallas 1984): 350–403.
28. Rice 1998, esp. ch. 6.
29. Midant-Reynes 2000: 126–41, 225–30.
30. As in P. Lhote, *The Search for the Tassili Frescoes* (New York 1959), which did much to introduce this extraordinary reserve of art to the world outside the Sahara.
31. A.E.P. Weigall, *Travels in the Upper Egyptian Deserts* (Edinburgh and London 1909): Pls XXIX, XXX.16.
32. H.A. Winkler, *Rock Drawings of Southern Upper Egypt I: Sir Robert Mond Expedition*, vols I and II London (1938/9).
33. Ibid., vol. I: 26, Pl. XXV.
34. J.H. Dunbar *The Rock Pictures of Lower Nubia* (Cairo 1941).
35. Ibid.: 52, Pl. XII.
36. Ibid.: Pl. II.ii.
37. Ibid.: 46.
38. See below, ch. 2 n46.
39. J. Zarins, A. Murad and Kh. Al-Yaish, 'The Second Preliminary Report on the South Western Province', *ATLAL* 5 (1981): Figs 34a, 34b.
40. Dunbar, *The Rock Pictures of Lower Nubia*: 46–7.
41. Ibid.
42. Ibid.

43. G. Fuchs, 'Rock Engravings in the Wadi el-Barramiya, Eastern Desert of Egypt', *African Archaeological Review* 7 (1989): 127–54.

44. Ibid.: ET-A/WB3 Fig. 8.

45. Ibid.: ET-A/WB5 Fig. 29.

46. D. Rohl, *The Followers of Horus: Eastern Desert Survey Report*, vol. 1 (Institute for the Study of Interdisciplinary Sciences, London 2000).

47. Ibid.: DR-1(11). Note: figures in parenthesis represent drawings of the engravings.

48. Ibid.: DR-2.11(12).

49. Lhote, *The Search for the Tassili Frescoes*, 'Style of the Round-headed Men (Egyptian Influence)', Notes on the Plates 26, 30, 33, 35, 36, 48, 51, 52 and 53, 60.

50. M. Khan et al., 'Preliminary Report on the Second Phase of Comprehensive Rock Art and Epigraphic Survey of Northern Province', *ATLAL* 11 (1986): 173–4.

51. Clutton-Brock 1995: 79.

52. A. Scharf, 'Some Prehistoric Vases in the British Museum and Remarks on Egyptian Prehistory', *Journal of Egyptian Archaeology* 14 (1928): 261–7, fig.

53. See n19 above.

54. Elise J. Baumgartel, *The Cultures of Prehistoric Egypt*, vol. I (London 1947): 30.

55. Hilzheimer 1932: 418.

56. Ibid.

57. Midant-Reynes 2000: 106, 111; citing A. von den Driesch and J. Boessneck, *Die Tierknochenfunde aus der neolithischen Siedlung von Merimde Benisalâme am westlichen Nildelta* (Munich 1985).

58. Ibid.: 216.

59. H. Epstein, *The Origins of the Domestic Animals of Africa* (New York 1971): 53.

60. Galant 2002.

61. For example, in the *Tale of the Shipwrecked Sailor*, a kindly snake, 'The Lord of Punt', cares for the sailor who is thrown up on his magical island. He smothers him with gifts, the products of his island, including 'greyhounds'. Lichtheim 1975: 211–15.

62. Asselberghs 1961: 277, Pl. XL.

63. Viz. Osborn and Osbornovà, 'resembles Gilgamesh, the Mesopotamian Lord of the Beasts' (1998: 4). The figure on the Gebel el-Arak knife is not Gilgamesh. Gilgamesh was king of Uruk in Southern Mesopotamia several hundred years after the date at which the knife is thought to have been made; nor was he ever represented as 'Lord of the Beasts' as the man (or god) on the knife hilt seems to be.

64. G. Dryer et al., 'Umm el-Qa'ab: Nachtuntersuchungen in frühzeitlichen Königsfriedhof', 5/6 Vorbericht, *MDAIK* 49 (1993): 23–62.

65. Asselberghs 1961: 272–3, Pl. XXIV.

66. Kemp 1979: 36–43.

67. B. Adams, Unprecedented Discoveries at Hierakonpolis, *Egyptian Archaeology* 15 (1999): 29–31.

68. Elise J. Baumgartel, *The Cultures of Prehistoric Egypt*, vol. II (London 1960): 128.

69. Ibid.: 127.

70. D.V. Flores, *Funerary Sacrifices of Animals in the Egyptian Predynastic Period* (London 2003).

71. Ibid.: 73–4.
72. B. Midant-Reynes, E. Crubézy and T. Janin, 'The Predynastic Site of Adaïma', *Egyptian Archaeology* 9 (1996): 13–15.
73. Baumgartel, *The Cultures of Prehistoric Egypt*, vol. II: 128.
74. Clutton-Brock 1995: 79.
75. D. O'Connor, *Ancient Nubia: Egypt's Rival in Africa* (Philadelphia 1993): xix.
76. Williams 1986: 172–82.
77. Ibid.: Fig. 58.
78. G.A. Reisner, *The Archaeological Survey of Nubia: Report for 1907–8*, vol. I (Cairo 1910).

Chapter 2

1. Hoffman 1982: 275–9, 284; Wilkinson 1999: 227, 265–7.
2. Emery 1958: ch. IX et seq., 73–109; Pl. 91.
3. Wilkinson 1999: 126.
4. B. Adams, *Ancient Nekhen: Garstang in the City of Hierakonpolis* (New Malden 1995): 66.
5. Zeuner 1963: 92, Fig. 4.15.
6. M. Rice, 'Al Hajjar Revisited: The Grave Complex at Al Hajjar, Bahrain. Revised with Photographs', *Proceedings of the Seminar for Arabian Studies* 18 (1988): 79–95; Pl. XIX.
7. Reisner 1923.
8. Midant-Reynes 2000: 227.
9. Emery 1949, 1953, 1958.
10. W.B. Emery, *Excavations at Saqqara: The Tomb of Hemaka* (Cairo 1938): Frontispiece, The Disk.
11. Petrie 1900: Pl. XXXII, 10, 11, 12; J.L. de Cenival, 'Stèle du chien Sed', in *Un Siècle de Fouilles Françaises en Égypte 1880–1980* (IFAO, Paris 1981): 5.
12. Petrie 1900: Pl. XXXIII.
13. C.M. Firth, J.E. Quibell, with plans by J.-P. Lauer, *Excavations at Saqqara; The Step Pyramid*, 2 vols (Cairo 1935).
14. M. Lehner, *The Complete Pyramids* (London 1997): 96–102.
15. H. Junker, *Giza I–XII* (Vienna and Leipzig 1929–55): vol. I, 148–61.
16. W. Stevenson Smith, *The Art and Architecture of Ancient Egypt* (1981): 80–81, 83–4, 94; ill. 71–3, 74, 75, 88.
17. Lehner, *The Complete Pyramids*: 106–9. For a useful if sometimes winsomely written demolition of the arguments for a construction date for the Giza pyramids earlier than the Fourth Dynasty, see I. Lawton and C. Ogilvie-Herald, *Giza: The Truth* (London 1999): ch. 2, 77–126.
18. G.A. Reisner, 'The Dog that was Honoured by the King of Egypt', *MFA Bulletin*, XXXIV (1936): 96–9.
19. P. Duell, *The Mastaba of Mereruka*, parts 1 and 2 (Chicago 1938).
20. A.M. Moussa and H. Altenmüller, *Des Grab des Nianchnum und Chnumhotep* (Mainz-am-Rhein 1977).
21. Ibid.: 10.
22. Ibid.: Pl. 2.

23. Ibid.: Pl. 12.

24. Ibid.: Pl. 23.

25. Moussa and Altenmüller, Des Grab des Nianchnum und Chnumhotep.

26. Murray 1904: 10, §19. Pl. VII.

27. Ibid.: 9, §18.

28. A. Piankoff, The Pyramid of Unas (Princeton 1968).

29. H.E. Winlock, The Rise and Fall of the Middle Kingdom in Thebes (New York 1947): 12–17.

30. H.G. Fischer, 'More Ancient Egyptian Names of Dogs and Other Animals', Metropolitan Museum Journal, vol. 12, no. 969 (1977): 176.

31. R.B. Parkinson, Voices from Ancient Egypt (London 1991): 112–13, Pl. 39a.

32. Tooley 1988: 211; see also n39 below.

33. H.G. Fischer, 'The Nubian Mercenaries of Gebelein during the First Intermediate Period', Kush 9 (1938): 44–80.

34. J.C. Darnell, with the assistance of D. Darnell, 'Opening the Narrow Doors of the Desert: Discoveries of the Theban Road Survey', in R. Friedman, ed., Egypt and Nubia: Gifts of the Desert (1941): 132–55; Fig. 14.

35. Parkinson, Voices from Ancient Egypt: 114, Fig. 39f; A.M. Blackman, 'The Rock Tombs of Meir I: The Tomb Chapel of Ukh-Hotep's Son Senbi' (London 1914): Pl. IX.

36. P.E. Newberry et al., Beni Hasan (London 1893–1900): Pls I–IV.

37. F.W. Griffith and P.E. Newberry, El Bersheh II (London 1895): Pls xii, xiii, xiv, xv.

38. B.G. Trigger, 'Kerma, the Rise of an African Civilization', International Journal of African Historical Studies 9 (1976): 1–21; Stevenson Smith, The Art and Architecture of Ancient Egypt: Pls 180, 181.

39. F. Tiradritti, 'The Coffin of Khui', in The Cairo Museum: Masterpieces of Egyptian Art (London 1998): 126, Journal d'Entrée 36445.

40. A.M.J. Tooley, 'Coffin of a Dog from Beni Hasan', Journal of Egyptian Archaeology 74 (1988): 207–11; Pl. xxxviii 1 and 2.

41. W.C. Hayes, The Scepter of Egypt: A Background for the Study of the Egyptian Antiquities in the Metropolitan Museum of Art (New York [1953] 1990): 250, Fig. 160.

42. V. Loret and G. Daressy, Fouilles de la Vallée des Rois 1898–9 (Cairo 1899): 1–62, 43; Reeves and Wilkinson 1996: 179–82.

44. Reeves and Wilkinson 1996: 185 (from a painting by Harold Jones).

45. N. De Garis Davis, Two Ramesside Tombs at Thebes (New York 1927): Pl. XXIX; A. Wilkinson, The Garden in Ancient Egypt (London 1998): 48, 59, 110, 105; Pl. XIX.

46. Fischer, 'The Nubian Mercenaries of Gebelein': 176: Fig. 3.

47. Sir J. Gardner Wilkinson, A Popular Account of the Ancient Egyptians, rev. and abd, 2 vols (London 1854 [1836]).

48. Ibid.: Vol. I, Fig. 245.

49. Ibid.: 231.

50. Quoted in C.S. Churcher, 'Dogs from Ein Tirghi cemetery, Balat, Dakhleh Oasis, Western Desert of Egypt', in Clason, Payne and Uerpermann 1993.

51. Ibid.: Tables 1, 2 3 (Tibia).

52. L. Chaix and J. Olive, 'Annexe II: La faune du Mastaba V (2200 BC) à Balat', in M. Vallogia with N.H. Heinen, eds, Balat: Le Mastaba du Medou-Nefer. Fasc.1. Fouiles de l'Institut Français d'Archéologie Orientale 31 (1986): 201–13.

Chapter 3

1. Wilkinson 1999: 68, 70–71.
2. A. Wilkinson, *The Garden in Ancient Egypt* (London 1998).
3. G. Dryer, 'Abydos and Umm al Qa'ab', in Bard 1999.
4. Faulkner 1969: 80–83, Utterances 273–4, 'The King Hunts and Eats the Gods'.
5. Wilkinson 1999: 36–41.
6. Asselberghs 1961: 284; Pls LXV–LXVII ('Lion-Hunt Palette'); Petrie 1953: 12, Pl. 3A ('The Hunters' Palette').
7. Osborn with Osbornovà 1998: 3, Ills 1–3.
8. Zarins et al. 1981: 35; Pls 34A, 34B, 35A.
9. W.M.F. Petrie, *Deshasheh* (London 1898): Pl. IX. The same publication portrays two handsome *tjesm*.
10. Asselberghs 1961: 285, 286; Pls LXX, LXXI.
11. There is now a substantial bibliography on the Mesopotamian (and Elamite) influences on late predynastic Egypt. H.S. Smith, 'The Making of Egypt: A Review of Influences of Sumer and Susa on Upper Egypt and Lower Nubia in the Fourth Millennium BC', in R. Friedman and B. Adams, eds, *The Followers of Horus* (Oxford 1992); Wilkinson 1999: 32, 224–5; Rice 2003: 68–9, 230–32.
12. Asselburghs 1961: Pl. LXXI; Midant-Reynes 2000: 240.
13. Budge 1920, vol. I: 352A (note: references to Budge 1920, vols 1 and 2 give volume, page and column numbers).
14. 'Scientific Correspondence', *Nature* 2 (June 1994): 364, 'Mammoths in Ancient Egypt'.
15. A.H. Simmons, 'Humans, Island Colonization and Pleistocene Extinctions in the Mediterranean: The View from Akrotiri, Cyprus', *Antiquity* LXV (1991): 249; A.H. Simmons and D.R. Reese, 'Hippo Hunters of Akrotiri', *Archaeology* (September/October 1993): 40–43.
16. Nunn 1996: 128–9, Fig. 6.10.
17. F.Ll. Griffith, *Hieratic Papyri from Kahun and Gorob* (London 1898).

Chapter 4

1. Parker et al. 2004.
2. Masson 1998; Sheldrake 1999: *passim*.
3. Linnaeus 1758.
4. Clutton-Brock 1984: 199, 'There are probably more than 400 breeds of dogs in the world today.' The British Kennel Club recognises 183 breeds (Kennel Club 1998: 8).
5. C. Darwin, *Animals and Plants under Domestication* (New York 1868).
6. Clutton-Brock 1984: 202.
7. Hilzheimer 1932: 412.
8. K. Lorenz, *Man Meets Dog* (London 1954).
9. Clutton-Brock 1984: 202, quoting A.B. Chiarelli, 'The Chromosomes of the Canidae', in M. Fox, ed., *The Wild Canids* (New York 1975): 40–53; N.B. Todd, 'Karyotypic Fissioning and Canid Phylogeny', *Journal of Theoretical Biology* 26 (1970): 445–80.
10. I. Dunbar, *Dog Behaviour* (New Jersey 1979): 178; cited by Masson 1998: 143.

11. Osborn with Osbornovà 1998: 57; they cite Lawrence 1967 and 'Clutton-Brock 1987' (sic). This last appears to be a misattribution for Clutton-Brock 1984: 34, which is correctly cited in the bibliography, though page 34 of the first edition of the work to which reference is made does not appear to support the attribution Osborn gives to it. Nowhere does Clutton-Brock support the idea of an exclusive descent from the wolf, though she accepts that it is probably the most important of the domesticated dog's progenitors.

12. Clutton-Brock 1984: 203.

13. See Galant 2002.

14. Clutton-Brock 1984: 206.

15. These characteristics and the others which are referred to here in relation to the golden jackal's social behaviour, vocalisation and other traits appear in a remarkable film made by BBC Bristol and shown in their series *The World About Us*. The film, televised in 1981 and based on the research of Dr P.D. Moehlman, was entitled 'Days of the Jackal', and was broadcast on BBC2, 20 September 1981, Prog. No. NB 5D1007.

16. Ibid.

17. Personal communication, Dr J. Druce, breeder of the Merymut Pharaoh Hounds, who has done so much to stabilise the breed in Britain.

18. Ibid.

19. Kennel Club 1998: 58–9, 'The Pharaoh Hound'.

20. Camilleri 1995: 73–8.

21. The hound was owned by Dr J. Druce, referred to in n17 above.

22. The comments here, relating to Pharaoh Hound behaviour, are based on personal observation by the writer over the course of nine years.

23. Block and Sacks 1983: 87.

24. Ibid.: 18–19.

25. J. Moore, *About the Cirneco: The Italian Greyhound and Cirneco dell'Etna Club of Finland*, Federation Cynologique Internationale Inka Luomanmäki 1998–2000 (n.d.); see also n35 below.

26. C.M. Kraay and M. Hirmer, *Greek Coins* (London 1966), especially 'Sicily'.

27. R.R. Holloway, *The Archaeology of Ancient Sicily* (London 1991): 43, 155–6.

28. R. Leighton, *Sicily Before History: An Archaeological Survey from the Palaeolithic to the Iron Age* (Ithaca 1999): 59.

29. Hilzheimer 1932: Pl. I Fig. 3, facing p. 416.

30. Kraay and Hirmer, *Greek Coins*: Pl. 193.

31. Ibid.: Pl. 194

32. Ibid.: Pl. 202.

33. Also Aegesta. Virgil, *Æneid* I, v, 554; Dio. 10.

34. See below, n37.

35. I am indebted to Mrs Jane Moore and Mrs Maureen Foley for much helpful background on the popular history of the Cirneco.

36. 'Cirneco dell'Etna', Ente Nazionale delle Cinofilia Italiana.

37. Cirneco dell'Etna Club of America: from the breed standard 'Primitive type of dog of elegant and slender shape'.

38. L.B. Brea, *Sicily before the Greeks* (London 1957): 38–46; Holloway, *The Archaeology of Ancient Sicily*: 8–10.

39. Holloway, The Archaeology of Ancient Sicily: Pl. 10.

40. Kennel Club 1998: 48.

41. Clutton-Brock 1981: 45.

42. G. Goodman in G. Goodman, ed., The Saluqi: Coursing Hound of the East (Arizona 1995): 40.

43. Parker et al. 2004: 1164.

44. D. Trump, Malta: Prehistory and Temples (Malta 2002): 9, 20–21, 26, Chronology 54.

45. D.B. Redford, Egypt, Canaan and Israel in Ancient Times (Princeton 1992); M. Bietak, Avaris, the Capital of the Hyksos: New Excavation Results (London 1996).

46. See Sir T.J. Clark, 'Saluqis in Iraq', in Goodman, ed., The Saluqi: 128–68, especially 164–5.

47. G.R. Smith and M.A.S. Abdel Haleem, eds and trans., The Book of the Superiority of Dogs over Many of Those Who Wear Clothes, from the Arabic of Ibn al Marzuban (Warminster 1978). See also Professor Smith's chapter 'The Saluqi in Islam', in Goodman, ed., The Saluqi.

48. O. El Daly, Egyptology: The Missing Millennium. Ancient Egypt in Medieval Arabic Writings (London 2005): 169–70.

Chapter 5

1. Gardiner 1957: R8.

2. Ibid.: A40.

3. C.G. Jung, Collected Works, vol. 5: §§24, 89, 505; vol. 14: §4; J.D. Lewis Williams and T.A. Dowson, Images of Power: Understanding Bushman Rock Art (Johannesburg 1989).

4. For example, the Egypt Exploration Society, London and the Palestine Exploration Fund, London.

5. From a seminar by Jung quoted by James Hillman, 'Senex and Puer', in Puer Papers (Dallas 1989): 44.

6. Jung, Collected Works, vol. 5, 'The Origin of the Hero': §264.

7. Jung, Collected Works, vol. 9, pt I: §3.

8. A valuable summary of the present state of research into these areas is contained in J.D. Lewis Williams, The Mind in the Cave (London 2002).

9. J.D. Lewis-Williams, The Rock Art of Southern Africa (Johannesburg 1983); Lewis-Williams and Dowson, Images of Power.

10. J.D. Lewis-Williams and T.A. Dowson, 'The Signs of the Times: Entoptic Phenomena in Upper Palaeolithic Art', Current Anthropology 24 (1988): 201–45.

11. J.D. Lewis-Williams, 'A Visit to the Lion's House: Structures, Metaphors and Socio-political Significance in a Nineteenth Century Bushman's Myth', in J. Deacon and T.A. Dowson, eds, Voices from the Past: !Xam Bushmen and the Bleek and Lloyd Collection (Johannesburg 1996): 56–7.

12. Lewis-Williams and Dowson, Images of Power: passim.

13. Nunn 1996: 168–9.

14. P. Brunton, A Search in Secret Egypt (London 1935); W.H. Biegman, Egypt, Moulids, Saints, Sufis (London 1990).

15. Rice 1998: ch. 10.

16. Jung, Collected Works, vol. 9, pt I: §6.
17. Manetho gives Anubis third place in the list of 'Demi-Gods' who ruled Egypt in legendary times. He reigned for 17 years according to one recension; according to another for 83 years.
18. Wilkinson 1999: 280–81, 'Anubis'.
19. DuQuesne 1996 cites DMP XIV 28, 'son of a jackal (wns) and a dog (whr)'.
20. Plutarch 1957: 39, §14.
21. Gardiner 1957: D15, D16.
22. G. Dryer, 'Ein Siegal der früzeitlichen Königsnekropole von Abydos', MDAIK 43 (1987).
23. Gardiner 1957: G18.
24. O. Keller, Die Antike Tierwelt I (Leipzig 1909): Fig. 5.
25. D. Morris, How Well Do Dogs See? (London 1986): 55.
26. D. Alderton, The Dog: The Complete Guide to Dogs and Their World (London 1987): 18–19.
27. Examples of Old Kingdom mummies that have subjected to this technique include 'Waty' in Moussa and Altenmüller 1971: Pl. 40a and b, and 'Revêtment de momie', from the Boston Museum of Fine Arts, in L'Art Égyptien au temps des pyramides (Paris 1999): 382, Pl. 196.
28. Bernal 1987: passim.
29. Plutarch 1957: 107, §44.
30. See 'Persians' in Bard 1999: 612. Herodotus relates the story, to Cambyses' disadvantage, in The Histories, Book 3, §27–§33.
31. Gardiner 1957: N14.
32. Much of the astronomical/astrological lore associated with Anubis is drawn from Allen 1963 and Sir Norman Lockyer, The Dawn of Astronomy (London 1892).
33. Apuleius, The Golden Ass, trans. Robert Graves (London 1950).
34. Ibid.: 276–7.
35. Wilkinson 1999: 280.
36. Murray 1904 (as Seker-Kha-Bau): 3–4; Pl. I.
37. G.A. Wainwright, The Sky Religion in Egypt (Cambridge 1938): 47.
38. Murray 1904, vol. I: 1–12; Pl. I.
39. Ibid.
40. J. Vandier, 'L'Anubis femile et la nome Cynopolite', in K. Michalowski, L'Art de l'ancienne Égypte (Paris 1968): 196–204; Egyptian Museum, Cairo JE=40679 Ill., in Tiradritti 1998: 71.
41. L. Borchardt, Das Grabdenkmal des Königs Ne-user-re' (Leipzig 1907–13).
42. Wainwright, The Sky Religion in Egypt: 47, 67.
43. T. DuQuesne, Black and Gold God: Colour Symbolism of the God Anubis with Observations on the Phenomenology of Colour in Egyptian and Comparative Religion (London 1996).
44. Gardiner 1957: C6.
45. Carter 1954, vol. 3: Pl. II.
46. Carter and Mace 1954; Carter 1954.
47. Carter 1954, vol. 3: 41.
48. Ibid.
49. Ibid.
50. Ibid.: 45.

51. Ibid.
52. Ibid.: 42–3.
53. Ibid.: 43–4.
54. This encounter took place at a breeding kennels in Bedfordshire in 1978. Among a melée of golden-red Pharaoh Hounds was one jet-black individual, morphologically identical to his half-siblings, other than in his coloration.
55. Clutton-Brock 1984: 209.
56. Carter and Mace 1954, vol. 1: Pl. XIV.
57. Dryer, 'Ein Siegal der früzeitlichen Königsnekropole von Abydos': Fig. 3.
58. Gardiner 1957: E18.
59. Ibid.
60. Description de l'Égypt: publiée par les ordres de Napoleon Bonaparte, vol. VI: Pls 43–49.
61. Asselberghs 1961: Pl. XCV Afb. 169; 258, 291.
62. Frankfurt 1948. He uses the transliteration 'Upwaut' throughout.
63. Ibid.: 94.
64. Ibid.: 203–5.
65. Lichtheim 1975: 123.
66. Ibid.
67. Tony A.H. Wilkinson, Early Dynastic Egypt (London 1999).
68. J. Bourriau, Pharaohs and Mortals (Cambridge 1988): 72; Pl. 58. BM EA 969.
69. Lichtheim 1976: 37, Ill. 26–7.
70. Much of the material here is derived from R. David, A Guide to Religious Ritual at Abydos (Warminster 1981).
71. Ibid.: West Wall South Section.
72. Bernal 1987.
73. Griffiths 1960.
74. Te Velde 1977: 56–84.
75. Ibid.: 10–11.
76. Ibid.
77. Asselberghs 1961: 172–6, Pls XCVII–XCIX.
78. Ibid.; Te Velde 1977.
79. Budge 1920: 624.
80. Ibid.: I 25 B.
81. Te Velde 1977: 27–8.
82. Ibid.: 7–26.
83. Petrie 1900: 179; Pl. XXII.
84. Gardiner 1957: G.E21.
85. Ibid.: G.E20.
86. Te Velde 1977: 13–16.
87. P.E. Newberry, 'The Pig and the Cult of Set', Journal of Egyptian Archaeology 14 (1928): 211–25.
88. Te Velde 1977: 22 no. 6.
89. Allen 1963: 123–4.
90. P. Jumilhac XVII 6–14, quoted in DuQuesne 1996: 47 n278.
91. Wilkinson 1999: 82–94.
92. Newberry 1922: 40–46.
93. Wilkinson 1999: 90–91.

94. Te Velde 1977: 72.
95. Petrie 1900: 173, Pl. XXI.
96. Wilkinson 1999: 91–4.
97. Te Velde 1977: 20.
98. Rubanus Maurus of Monte Casino in J. Seznic, *The Survival of the Pagan Gods* (New York 1953): 62, 238.
99. Rice 1997: 6, 10, 104, 262, 272–3.

Chapter 6

1. Zeuner 1963.
2. Ibid.: 107–8.

Bibliography

Allen, R.H. (1963 [1899]) *Star Names: Their Lore and Meaning*. New York.

Asselberghs, H. (1961) *Chaos en Beheersing: Documenten in Aeneolithisch Egypte*. Leiden.

Bard, K.A. (ed.) (1999) *Encyclopaedia of the Archaeology of Ancient Egypt*. London.

Bernal, M. (1987, 1991) *Black Athena: The Afroasiatic Roots of Classical Civilization*, vol. I, *The Fabrication of Ancient Greece 1785–1985* (1987); vol. II, *The Archaeological and Documentary Evidence* (1991). London.

Block, P., and Sacks, R.L. (1983) *The Pharaoh Hound*, ed. W.W. Denlinger and R.A. Rathman. Fairfax VA.

Brewer, D.J., Redford, D.B., and Redford, S. (n.d.) *Domestic Plants and Animals: The Egyptian Origin*, Warminster.

Budge, E.A.W. (1920) *An Egyptian Hieroglyphic Dictionary*, 2 vols. London.

Camilleri, C. (1995) *A Study of the Maltese Kelb tal-Fenek*. Valetta.

Carter, H. (1954) *The Tomb of Tut.Ankh.Amen*, vols 2 and 3. New York.

Carter, H., and Mace, A.C. (1954) *The Tomb of Tut.Ankh.Amen*, vol. 1. New York.

Clason, A., Payne, S., and Uepermann, H.-P. (eds) (1993) *Skeletons in Her Cupboard: Festschrift for Juliet Clutton-Brock*. Oxford.

Clutton-Brock, J. (1979) 'Mammalian Remains from the Jericho Tell', *Proceedings of the Prehistoric Society 45*.

―――― (1981) *Domesticated Animals from Early Times*. London.

―――― (1984) 'Dog', in I. Mason, ed., *Evolution of Domestic Animals*. London.

―――― (1995) 'Early Origins of the Saluqi', in G. Goodman, ed., *The Saluqi: Coursing Hound of the East*. Arizona.

Cockroft, S.J.(ed.) (2000) *Dogs through Time: An Archaeological Perspective. Proceedings of the 1st ICAZ Symposium on the History of the Domestic Dog*, Eighth Congress of the International Council for Archaeozoology, Vancouver. Oxford.

Davis, S.J.M., and Valla, F.R. (1978) 'Evidence for the Domestication of the Dog 12000 years ago in the Natufian of Israel', *Nature*, vol. 276, no. 5688: 608–10.

Douglas, K. (2000) 'Mind of a Dog', *New Scientist*, 4 March: 22–7.

DuQuesne, T. (1991) *The Jackal at the Shaman's Gate*. Thame.
——— (1996) *Black and Gold God: Colour Symbolism of the God Anubis with Observations on the Phenomenology of Colour in Egyptian and Comparative Religion*. London.
Emery, W.B. (1949–58) *Great Tombs of the First Dynasty*, vol. I, 1949, Cairo; vol. II, 1953, London; vol. III, 1958. London.
Faulkner, R.O. (1969) *The Ancient Egyptian Pyramid Texts*. Oxford.
Fischer, H.G. (1978) 'More Ancient Egyptian Names of Dogs and Other Animals', *Metropolitan Museum Journal* 12: 173–7.
Flores, D.V. (2003) *Funerary Sacrifices of Animals in the Egyptian Predynastic Period*. Oxford.
Frankfort, H. (1948) *Kingship and the Gods*. Chicago.
Galant, J. (2002) *The Story of the African Dog*. Pietermaritzburg.
Gardiner, Sir A. (1957) *Egyptian Grammar*, 3rd edn. London.
Gransard-Desmond, J.-O. (2004) *Étude sur les Canidae des temps pré-pharaonique en Égypte et au Soudan*. Oxford.
Griffiths, J.G. (1960) *The Conflict of Horus and Seth*. Liverpool.
——— (1966) *The Origins of Horus*. Munich.
Herodotus (1998) *Histories*, trans. Robin Waterfield. Oxford.
Hilzheimer, M. (1932) 'The Dog', *Antiquity*, vol. VI, no. 24: 411–19; trans. with annotations by Roland G. Austin, Glasgow University.
Hoffman, M.A. (1979) *Egypt before the Pharaohs: the Predynastic Foundation of Egyptian Civilization*, New York; 2nd edn 1991.
——— (1982) *The Predynastic of Hierakonpolis: An Interim Report*.
Jung, C.G. (1956) *Collected Works*, vol. 5, *Symbols of Transformation*; vol. 9, pt. 1, *The Archetypes and the Collective Unconscious*, trans. R.F.C. Hall. London.
Kemp, B.J. (1979) 'Photographs of the Decorated Tomb at Hierakonpolis', *Journal of Egyptian Archaeology* 59: 36–43.
Kennel Club (1998) *The Kennel Club's Illustrated Breed Standards*. London.
Lawrence, B. (1967) 'Early Domestic Dogs', *Zeitschchrift für Saugetierkunde* 32: 44–59.
Lichtheim, M. (1975–1980) *Ancient Egyptian Literature*: vol. I, *The Old and Middle Kingdoms* (1975); vol. II, *The New Kingdom* (1976); vol. III, *The Late Period* (1980). Berkeley.
Linnaeus, C. (1758) *Systema Naturae*.
Masson, J.M. (1998) *Dogs Never Lie about Love*. London.
Mellaart, J. (1967) *Catal Hüyük*. London.
——— (1975) *The Neolithic of the Near East*. London.
Midant-Reynes, B. (2000) *The Prehistory of Egypt: From the First Egyptions to the First Pharaohs*. Oxford.
Moussa, A.M., and Altenmüller, H. (1971) *The Tomb of Nefer and Ka-Hay*. Mainz-am-Rhein.
Murray, M.A. (1904) *Saqqara Mastabas*, Part 1. London.
Newberry, P.E. (1893) 'Beni Hasan', Part 2, in *Archaeological Survey of Egypt*, ed. F.Ll. Griffith. London.
——— (1922) 'The Set Rebellion of the IInd Dynasty', *Ancient Egypt*, Part 2.
Nunn, J.F. (1996) *Ancient Egyptian Medicine*. London.
Osborn, D.J., with Osbornovà, J. (1998) *The Mammals of Ancient Egypt*. Warminster.
Parker, H.G., Kim, L.V., Sutter, N.B., Carlson, S., Lorentzen, T.D., Malek, T.B., Johnson, G.S., DeFrance, H.B., Ostrander, E.A., and Kruglyak, L. (2004) 'Genetic Structure of the Purebred Domestic Dog', *Science* 304, 21 May.

Petrie, W.M.F. (1900) *The Royal Tombs of the Earliest Dynasties Part I.* London.
——— (1901) *The Royal Tombs of the Earliest Dynasties Part II.* London.
——— (1925) *Tombs of the Courtiers and Oxyrhynkhos.* London.
——— (1953) *Ceremonial Slate Palettes: Corpus of Predynastic Pottery.* London.
Plutarch (1957) *Moralia*, trans. Frank Cole Babbitt. Cambridge MA.
Reeves, N. and Wilkinson, R.H. (1996) *The Complete Valley of the Kings.* London.
Reisner, G.A. (1918) 'The Tomb of Hepzefa, Nomarch of Siut', *Journal of Egyptian Archaeology* vol. 5, no. I: 79–98.
——— (1923) *Excavations at Kerma*, Parts 1–5. Cambridge MA.
Rice, M. (1997) *Egypt's Legacy: The Archetypes of Western Civilization 3000–30 BC.* London.
——— (1998) *The Power of the Bull.* London.
——— (2003) *Egypt's Making: The Origins of Ancient Egypt 5000–2000 BC* (1990), revised and extended edition. London.
Rohl, D. (2000) *The Followers of Horus, Eastern Desert Survey Report*, vol. I. Basingstoke.
Savolainen, P., Ya-ping, Z., Jing L., Lundeberg, J., and Leitner, T. (2002) 'Genetic Evidence for an East Asian Origin of Domestic Dogs', *Science* 298, 22 November.
Serpell, J. (ed.) (1995) *The Domestic Dog: Its Evolution, Behaviour and Interactions with People.* Cambridge.
Sheldrake, R. (1999) *Dogs That Know When Their Owners Are Coming Home, and Other Unexplained Powers of Animals.* London.
Stevenson Smith, W. (1946) *A History of Painting and Sculpture in the Old Kingdom.* London.
Te Velde, H. (1977) *Seth God of Confusion: A Study of His Role in Egyptian Mythology and Religion.* London.
Tiradritti, F. (1998) *The Cairo Museum: Masterpieces of Egyptian Art.* London.
Tooley, A.M.J. (1988) 'Coffin of a Dog from Beni Hasan', *Journal of Egyptian Archaeology* 74: 207–11.
Vilà, C., Savolainen P., Maldonado, J.E., Amorim, I.R., Rice, J.E., Honeycutt, R.L., Crandall, K.A., Lundeberg, J., and Wayne, R.K. (1997) 'Multiple and Ancient Origins of the Domestic Dog', *Science* 276.
Waddell, W.G. (1940) *Manetho* (trans.). Cambridge MA and London.
Wilkinson, T.A.H. (1999) *Early Dynastic Egypt.* London.
Williams, B. (1986) *Excavations between Abu Simbel and the Sudan Frontier.* Chicago.
Winkler H. (1938–9) *Rock Drawings of Southern Upper Egypt*, 2 vols. London.
Zarins, J., et al. (1981) 'Second Preliminary Report on the Southwestern Province', *ATLAL* 5, Riyadh.
Zeuner, F.E. (1963) *A History of Domesticated Animals.* London.

Picture Sources and Acknowledgements

Frontispiece W.B. Emery, *Excavations at Saqqara: The Tomb of Hemaka* (Cairo 1938): Frontispiece.

Figure 1 a, b: H.A. Winkler, *The Rock-Drawings of Southern Upper Egypt. Sir Robert Mond Expedition* (London 1938): Pls XXIII, XXIII.3; c: from H.A. Winkler, *Rock-Drawings of Southern Upper Egypt II. Sir Robert Mond Desert Expedition* (London 1939): Pl. LV.2. All by kind permission of the Committee of the Egypt Exploration Society, London.

Figure 2 J.H. Dunbar, *The Rock Pictures of Lower Nubia* (Cairo 1941): Pl. XII, Figs 52–7.

Figure 3 D.R. Rohl (ed), *The Followers of Horus: The Eastern Desert Survey Report*, vol. I (Basingstoke 2000). Drawings reproduced by kind permission of D.R. Rohl.

Figure 4 H. Müller-Karpe, *Handbuch der Vorgesischte* (1968), vol. II: Tfl. 18. B3

Figure 5 Excavations at Abydos of the Deutsches Archäologisches Institut Kairo; reproduction of the labels by kind permission of Professor G. Dreyer and by courtesy of Kathryn Piquette, the Institute of Archaeology, University College, London. G. Dreyer, *Das prädynastische Königsgrab U-j und seine frühen Schriftzeugnisse* (Mainz 1998).

Figure 6 Williams 1986: Figure 58, after Reisner 1910: Pl. 65f. Reproduced by courtesy of the Oriental Institute of the University of Chicago.

Figure 7 Petrie 1901: Pl. XV.108. By permission of the Committee of the Egypt Exploration Society, London.

Figure 8 Emery 1958, vol. III: Pl. 91b. By permission of the Committee of the Egypt Exploration Society, London.

Figure 9 M. Rice, 'Al-Hajjar Revisited: The Grave Complex at Al-Hajjar Bahrain' (rev. with photographs), *Proceedings of the Society for Arabian Studies* 18 (1988): Pl. 7.29.

Figure 10 Photograph by courtesy of John. R. Ross.

Figure 11 Petrie 1900: Part I, Pl. XXXII.10, 11, 12.

Figure 12 a: Photograph: Robert Partridge, Ancient Egypt Picture Library; b: R.F.E Paget and A.A. Pirie, *The Tomb of Ptah-hetep* (London 1898): Pl. XXXV (detail).

Figure 13　From Moussa and Altenmüller 1971: Pl. 2. Print from Deutsches Archäolo-gisches Institut, Abteilung Kairo.

Figure 14　From Murray 1904: Pl. VII. By kind permission of the Petrie Museum of Egyptian Archaeology, University College, London.

Figure 15　Reproduced from R.B. Parkinson, *Voices from Ancient Egypt* (London 1991), with transliterations from the same source. Reproduced by permission of the British Museum Press.

Figure 16　Museum of Fine Arts, Boston. Photograph © Museum of Fine Arts Boston.

Figure 17　A.M. Blackman, *The Rock Tombs of Meir*, Part 1 (1914): Pl. XI. Reproduced by permission of the Committee of the Egypt Exploration Society, London.

Figure 18　P.E. Newberry, El Bersheh I (London 1896), Pls XXIV, XXIX. By permission of the Committee of the Egypt Exploration Society, London.

Figure 19　Asyut IFAO Excavations 1910, Egyptian Museum, Cairo. Photograph: Robert Partridge, Ancient Egypt Picture Library.

Figure 20　Private collection.

Figure 21　V. Loret 1899 for the Service des Antiquities. G. Daressy, *Fouilles des Vallé des Rois 1898–1899* (Cairo): 1–62. Photograph: Robert Partridge Ancient Egypt Picture Library.

Figure 22　The Egyptian Museum, Cairo CG 29836. T.M. Davis, *The Tomb of Siptah: The Monkey Tomb and the Gold Tomb* (London 1908): 4–5, 17; Reeves and Wilkinson 1996: 185; S. Ikram and N. Iskander, *Catalogue Général of Egyptian Antiquities in the Cairo Museum: Non-Human Mummies* (Cairo 2002): 26–7; 85. Photograph: Robert Partridge Ancient Egypt Picture Library.

Figure 23　Gardner Wilkinson, *A Popular Account of the Ancient Egyptians*, vol. I (London 1856): Pl. 245.

Figure 24　N. De G. Davis, *The Mastaba of Ptahhetep and Akhethetep at Saqqareh*, Part I, *The Chapel of Ptahhetep and the Hieroglyphs* (London 1900): Pl. XXI. Reproduced by permission of the Committee of the Egypt Exploration Society, London.

Figure 25　Reproduced by permission of the Ashmolean Museum, Oxford.

Figure 26　Photograph by courtesy of Mrs S.M. Simm.

Figure 27　Photograph by courtesy of Mrs Jane Moore.

Figure 28　Reproduced by permission from Max Hilzheimer, 'Dogs', *Antiquity*, vol. VI, no. 24 (1932): 411–19, Pl. I

Figure 29　From Reginald Stuart Poole, ed., *Catalogue of Greek Coins: Sicily* (London 1876). Images reproduced by courtesy of the Department of Coins and Medals, British Museum.

Figure 30　Photograph by courtesy of Mr and Mrs Simm.

Figure 31　Photograph by courtesy of Rupert Wace Ancient Art, *Pharaoh's Creatures: Animals from Ancient Egypt* (Exhibition Catalogue, n.d.): no. 98.

Figure 32　Murray 1904: Pl. I. Reproduced by permission of the Petrie Museum of Egyptian Archaeology, University College, London.

Figure 33　A.J. Spencer, *Early Egypt: The Rise of Civilisation in the Nile Valley* (London 1993), Fig. 43. By kind permission of the British Museum Press.

Figure 34　Photograph: Robert Partridge Ancient Egypt Picture Library.

Figure 35　Ashmolean Museum, Oxford. Detail supplied by the Ashmolean.

Figure 36　Murray 1904: Pl. XXXVIII.24. By permission of the Petrie Museum of Egyptian Archaeology, University College, London.

Figure 37　Petrie 1901: Pl. XXII.179. By permission of the Committee of the Egypt Exploration Society, London.

Figure 38　Petrie 1901: Pl. XXIII.197.

Index